Keepers of the Wolves

Richard P. Thiel

Keepers of
the Wolves

The Early Years of Wolf
Recovery in Wisconsin

The University of Wisconsin Press

The University of Wisconsin Press
1930 Monroe Street
Madison, Wisconsin 53711

www.wisc.edu/wisconsinpress/

3 Henrietta Street
London WC2E 8LU, England

5   4   3   2   1

Printed in the United States of America

Library of Congress Cataloging-in-Publication Data
Thiel, Richard P.
    Keepers of the wolves : the early years of wolf recovery
in Wisconsin / Richard P. Thiel.
    242 pp.   cm.
    Includes index.
    ISBN 0-299-17470-0 (cloth: alk. paper)
    ISBN 0-299-17474-3 (pbk.: alk. paper)
    1. Wolves—Wisconsin.
    2. Endangered species—Wisconsin.   I. Title.
    QL737.C22 T474   2001
    333.95′9773′09775—dc21   2001000715

To Deborah Jean Thiel, who has allowed me to live my dream and who has shared with me the trials and triumphs of this life's journey as my best friend, confidante, and lover

Contents

Illustrations

Figures

Maps

Acknowledgments

Between January 1980 and November 1989, I directed the wolf recovery program in the state of Wisconsin. Over the years since, friends and strangers alike have asked when I was going to write a book about my experiences as Wisconsin's wolf biologist. I imagined this would make for a fine project in my retirement, which was then quite a few years distant. One acquaintance urged me not to wait. By that time, it had already been four years since I had left the program. I began to write almost immediately.

My intentions in writing this book are (1) to compliment the historical treatise *The Timber Wolf in Wisconsin: The Death and Life of a Majestic Predator*, which I wrote and the University of Wisconsin Press published in 1993, (2) to provide factual information on aspects of the biology of the wolf living in the frontier of its North American range, and (3) to provide the reader with a view of the volatility of the issues that confront and confound government workers' efforts to preserve a species and move it off the endangered species list.

This story has a happy ending. The wolf population has rebounded with an unprecedented vitality in Minnesota, Wisconsin, and the Upper Peninsula of Michigan. In the span of a few decades, wolves have managed to reclaim much of the suitable habitat that remains in these regions. I am convinced that this was made possible only because of the federal Endangered Species Act.

By the time this book is published, it will be twelve years since I left the project. It is truly amazing how quickly one's memory can falter. Were it not for my diaries, field notebooks, and the conversations I held over the ensuing years with many of the individuals who assisted in the Wisconsin wolf-recovery work, it would have been nearly impossible to put words on paper with any degree of accuracy.

The events portrayed in this book actually happened. I have taken care to retell them as accurately as memory, notes scribbled in field books, newspaper articles, and recollections of others would allow. I take full responsibility for any omissions or errors in the portrayal of events depicted in this book.

Conversations in the following pages should not be taken literally. I attempted to re-create these based on my knowledge of the events, the surrounding circumstances, and the mannerisms of the people involved. I have chosen to use pseudonyms for the private citizens I encountered and in some cases intentionally obscured various facts to preserve their anonymity. The government workers within the Wisconsin and Michigan Departments of

Natural Resources, the U.S. Fish and Wildlife Service, and the U.S. Forest Service and friends are real. A fair number of these people are retired; a handful, deceased. They are all listed below.

I would like to thank my family—Debbie, Allison, and Cassie—for their support during numerous drafts and rewrites as I maneuvered the manuscript into final form. Thanks also go to our friend John Archer for allowing me to use his photograph of Sharon, a wild Wisconsin timber wolf, which has been used on the cover of this book. Blackwell Science, Inc., kindly gave me permission to reprint with minor alterations David Mladenoff's map of suitable Wisconsin wolf habitat (p. 211), which first appeared in "A Regional Landscape Analysis and Prediction of Favorable Wolf Habitat in the Northern Great Lakes Region," *Conservation Biology* 9 (1995): 279–94.

I would like to express my appreciation to the following individuals who directly or indirectly contributed to making the Wisconsin Wolf Recovery program a reality and a success. It was truly a privilege to work and share time with each of you:

John Archer
Jeff Beringer
Steve Beuchel
Chet Botwinski
Diane Boyd
Lori and Mike Bronk
Don Bublitz
Joe Davidowski
Jim Dienstl
Dan Doberstein
Bob Dreis
Ruth, Hip, and Lynn Dudeck
Dave Duncan
Ron Eckstein
Eric Epstein
Mike Fairchild
Steve Fritts
Dan Grubner
Jim Hale
"Yukon" John Hanson
Bob Hayes
Ruth Hine
Frank Iwen
Joe Jochem
Randy Jurewicz

Marty Kasinskas
Jim Knuteson
Ron Kofal
Fred Kruger
Arlyn Loomans
Bob MacGilligott
Larry Martoglio
Ray Marvin
Dave Mech
Bill Meier
Tom Meier
Kim Mello
Vicky Mello
Sue Nelson
Larry and Kathy Prenn
Georgine Price
Bob Ream
Tony Rinaldi
Ernie Rozelle
Ron, Carol, and Christopher Schultz
Bill Scott
Greg Sevener
Howard Sheldon
Barry Stanek
Fred Strand

Dick Stroud

Allison and Cassie Thiel

Bill Thiel

Deborah Thiel

Ray and Fayne Thiel

Scott Thiel

Nancy Thomas

Terry Valen

Ron VanderVelden

Rick Vincent

Norm Weiland

Bob Welch

Jim Welch

Ed Wenger

Tom White

Cliff Wiita

Adrian Wydeven

Jeff Zuba

Keepers of the Wolves

Phantoms of the Forest

We still get reports each year on timber wolves in the state.
Most are sightings of coyote or brush wolves. Occasionally a dog
is mistaken for a timber wolf. In-so-far as we can determine
there are no resident timber wolves in . . . Wisconsin. Any found
in our state are probably drifters from Michigan and Minnesota.
Wisconsin Conservation Department official, May 1969

TIMBER WOLVES ARE ALREADY PROTECTED in Wisconsin,
but the term "protect" is relative since there are no wolves
remaining in the state. They have all been killed or run off by
the encroachment of civilization.
Jay Reed, Milwaukee Journal, October 8, 1972

THE ASSOCIATED PRESS recently sent out a story detailing
fears of Minnesota residents about the return of the eastern
timber wolf. Once nearly extinct, the animals now number an
estimated 1,200 to 1,500 in that state and a few have reportedly
been spotted in Northern Wisconsin.
Editorial, Capital Times (Madison), January 29, 1977

It was January 28, 1978, at 4:30 P.M.

My good friend Bob Welch and I were on the last leg of a twelve-mile
snowshoe trek along a decrepit fire lane that cut through the heavily forested
border country separating the states of Minnesota and Wisconsin. We were
on the Wisconsin side, looking for some sort of sign of timber wolves—Wisconsin's north woods' phantoms that many claimed no longer existed. Bob's
brother Jim and two buddies were searching another area nearby.

Early that morning, before we left the cabin, we had made arrangements
for the other group to pick us up at 4 P.M. where the fire lane intersected a
plowed town road. It was now 4:30 and, although thoroughly exhausted, we
plodded on, aware that another painful mile separated us from the rendezvous point.

It was only 5 degrees Fahrenheit, and the sky, totally devoid of clouds, foretold of temperatures that would fall well below zero as darkness enveloped
the rugged scenery through which we had been trudging these past six hours.
As we neared the top of another of those innumerable hills, we made silent
prayer that our ride awaited us. I was acutely aware that our friends probably

3

had had a busy day searching their area for signs of wolves. Then, too, because this was unfamiliar territory, our friends might not be at the right spot.

The gremlins in my mind kept conjuring pessimistic visions that no one would be there to greet us. To override that painful thought, I concentrated on the cramping in my legs.

For all our labor, Bob and I could not report anything promising from our long hike. Our findings, which we scribbled into a notebook, included 311 sets of snowshoe hare tracks, 41 deer tracks, 15 coyote tracks, and 2 bobcat tracks. We'd also run into—or, more precisely, nearly been run over by—twenty-five snowmobilers and even four 4-wheel-drive Jeep enthusiasts. But no wolves. It was, to say the least, discouraging.

As we reached the top of a large hill, we saw a tiny figure on a distant hill about a half-mile down the lane. It was our friend "Yukon" John Hanson, and he was waving with outstretched arms and shouting. "Did you hear that? Yukon's saying something about *wolves*," Bob said to me. The news jump-started our aching muscles and, ignoring our fatigue, we quickened our pace. As the distance between us and Yukon slowly decreased, my mind drifted back over the many crazy years that had led to our searches that day.

Wolves disappeared from Wisconsin during my childhood in the 1950s; mine was the first generation of Wisconsinites unable to "experience" wolves. In 1966, when I was thirteen and growing up in suburban Milwaukee, I read Ernest Thompson Seton's story about Lobo. Then, while searching through several mammal books at the local library, I came across a map showing that wolves supposedly lived in Wisconsin. I learned that the state was responsible for managing its wildlife, and I wrote to the Wisconsin Conservation Department to get information about the status of rare wildlife. I found the response regarding timber wolves especially disturbing. Wildlife officials weren't sure whether any remained in the state, but they were fairly certain the species had been all but eradicated from the lower forty-eight states, with the sole exception of a small population that persisted in northeastern Minnesota.

I kept asking questions and learned that many believed that the wolves' ruin was connected to both publicly funded wolf bounties and the wolves' need for "wilderness." I simply could not understand why generations of Wisconsinites apparently had condoned this creature's annihilation and how its obliteration had been accomplished. No one could tell me.

I taught myself how to identify wolf sign (tracks, urinations, and droppings) and read every technical article and book about wolves that I could lay my

hands on while in high school. In the fall of 1971 I entered the University of Wisconsin–Stevens Point, which then, as now, had a preeminent department of wildlife biology, the area I had chosen for my major. I continued to privately research wolves, primarily by corresponding with people who were witnesses to or involved in the demise of wolves in the state. Some would tell me they would still occasionally see signs of wolves. One was Bert Dahlberg, who, as a young biologist in the Wisconsin Conservation Department in the late 1940s and early 1950s, witnessed the systematic elimination of the last few wolf packs.

In 1958 Dahlberg had been unwittingly involved in an investigation into the death of what would later be labeled the last timber wolf known to have lived in Wisconsin. Dahlberg knew the wolf. He had first seen its peculiar tracks in 1954—it had lost some toes, probably in a trap—in remote forested land at the tip of Wisconsin's Bayfield Peninsula, which juts into Lake Superior about midway between Duluth and the Wisconsin–Michigan state line. In subsequent years, Dahlberg dutifully recorded information in his field notebook each time he encountered the animal's tracks.

On a snowy evening in January 1958, a year after the state eliminated wolf bounties in Wisconsin, Old Two Toes, as he was called, was struck and killed by a car. This seemed to confirm that, indeed, Wisconsin had no room for wolves.

By the end of the 1950s no packs seemed to remain, and biologists could find no indication of breeding. However, every once in a while someone would spy the tracks of a lone wolf and, just as mysteriously, all sign of the animal would vanish.

Cliff Wiita, a wildlife manager in the Park Falls area, found a 5.5-inch wolf track near Hoffman Lake in northeastern Price County in 1960. Chet Botwinski, a wildlife manager in the Woodruff area, found tracks of a pair of wolves near western Oneida County's Stone Lake in 1962, but several trips back to that area revealed no further evidence of their presence. Wildlife officials dismissed these apparitions as loners passing through en route to or from Michigan or Minnesota.

Bert Dahlberg had one last encounter with a Wisconsin wolf. In the winter of 1962, while he was conducting scientific surveys within deer-yarding areas along the eastern flank of Ashland County, not far from the Michigan state line, Dahlberg stumbled across the tracks of a single wolf.[1] He and his crew followed the trail eastward toward Iron County because some of the younger biologists had never seen a wolf's tracks before. The trail led them into the jurisdiction of the wildlife biologist from a neighboring district. They figured they could gain nothing by continuing to follow the trail, so they gave up the hunt at the county line and returned to their responsibilities, measuring the effects of deer overpopulation on forest vegetation.

Forest and Florence Counties in the Nicolet National Forest in northeastern Wisconsin, Oneida County's Willow Flowage region, and the central block of forest in Iron County were widely known among bounty trappers and older wildlife biologists as the last wolf strongholds.[2] All agreed the last family groups of wolves in these areas had been bountied into extinction by the mid- to late 1950s. I firmly believed a few wolves had managed to elude the bounty trappers and hunters.

In the summer of 1973, between my sophomore and junior years in college, I bought a car. That gave me the means to visit northern Wisconsin's forest regions to search for the presence of wolves.

I knew that trying to prove the existence of wolves in Wisconsin would not be easy. In fact, it would be the proverbial search for the needle in the haystack. Seventeen thousand square miles of northern Wisconsin forest lay between Lake Superior and Wausau and from east-central Minnesota to the Upper Peninsula of Michigan.

I decided to concentrate my survey work in the northern Nicolet National Forest. This area was fairly remote and was not widely used by humans—and the last report of timber wolf pack activity came from the Pine River headwaters country in the Nicolet around 1958. I would typically spend one or two days at a time during summer and winter, establishing base camps along the Pine River, a popular trout stream.

I was convinced the wolves were there. It was just a matter of knowing what to look for and when to look for it. I did not hope to actually see any wolves. Wolves are too wary. Besides, had I seen one, it would be my word against the state's wildlife biologists—their experience and opinions against the word of a total greenhorn. I needed to find irrefutable evidence, such as tracks and droppings.

But in Wisconsin I had the problem of discriminating the tracks and droppings of wolves from those of coyotes, smaller cousins of wolves, which are abundant in the state's northern forests, as well as telling the difference between wolf sign and dog sign.

Coyote tracks are half the size of wolf tracks. They rarely are longer than three inches. Wolf tracks, on the other hand, stretch a good four to five inches. Dog tracks can be smaller than a coyote's or larger than a wolf's. Of the three canids—dogs, wolves, and coyotes—dogs are by far the most abundant in Wisconsin, where an estimated 1.2 million live the golden life. Then there are feral dogs, domesticated animals occasionally abandoned in remote places by unscrupulous people who think their former pets can eke out a living White Fang–style.

Droppings provide the most definitive evidence. A Wisconsin study of the food habits of wolves in the mid-1940s told how to differentiate between coyote and timber wolf droppings. All an exuberant biologist had to do was get down on all fours, knuckle up to the feces in question, and measure its diameter — a formidable task to some. Not to me. Less than thirty-two millimeters — a coyote; larger — a timber wolf . . . or dog.

To differentiate between the feces of a wolf and that of a similar-sized dog, all one has to do is pin the pile down with one stick and pull it apart with another. Kibble in, kibble out — if the droppings look like dog food, they're usually from a dog. Deer hair, rabbit fur, or the remains of some other wild animal indicates wolf — or perhaps feral dog.

The data came in slowly — and mostly not at all. In 1973 I captured on film two paw prints in a muddy rut on a woods trail near Briss Lake in Forest County. On another occasion I found a dropping full of deer hair that was way too large to have been deposited by a coyote.

In 1974 I was able to secure grants from my university and the U.S. Forest Service, which helped defray the money my friends and I were laying out to look for wolves. I worked primarily at night, regularly driving "howl survey routes" along the fire lanes in the northern Nicolet, stopping at one-mile intervals and blasting tape-recorded wolf howls out of several speakers mounted to the roof of my two-door Rambler. My hope was that any wolves who happened to be passing through the neighborhood would oblige me and return a howl or two.

Wolves can easily hear sounds over a distance of two or three miles, but the human ear (in this case, mine) is limited to less than 1.5 miles.[3] So for me to know they were out there, any wolves responding to my broadcast howls had to be within earshot of the roads I was driving. And the area I was trying to survey had a five-mile core of roadless forest.

It was lonely work and fairly boring because mile after mile, night after night, only an occasional coyote's yip-yapping call broke the silence of the forest. Late in August my college roommate, Steve Beuchel, drove up for a two-day visit to help out.

On his first night there we decided to canoe upstream along the forested banks of the Pine River to check the big area that I could not penetrate in the Rambler.

Hauling all that electronic equipment in our canoe was impractical, so I decided to use my own voice instead. Around 11 P.M. we stopped among the tag alders and listened for perhaps a minute or so. I let out a single howl, then another. After about a minute a howl suddenly drifted up out of the blackness somewhere off to the east. It was the plaintive howl of a lone timber wolf.

Astonished, I muttered, "Steve, did you hear that?"

"I sure did!" he replied.

I howled back, obtaining one additional reply. Further howling elicited nothing. But the wolf had replied twice—and that was enough for us.

We promptly turned our canoe around, paddled back to my car, and did precisely what most college kids would do; we headed to the nearest bar to celebrate.

In 1974 the wolf was not on the state's endangered species list; it was considered extirpated. Back at the university, I carefully assembled my evidence and prepared a report. One of my professors forwarded it to the Department of Natural Resources' Endangered Species Committee, which periodically reviewed records and reports of state and federally threatened and endangered species.[4] My information then was presented at a formal hearing of the Endangered Species Committee in the spring of 1975. As a result, Wisconsin reclassified the timber wolf as an endangered species.

The professional wildlife management community was unmoved by my report and the state's reclassification of Wisconsin's wolves. The presence of lone wolves proved nothing. None of the evidence remotely suggested that wolves were breeding within the state. Without packs, the chances wolves would return to the state were slim. And because a viable population did not exist, the wolf had no hope for a future in Wisconsin. And despite the timber wolf's official recognition as an endangered species in Wisconsin, no one in a position of authority was seriously interested in conducting surveys to determine the wolves' status. The collective opinion of the state's wildlife professionals was that Wisconsin no longer offered this species the solitude it seemed to require. As a DNR official wrote to me, "This creature is specifically adapted to vast wilderness areas and it simply cannot tolerate the ever-extending influence of man."

The official skepticism was understandable. Up to now my friends and I had found sign made only by single wolves. In March 1975 we had encountered— or, in the jargon of biologists, "cut tracks" of—two wolves on Kimball Creek in the northern Nicolet. But the association of the two wolves was apparently fleeting—or interrupted by unscrupulous individuals who sometimes shot wolves. We never found sign of the pair again.

I graduated from college in May 1975. Then, as now, jobs in my field were scarce. My small group of friends scattered across the upper Midwest in search of graduate schools and employment opportunities. Debbie and I married in 1976 and moved to Arkansas, where Deb completed an internship and I worked for the public schools as an environmental educator. Despite the distance, my thoughts were never far from the wolves and Wisconsin. We moved back in the early summer of 1977, settling in Tomah, a community in west-central Wisconsin, where Deb secured permanent employment as a dietitian at the Veterans Administration Hospital. I found temporary seasonal work as a biologist assistant with the DNR at the nearby Sandhill Wildlife Area. It was good to be home. I was certainly itching to renew my fieldwork.

I set my sights on finding evidence of a pack. A pack would mean that the wolves had established a territory and perhaps were attempting to breed. Finding sign of one or more packs would perhaps cause DNR administrators to change their thinking about wolves in Wisconsin.

Neither I nor my friends had ever seen sign of a pack, so we were uncertain just how to recognize what we were searching for. I shifted our focus to the border south of Duluth-Superior, the natural gateway to Minnesota's wolf country and home to a fairly respectable concentration of wolves. I reasoned that if some animals could somehow navigate around the developed west end of Lake Superior, switch directions, and head southeast, they might just find the heavily forested border country of Douglas County appealing.

I had some reason to think that I was right. In August 1975 a motorist accidentally struck a yearling female timber wolf along Highway 35, six miles east of the state line. The following year, a few miles to the south, a sheep farmer shot and killed a seventy-six-pound male wolf in one of his pastures. I had mulled these locations as I tried to figure out where we would be likely to find signs of a pack. In November 1977, just a few months after Deb and I moved back, my college friend Yukon John made arrangements to use a friend's cabin in Douglas County. We made plans to survey the region on the weekend of January 28 and 29, 1978.

That was how Bob Welch and I came to be snowshoeing that desolate stretch of fire lane that straddled the state line. Meanwhile, Yukon, Jim Knuteson, and Jim Welch had cruised a series of fire lanes east of Highway 35 in an area Bob and I privately felt would be less likely to have wolves (of course, we didn't tell them that).

We finally reached Yukon, who had decided to hike in and greet us with some interesting news. We listened intently as we hiked back to the car.

Around ten that morning he and the two Jims had encountered some very large canid tracks while checking out a series of plowed lanes near Bear Lake. One track measured nearly 5.5 inches from the base of the heel pad to the tip of the nails.

"There were three of them," Yukon told us. "They cut right across the fire tower lane on a deer trail. We measured their tracks. Excepting the big one, the other two measured three and a quarter by four and a quarter inches, with a stride averaging nineteen inches. We also found several BIG scats full of deer hair and fifteen urinations."

"What were the diameters of the droppings?" I asked. John replied, "Thirty-five to forty-two millimeters." These were much bigger than coyote droppings.

The tracks and stride were definitely within the wolf's range. They were also within the range of the dog, so my friends had had to scrutinize the evidence carefully. The scats—full of deer hair—and especially the urinations, were telltale tokens of wolves.

The trio had followed the animals' trail north into a large tract of balsam fir and black ash. The wolves had coursed through a deer yard, which made tracking them difficult because the deer trails were so numerous. On occasion, deer had walked along the trail after the wolves had moved through, all but obliterating their tracks. Yukon and the Jims had finally lost the beasts in an especially dense stand of spruce where deer sign was so profuse, Yukon exclaimed, that they could hardly find their own tracks, even though they were still standing in them.

"None of us has ever seen sign of a timber wolf—let alone a pack. So, tell us, do you think these were wolves?"

We couldn't be sure, either. I replied, "Only one way to tell. We'll all return to the spot tomorrow morning, first thing, and take a look."

The sun was down and the light was fading fast by the time we arrived at the car. Exhausted, Bob and I were thankful to be headed back to a warm cabin, a good meal, a couple of cases of beer, and the excitement that we might well have found what we'd been searching for since 1972—a timber wolf pack inside Wisconsin.

Before daybreak the oatmeal was boiling on the camp stove. We intended to get out by daylight, check the signs the guys had found the previous day, determine whether they were from wolves, and follow the wolves' tracks cross-country on snowshoes to figure out where the animals were ranging. It was Sunday. We would have to break camp around noon and head south to our homes and Monday morning jobs.

An hour after we rolled out of bed, just as the sun crested the horizon and illuminated the spires of the spruces in hues of yellow and orange, we pulled up to where the guys had found the tracks the day before. Softly etched in the snow along the shoulder of the road was the unmistakable outline of three sets of large paw prints. The animals had crossed the trail in a swampy patch of balsam fir, heading north toward Lake Seventeen, a small bog lake surrounded by open sphagnum bog and lowland forest.

The tracks were huge: toe pads the size of my thumbs and a heel pad not much smaller than the palm of my hand. I had never seen a domesticated dog put down such a track. They were wolves' tracks.

I unfolded a map on the hood of the car and laid out a plan of action. "They're headed north into this block. Let's circle around to the road north of here a few miles and see if they crossed it during the night. If they have, we'll follow 'em from that point on snowshoes. If they didn't cross, we'll return to this spot and follow their back trail a ways since you fellows lost sign of them on the front trail."

We jumped back in the car and continued down the fire lane, driving slowly, looking for tracks in the dusting of snow that covered the road. The temperature was 15 degrees below zero. The five of us hopelessly fogged up the windows as we crowded into Bob's old Buick. We were forced to proceed with our windows rolled down, heat on full blast. According to the map, the next road paralleling the one the wolves had crossed lay about three miles north of our position. Bob meticulously calculated where they should have crossed the night before, if they had gotten that far. He was right on.

We cut tracks of at least three wolves about a mile and a half east of Highway 35. The wolves didn't spend any time loafing on this town road and instead cut right across. It took Bob's sharp eyes to discern the scanty spoor that ever so slightly marred the cold, hardened surface of the plowed road.

We lost no time. Bob and Jim Knuteson teamed up to follow the wolves' back trail. Jim Welch, Yukon John, and I followed their front trail north across the Pioneer Road into the forest that blankets this desolate corner of Douglas County.

The going was slow, through sugary snow piled twenty-five inches deep. My snowshoes sank way down with each step. With every step forward they picked up a foot of snow as it caved in. We toiled along, weaving in and out among the trees and brush that the wolves had negotiated so easily. Despite the biting cold, we were soon drenched in sweat.

Not far from the road, the wolves had crossed a small open sphagnum bog.

There, the trails of the animals fanned out, providing a perfect opportunity to obtain a minimum count of the wolves we were following. I counted at least four different sets of tracks.

Their trails met in the brush at the far end of the bog. The pack continued single file up an esker covered with small birch, aspen, and an occasional balsam fir. They meandered through two thickets of deciduous trees and conifers and cut across two more eskers.

The second esker was steep and presented some difficulty as we climbed it. From the summit we were able to canvass quite a bit of the surrounding forest. At the esker's base was a stand of trees that was being harvested. To our astonishment, the wolves' trail seemed to pass right through it. We had assumed that these wary creatures would avoid any contact with humans. We based this on observations from biologists in upper Michigan and Wisconsin back in the 1940s and 1950s. In those days wolves went out of their way to avoid, among other things, tree-cutting operations.

We were naive. These wolves, of course, had never experienced the intense extermination pressures their forebears had suffered thirty years earlier and therefore did not mistrust things tainted by humans. Then too, if these wolves were going to make a living in a place as peopled as modern-day Wisconsin, they were going to have to learn to ignore some of Homo sapiens' activities.

Sorting out the mix of deer, people, and wolf tracks in the cutting area was more difficult than we had envisioned. Although we spent a considerable amount of time deciphering tracks, we lost the wolves in a maze of trails where deer had congregated to chew the tender twigs of felled treetops. We retreated to the surrounding forest and circled the entire clear-cut, hoping to encounter some sign of the wolves. But the deer traffic in this area was too intense. Disheartened, we headed back to the car hoping that the other guys had had some excitement.

Bob and Jim had followed the wolf trail as it dropped into a dense cedar swamp. There, the dense conifer foliage diffused what little light was available—and an ominous bank of clouds, blowing in off Lake Superior, had obscured the sun. The clouds foretold a change in weather. More snow was in store.

The cedars' branches held a significant amount of snow aloft. Snow depth beneath the cedars was half the depth we had been wading through, and Bob and Jim had a considerably easier trip.

They followed the wolves for perhaps an hour, noting that they had been walking single file, stepping precisely within the footsteps of the lead animal. This made it difficult to count the number of animals in the pack. Bob and Jim had been forced to walk bent over most of the way in order to duck beneath the branches.

Eventually, Bob came to a small opening, not more than twenty feet in diameter, created long before by two cedars that had toppled in a windstorm. In the middle of the opening stood another cedar.

As he entered the opening, Bob noticed the snow was crusted, padded down as if compressed by a giant steamroller. Testing his weight on its surface, Bob found it supported him easily. He hollered to Jim, who was some distance behind, urging him to move forward.

Something was odd about this place. Tiny crimson speckles were scattered across the padded snow. Blood. "Gotta be a deer kill around here somewhere," Bob said. They searched the surrounding forest but found no sign of a struggle, no deer hair, and no other sign of blood.

Perplexed, Bob and Jim returned to the lone cedar. Clearly, the wolves had spent quite some time in the opening. They were responsible for padding down the snow. The outlines of wolf paws were etched in the snow everywhere. The blood was not from a deer, and Bob was sure it wasn't coming from a wolf.

Bob leaned up against the tree, pausing to take in the scene of the crime. A few seconds later he heard a faint splat. It seemed to come from the surface of the snow, just a few feet to his right. He peered intently in the general direction, waiting for the sound to be repeated, hoping to catch some type of movement that might provide a clue.

Splat.

A steaming hot droplet of blood fell from the tree, exploding into tiny particles as it hit the cold snow.

"I'll be damned. Jim, come here and look at this," Bob called as he looked up. A porcupine was peering down at them from high in the branches of the cedar. A sizable chunk of the porky's hide had been ripped from its back and was dangling to one side, raw and ragged, exposing the flesh and muscles beneath.

Bob turned toward the trunk to examine any evidence that might reveal what had happened here. He found large scrape marks that had been left by claws furiously digging into the scrappy bark of the cedar.

The wolves had evidently surprised the porcupine on the ground. As it scrambled for the safety of the cedar, a wolf had lunged, grabbing the back of the spiny creature as it tried to reach a safe haven above its tormentors. The porcupine's sharp, barbed quills had given the wolf something else to contend with.

The porky had retreated again, trying desperately to make good its escape.

Once again a wolf had leaped into the air, caught the porcupine nearly six feet off the ground, and plucked it from the tree trunk.

It had been a standoff. The wolves had yielded, and the porcupine had clambered high into the cedar to avoid further assault, there to await its inevitable ruin, drop by drop, in the cold, snowy world that was its home.

By the time Bob and Jim got back to the car, flurries were falling. Time to head back to the cabin, pack up, and make plans for a return trip. Our success this weekend had been beyond our wildest expectations. We had not only discovered a *pack* but had begun the arduous process of counting the number of wolves in the pack, tracking their movements, determining the size of the pack's territory, and collecting information on the wolves' behavior in response to human activity.

We decided to name this pack the Bear Lake Pack. We returned to the area twice more that winter and found evidence of a second pack in the area straddling the state line that Bob and I had snowshoed that fateful day in January. At least seven wolves were present in the Bear Lake Pack that winter, and we counted three in the second pack, which we named the Stateline Flowage Pack after a man-made flowage located on the border.

We were elated with the winter's work. Our small crew had found wolf packs in Wisconsin. All that remained was to find evidence that they were producing pups. This would be much more difficult than finding tracks in the snow. Wolf pups are born in April and develop rapidly. But throughout the summer months they are still too small to accompany the adults in their nightly forays for food.

After considering our options, we decided to wait until mid-August to conduct our searches. We reasoned that the pups—should they exist—would be large enough by then to wander out onto some of the few fire lanes that crisscross both packs' areas and leave behind some tracks.

Late in August 1978, Debbie, Bob Welch, and I headed north to Douglas County to find evidence of wolf pups in our two packs.

Two days before we arrived, the region had received quite a bit of rainfall that turned the surface of the clay-based fire lanes into a mud slick.

We drove nearly all day that first day in search of wolf sign and found nothing. Then, late in the afternoon, we rounded a bend in the West Moose Road and spied the zipperlike pattern of wolf tracks dotting the edge of the lane. We stopped, got out, and walked forward to inspect the tracks. It was the faint imprint of an adult wolf heading west. Bob walked ahead while I looked for signs of any additional wolves.

"Dick. Deb. Come here and look at this!" Bob exclaimed as he knelt in the soft clay and stared intently at an imprint that paralleled the tracks of the adult wolf.

From ten feet away I could see the outline of the paw print. Smaller than the adult's but the toes and heel pad were nicely pronounced, thanks to the rain earlier in the week. The print was a little larger than a coyote's track but definitely did not contain the dainty features characteristic of coyotes.

"Whaddya think?" Bob asked carefully.

Deb and I stood beside him and peered at the track. We cautiously exclaimed that it certainly *looked* like a wolf track, but we felt our case would be more solid if we could find more tracks from this individual. One hundred yards farther up the road, we found a series of tracks. It was obvious that two adults and a single wolf pup had walked down the lane sometime after the rain had stopped. We followed their trails, uninterrupted, for more than a mile.

The next day, Sunday, August 20, 1978, we encountered similar trails made by two adults and two pups within the Bear Lake territory. We were elated. We had found what we had sought for so long: evidence that wolves were successfully breeding in Wisconsin.[5]

It took only two more years to convince Wisconsin DNR officials that wolf packs were living in the state and persuade them to support a formal field investigation of the status and distribution of Wisconsin's timber wolves.

Beginnings

At 10:45 A.M. on January 28, 1980, I pulled into the parking lot of the Northwest District headquarters of the Wisconsin Department of Natural Resources. A few minutes later I reported to my supervisor, the district wildlife staff specialist. The Wisconsin DNR's wolf project officially began on that very cold day, exactly two years to the day after Yukon John Hanson, Jim Welch, and Jim Knuteson had discovered the tracks of the Bear Lake Pack in western Douglas County. The resort town of Spooner was to be my home for the next several years.

The previous fall, the agency's Office of Endangered Species (later to be reorganized as the Bureau of Endangered Resources) obtained approval from the DNR to begin a two-year investigation of the status of the timber wolf in Wisconsin. Jim Hale, director of the office, had offered me the job of conducting the study, and I cheerfully accepted.

There were several glitches. First, the job was only a temporary assignment, known in state service as an LTE (limited term employee) position. Because of this Deb and I had wisely decided not to leave Tomah, where she continued to work at the VA hospital. Spooner was a three-hour drive north of Tomah, which meant I would have to live for extended periods away from home.

On the drive up to Spooner that morning, between choking back surges of separation anxiety, I thought about the equally cool reception I surely would receive from the Northwest District's administrative and wildlife staff. I was invading the district's sandbox. The Madison staff had hired me without the approval or participation of the Northwest District. In fact, Northwest officials had had to dismiss an LTE because Madison had hired me first.

The receptionist ushered me down the hall to Bob Dreis's office. He was assigned to supervise me. Bob was a widely respected biologist and an administrator of noteworthy achievement within the department. He had hired on with the Conservation Department in the early 1950s after receiving his master's degree in wildlife from Iowa State. Dreis, a short, slender man with close-cropped hair and a thin black moustache that fit his stern countenance, minced no words, as I was soon to find out.

He didn't get up from his chair when I walked into his small cluttered office to introduce myself. But he swept away a pile of folders and papers perched on top of the visitor's chair beside his desk and gestured for me to sit down.

18

No small talk. This man was all business, and I knew I was going to have to prove my worth to him if the wolf project were to succeed.

The first business we discussed was the rules—expected behavior, strictly minding my p's and q's, keeping up with the paperwork, and so on. Then he launched into a doomsday talk about what he thought of the wolf project.

After we found evidence of wolf pack activity within Wisconsin during our field trips in the winter and summer of 1978, Bob and Jim Welch and I had told DNR officials what we had learned. But they apparently were not interested in studying just what was going on with the state's endangered wolf population, so the three of us contacted world-renowned wolf authority Dr. L. David Mech, a research biologist then working with the U.S. Fish and Wildlife Service, and met with him at his office in Minneapolis–St. Paul in January 1979. Dave was impressed enough with our information that he promised to look into the possibility of conducting some type of study in Wisconsin, perhaps in the Minnesota border area.

Less than two weeks after we spoke with Mech, I got a call from Ron Nicotera, the DNR's assistant division administrator. He represented Wisconsin on the federal Eastern Timber Wolf Recovery Team. In the past, administrators had repeatedly proclaimed that a Wisconsin wolf study was of no value, which was exactly what had led us to Mech's door. Now the department was suddenly interested in investigating the status of wolves in the state.

A week later Nicotera and Jim Hale, director of the Office of Endangered Species, met me at my home in Tomah to discuss the details of a wolf study. Because they knew of my work with wolves in Wisconsin, they asked me to prepare a proposal and budget outline. They wanted to limit the study to winter tracking surveys. I encouraged them to consider radio telemetry work— monitoring the movements and fates of radio-collared wolves would yield information on their numbers, distribution, and mortality rates more efficiently than tracking, especially because they were talking about a two-year study.

I could not change their minds. As they envisioned it, the study would use the same winter ground-tracking techniques I'd been using for the past few winters in Douglas County. They agreed that no matter how we went about it, the work would be expensive. But they weren't interested in anything but more ground tracking.

I agreed to develop a budget proposal if they would give me fair consideration when hiring a person to do the work. Despite my misgivings that the budget I put together would be inadequate if they ultimately decided to use radio telemetry, I gave them a budget within a week.

Hale called me in August to say the project had been approved. He also informed me that he was going to start the paperwork for hiring a director and asked if I would still be interested in the position. He didn't seem surprised when I said, "Yes."

Somehow, I was not surprised to learn that in the seven or eight months since I had submitted the proposal, the agency had expanded the project to include telemetry work. Almost in passing, Jim pointed out that the budget had not changed to reflect this important strategic decision. The inadequate budget meant the person hired for the position would have to be laid off for four months in the first year of the project.

At about this time, a federal trapper, working under the newly approved cooperative agreement between the U.S. Fish and Wildlife Service and DNR to study Wisconsin's wolves, arrived to collar some wolves.

He succeeded. He captured three Wisconsin wolves within the Bear Lake territory in October 1979 and outfitted them with radios. Unfortunately, sometime shortly after the trapper left one wolf to sleep off the effects of the drugs used to safely handle and collar it, a grouse hunter shot the poor wolf. Another was shot illegally on the opening day of the state's annual deer season, and the third disappeared mysteriously a few weeks later. The signals of all three had gone dead within a month of the wolves' capture. These events turned the tepid support for a wolf telemetry study into resolute opposition from the district's wildlife management staff.

Yep, I thought, this is sure going to be fun. What the hell am I getting myself into?

Dreis reminded me that telemetry work was out of the question. "Not after that fiasco this fall," Bob said, pointing his finger at me in a warning of sorts.

He felt the radio collars made the wolves more conspicuous than usual and thus more likely to be targets. This, Bob assured me, was intolerable. I most certainly agreed that killing a species on both state and federal endangered species lists was intolerable. But I had the feeling Dreis was referring to the collars, whereas I was referring to the despicable act of killing an endangered animal.

Dreis, for all the rhetoric, was blowing smoke, though perhaps he didn't know it at the time. The collars were black and blended well with the wolf's grizzled grayish-brown coat, making it difficult to comprehend how an undiscriminating boor carrying a gun—who didn't give a rip about wolves—would somehow actually *notice* that the wolf was wearing a radio collar.

Concern over collars aside, Dreis and his staff took to heart their responsi-

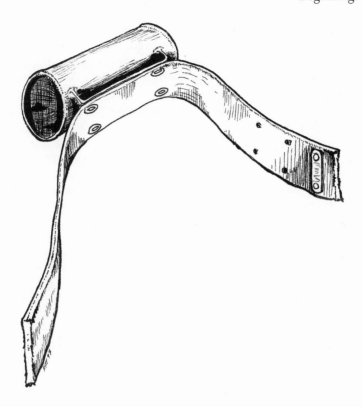

bility to this endangered resource. They were perhaps pessimistic about the prospects for the long-term survival of wolves in Wisconsin and felt that nothing short of Herculean protective efforts would do much good. They were afraid that doing anything that might publicize that a few wolves remained in the northwest corner of the state would only incense the public and probably accelerate their extinction.

I understood these apprehensions. Their misgivings about radio telemetry work revealed that these wildlife officials were not only frustrated but concerned about the wolves' welfare.

In my opinion, however, doing something was better than doing nothing at all. Besides, as employees of an agency whose mission it is to "preserve, protect and promote the wise use" of our state's natural resources, I felt (albeit naively) it was our duty to try anything that might prevent the timber wolf from once again disappearing from the state. Gaining knowledge was the first crucial step in preserving the wolves.

Dreis finished his monologue. I figured it wasn't the right time to argue about telemetry collars, so I mumbled a muffled "uh-huh" and let him think he was squelching my ambitions regarding telemetry. Then he gave me a tour of headquarters and briefly introduced me to the higher-ups.

After the tour he led me to a dilapidated two-story building behind a red pine plantation at the rear of the headquarters compound. Yellow paint hung in ragged sheets from the concrete block outer walls, a reminder of the building's better days as part of the old Wisconsin Conservation Department. Beneath the yellow paint was an even earlier government color—baby vomit green.

Dreis escorted me to the second floor (the first floor was a garage) where a motley collection of fish researchers, water quality biologists, and district pilots had their offices. These workers were gathered around a coffee table, trading opinions of the Super Bowl game, making Dreis's task of introducing me a bit easier.

Finally, I was shown to an empty desk in a bleak room on the east end of the building, across the stairway from the central meeting room where coffee breaks were obviously held. Stacked on my desk was an assortment of dusty cardboard boxes filled with ancient Wisconsin Conservation Department reports on fish. I tried to convince myself the worst was over, but somehow I knew this job would have its share of great challenges.

The first wolf study attempted within Wisconsin had occurred nearly thirty-five years earlier. In the mid-1940s a group of dedicated biologists had secretly monitored wolf activity while they were studying deer ecology. They included Bill Feeney, the deer project leader, and Bernie Bradle and Dan Thompson, both biologist assistants.

Feeney, Bradle, and a handful of other biologists kept their work secret because wolves were very unpopular among sportsmen of the day. In the mid-1970s I wrote to Feeney and he summarized their work for me:

> As you know, we did some extensive work on timber wolves back in the Forties, but my field notes and records were misplaced and some lost in a fire. We followed wolves in Iron Co., Vilas Co., Florence, Forest and Oneida Counties, and studied their movements, range, and feeding habits. I believe we estimated no more than twenty in Wisconsin at that time. Probably less. We found one den with 5 cubs in Iron Co. The work we did we considered very fascinating at the time. We were afraid that trappers would cause its extinction, but we thought it a most desirable predator and that it should be protected in the remote parts of Wisconsin as long as possible.

Bradle also had something to say about wolves in the twilight of their existence in northern Wisconsin:

You mention in your letter the status of the wolf here in the early 1950's; already this animal was badly on the way out at that time. Protection came too late as is always the case. Timber wolf sign and observations of any amount which I observed occurred before the mid 50's and then, too, it wasn't an occasional family group as did occur prior to 1950.

Dan Thompson completed his master's thesis on the food habits of two family groups of wolves living in western Oneida County and central Iron County. He published his results, along with a plea for the species' preservation, in the *Journal of Mammalogy* in 1952.

Writing in 1950, Thompson hit on perhaps the most important factor affecting the preservation of wolves—the effect of human access on wolf habitat:

In some instances these demands [to gain public access to state fire lanes] are justifiable in terms of the general public's transportation needs, but some of this pressure is from small local interests such as resorters, sportsmen and trappers who are anxious to have easy access by car into the few remaining natural areas. In the timber wolf range, the opening of each new section of closed fire lane area to public travel harasses the existence of the wolves. . . . If this trend continues, the timber wolf will eventually face extirpation in Wisconsin.[1]

Thompson became a professor of wildlife biology. Feeney left the Wisconsin Conservation Department in disgust in 1948, frustrated by the incessant bickering between wildlife administrators and hunters about the state's deer management policy. Bradle became one of the first Wisconsin game managers and was stationed in Crandon where, within ten years, he witnessed the demise of a local family group of wolves he had studied in the mid-1940s.

During the early 1950s Bradle frequently worked with a newcomer to the Conservation Department, John Keener, who had been hired as a forest habitat biologist. Both men kept track of the few family groups of wolves that remained in the state. They were discouraged by what they found. In 1955 Keener wrote a piece on the wolf entitled, "The Case for the Timber Wolf," in a popular outdoors magazine, the *Wisconsin Conservation Bulletin*. The opening paragraphs of Keener's article summed up the situation:

"To be or not to be" is the question presently facing the timber wolf in Wisconsin. . . .

In Wisconsin timber wolves are now found in only four or five localities of the northern counties. . . .[2]

Keener's article moved several state legislators, who attempted to enact laws to remove the timber wolf from the bounty list. They eventually succeeded but not before the last of Wisconsin's big wolves had been killed.

In a sense, these men had been the original keepers of the wolves. They were working to preserve the species in Wisconsin at a time when doing so was very unpopular. The hunting public, which footed the Conservation Department's bills through various license fees, loathed anyone who had anything good to say about a wolf. The views of Feeney, Bradle, Keener, and others regarding wolves also were unpopular with the department's upper management, which was ever sensitive to anything that riled the public, including the inevitable assault on that early rural welfare institution, the wolf bounty.

These pioneer biologists tried to persuade people that predators like wolves are not inherently bad. At that time society considered pro-predator philosophies heretical—radical thinking. In those days *conservation* was a word applied primarily to species that were considered game. Conservation leaders of that era thought they were doing good things for future generations by exterminating the wolf.

Thus the wolf disappeared. And we have inherited a far poorer natural world. Yet we are sometimes presented with opportunities to remedy a mistake of the past.

I thought about Feeney, Bradle, and the others as I cleaned off the desk and straightened out my quarters. If wolf recovery was possible in Wisconsin, now was the time to find out. The wolves were returning on their own. My task was to find out where they were, how many there were, and how well or poorly they were faring in the north woods.

One thing was obvious. Wisconsin had a rare shot at a second chance. This time, I thought, we had to be prepared to deal intelligently and effectively to ensure the wolves' conservation within the forested region south of Lake Superior. This time Wisconsin was *not* going to fail.

The First Winter

Two days after I arrived in Spooner, I made arrangements to board with an elderly lady who lived in a modest home there. I had a bedroom and kitchen privileges. This was to be my home for the next three months.

Bob Dreis had made arrangements for me to use a three-quarter-ton, 4-wheel-drive truck assigned to biologists working for the Bureau of Research in Rhinelander. Because they did not need the truck that winter, they had graciously agreed to lend it to Bob. After gasing up each morning at the pump next to the mechanics' shop behind the headquarters building, I would head north for the hourlong drive to the heart of Wisconsin's wolf country and return to Spooner each evening around 4:30 or 5 o'clock.

Tracking in winter is primarily an exercise in perseverance, mostly because of the light conditions. December and January, the dead of winter, provide adequate lighting for tracking for only about six hours a day. The extended twilight casts shadows, obscures tracks, and taunts one's eyes with imaginary wolf tracks, making it useless to track earlier than 9 A.M. or later than 3 P.M. Then there are soothingly pleasant sunny days when the mercury barely reaches 20 degrees below zero. On those days so much light reflects off the crystalline surface of the snowy landscape that it nearly sears your retinas, making tracking truly miserable, especially if the tracker is prone to forgetting his sunglasses.

Looking for timber wolf tracks is boring. You never know when or where you are likely to encounter signs. It doesn't help that this particular critter is exceedingly rare and roams huge parcels of forested land.

I literally spent hours, days, and sometimes a week or more cruising backcountry lanes, searching for faded footprints of the big wolves. Despite the tedium, I did encounter wolf sign. When I did, I pulled out my maps, plotted the wolves' location and direction of travel, and determined whether I should put on my snowshoes and trail the wolves cross-country or go around the block. By that I mean that if the wolf pack crossed into a block of forest I had

not known them to frequent before, I would drive the circuit of plowed lanes to determine whether and where the wolves had exited that block. This was how I learned the approximate boundaries and size of their territories.

Access to a few of the wolves' territories was a problem. The few fire lanes that transected the remote forests inhabited by the wolves were typically unplowed unless someone was harvesting logs from one of them. Using a snowmobile was out of the question because the budget did not have enough money to permit me to buy and operate one. Therefore, many of my daily searches for tracks were restricted to whatever ground I could cover on snowshoes or skis. As a result, I was unable to penetrate the heart of the wolves' domain.

A high priority that first winter was ascertaining how many family groups of wolves were present in Douglas County. I was fairly familiar with the Bear Lake Pack's range. On my first official day in the field I encountered their tracks and scribbled the following observation in my field book:

2 TW [timber wolf] tracks cross Rd heading S[outh]—exactly same place where they crossed in Jan. 1979.

I worked the Bear Lake country periodically throughout the winter and found signs that two or three wolves were still present, despite the loss of the three radioed wolves the previous fall. After verifying the presence of the Bear Lake wolves, I focused on surrounding areas that offered good prospects for finding wolf sign.

The Stateline Flowage Pack straddled the rugged border between Wisconsin and Minnesota. Only one dilapidated fire lane, the one Bob Welch and I had hiked two winters earlier, coursed through what I believed was really the eastern perimeter of their territory. Day after day I cruised fire lanes that penetrated the edges of that vast, roadless chunk of forest—to no avail. As winter progressed, I began to feel frustrated because I could not find the pack.

After several futile weeks I decided a little diversion was in order. During my first week on the job Pat Savage, a wildlife manager, had passed on what he considered a reliable report of wolf activity from a local hound hunter. Evidently, the fellow had encountered tracks of a pair of wolves below the Bear Lake Pack territory south of the St. Croix River and Highway T. The purported activity was not in a region that fit my preconceived notion of what wolf habitat should be, so I had put the report on the back burner.

On Friday, February 8, with the temperature hovering around 5 degrees and light snow falling, I drove out along Highway T toward the crossroads town of Dairyland, which is about the size of a postage stamp. Unlike the forested expanse immediately north of Highway T—where the wolves lived— the locale from which the report had come had quite a few roads. This was pine barrens country—sterile sandy soils covered by jack pine, commercially planted red pine plantations, and scrub oak. The landscape was fairly flat. It had few drainages but was pocked here and there by shallow lakes and ponds.

The roads crisscrossing the terrain gave the surface a checkerboard appearance. Aerial photographs of the region showed that everyone in the area who had ever owned a bulldozer had left their mark during the previous forty years. Solid town roads outlined every square mile. Logging roads carved up the landscape in between.

As I approached the area of the report, I grew more skeptical. Naturally enough, the roads attracted a lot of human activity. Not likely to attract wolves, I thought, as I pulled off blacktopped Highway T onto a well-traveled town road.

Not a hundred yards off the blacktop I found a set of tracks. I stopped the truck, got out, and walked to the edge of the road, stooping to get a closer look. "Wow," I said aloud.

I returned to the truck and continued to slowly drive the town road, stopping at intervals to get closer looks at some exceedingly interesting tracks left by a pair of very big canids.

I spent the rest of the day following their trails. By noon I was convinced that this sign had been made by a pair of timber wolves.

The high number of scent posts they left—urinations and droppings—told me they had recently settled this area. Dave Mech's students, studying newly formed pairs in Minnesota, found that the males raise their legs to urinate much more frequently than do males in established packs. This ensures that neighboring wolves will respect the territories being staked out by the newcomers. Settled packs apparently do not scent mark as frequently because the area they roam has garnered a reputation. I also observed blood in the urine of one of the wolves, indicating a female was present and in breeding condition.

I decided to call them the St. Croix Pair because most of their activity was near the St. Croix River. I was guardedly optimistic that they could survive and become parents. This pair certainly did not mind using the abundant roads. But this also meant the pair would be more visible and vulnerable than their counterparts in the relatively inaccessible forests nearby.

The citizen's report had expanded the number of known wolf groups in Douglas County to three: the Bear Lake Pack, the Stateline Flowage Pack, and the St. Croix Pair. An important find. I was pleased, to say the least.

Douglas County was not the only place that first winter with known wolf activity. We had information that led us to believe that another pack was living about one hundred miles to the east-southeast along the southern rim of Wisconsin's forested region. It was my job to determine wolf activity patterns there as well. I made plans to survey the area in late February.

I arrived in Merrill on Monday, February 25, and met Bill Meier, the wildlife manager in Lincoln County, at the DNR Ranger Station parking lot before I began my survey. Bill introduced me to the fire control staff, then ushered me into a modest meeting room in a corner of the second floor of the old building. There, I met Meier's technician and the Lincoln County forest administrator. I felt right at home—the walls were painted the same baby vomit green as the Fish Research building at Spooner, but the paint was definitely of more recent vintage.

The meeting began after Don Manthei, the wildlife warden, arrived. Meier

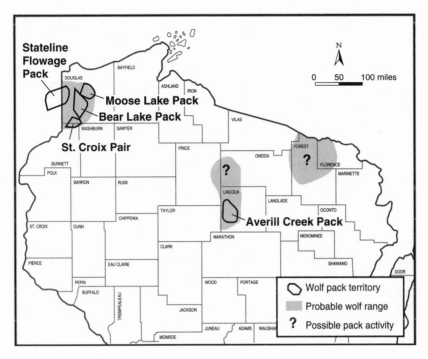

Gray wolf distribution in Wisconsin, winter 1979–80 (Wisconsin Department of Natural Resources)

liked to run a formal meeting and began by discussing its purpose. I was grateful. I had come here to get some fieldwork done and had no idea why Meier had called this meeting.

"I called you here today to provide an update on the status of the New Wood wolf pack, and to introduce Dick Thiel, who is working with wolves for the department up in Douglas County. He is going to be here throughout the week, working with us to get a better handle on things out in New Wood."

Bill reviewed the events that had led to my arrival in Merrill. In July 1979 a pulp cutter had struck a large coyote-like canid that bolted from the brush in front of his pickup truck on a dusty fire lane at midday. He brought the dead animal to the ranger station. Experts from the U.S. Fish and Wildlife Service identified the mysterious creature as a yearling female timber wolf. That November a youthful deer hunter had killed another yearling wolf from a deer stand about three miles west of where the first wolf had died.

In January Manthei and Meier had found signs that a good-sized pack was roaming the area, but they had no idea how many wolves there were.

Bill then turned the show over to me. I told the group that my work responsibilities included determining the status of wolves throughout the state. "I'm here to conduct some winter track surveys and to get familiar with the New Wood and its wolves."

The staff had set the week aside to work with me. I was happy to learn this, because running routes in unfamiliar terrain is slower work. We coordinated routes and laid out a plan to methodically survey the haunts of the mysterious pack.

That afternoon Manthei took me out for a view of this unique forested region. New Wood, as it is called, was so named because loggers turned to it in desperation at the turn of the century after the state's great pineries had been reduced to lumber, slash, and sawdust. White pine was not as common here as the hardwoods and hemlock that grew from its heavy clay soils. Termed *new wood,* the hardwoods could be marketed as veneer for furniture, and the bark of hemlock was rendered into tannins for use in the tanning industry.

New Wood's logging boom lasted from 1910 to the 1930s. Several logging companies had used narrow-gauge railroads to haul logs from the remote lumber camps to mills in nearby Rib Lake, Merrill, and distant Marshfield. The fire lanes we traversed were nearly all converted railroad grades. Most were closed off by huge steel gates maintained by private hunting estates and the Lincoln County Forest Administration, owners of the forested tracts within.

In many ways the place was similar to the Douglas County wolf range. Both were dominated by heavy clay soils and poorly drained landscape covered by hardwoods, aspen, and ash. Yet this locale seemed an unlikely place for wolves. More than one hundred miles separated New Wood from the Douglas County timber wolf groups. And, so far as anyone could tell, no wolves were living in the area in between.

Though New Wood was lightly roaded, it was far from isolated. This area was a peninsular extension of the more remote "North Woods," hemmed in on the south by the sedate and charming Marathon County dairy farm country and the rougher bush farms to the east and west.

The New Wood forest was also a well-known paradise for anglers and hunters in the Wisconsin River Valley, then populated by 175,000 souls and countless paper mills. It extends from Stevens Point, which is forty-five miles south of Merrill, to nearby Tomahawk. I wondered how long the wolves would persist amid all this human activity. In time we would perhaps learn the answer to this and other questions.

Three days after I arrived, I awoke to a dusting of snow. Enough to obliterate old sign and just enough to leave good imprints. It was still 5 degrees below zero and clear at 8 A.M. We'd found enough old sign in two days to convince me the wolves were there. But I had not been able to determine how many there were. Today we would hit pay dirt.

We split up. Manthei cut fresh tracks of two wolves, Meier found sign of five to seven animals traveling together, and I followed the trail of four wolves, including two that were raised-leg urinating (RLUing). We encountered all these in an area of about six miles square.

The profusion of wolf sign led Manthei and Meier to conclude that two or perhaps three distinct packs were living in the area. I was reluctant to accept this. Why would wolf packs operate so near to each other, especially in a place like Wisconsin, where space is free for the taking?

I mulled over the various options that evening back in my motel room. In my state of exhaustion, I could come up only with two explanations. Either the pack was getting so large (from several years of exceptional reproduction and survival of young) that an amiable split was just then occurring, or we had overlooked something. I opted to make no conclusions for the moment.

A full night's sleep provided for some clearer thinking, and the next morning I had an idea. Meier and Manthei hadn't mentioned the type of scent posts they had followed the previous day. That information just might be helpful in determining how many packs we were dealing with. I determined to reinspect the wolves' trails to find out.

In Wisconsin packs consist of an adult male and female wolf—the alphas—and their offspring. Because Wisconsin packs are essentially single families, the alphas are the only breeders. Wolves become sexually mature in two years, breed in February, and give birth to five or six pups in April. Two generations of offspring live with the parents: the newborns are called pups, and those born the previous year are called yearlings (they are between one and two years old). Also, only the alphas, both male and female, raise their legs to urinate; other wolves recognize this as part of the alphas' lexicon in maintaining their territory. Subordinate wolves in the pack—the pups and the yearlings—do not RLU. Irrespective of gender, they *squat* to urinate.

Meier and Manthei bowed out of Friday's surveys, and I took the opportunity to inspect the sign they had found. Manthei's pair and the group I had followed produced RLUs at regular intervals. These wolves behaved as alphas. The group of five to seven wolves followed by Meier produced only two squat urinations over a mile, although they had crossed two major fire lanes, where dominant wolves are likely to mark their territory.

Manthei encountered his wolves' RLUs in the forest west of Highway E. They had been traveling east toward the highway. Unfortunately, the road had been plowed, making it almost impossible to ascertain whether the pair had

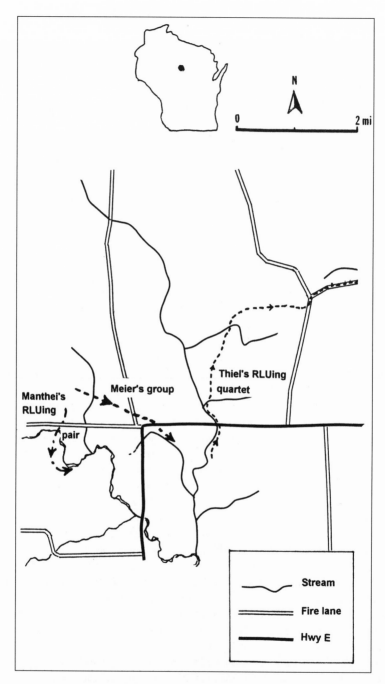

Averill Creek Pack movements, 29 February 1980

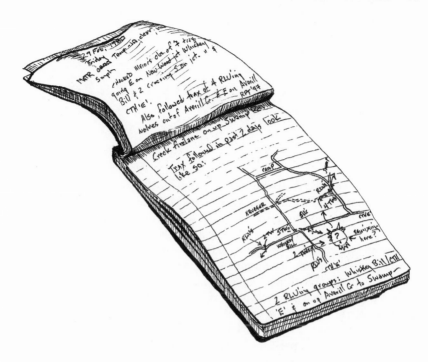

crossed east of Highway E into the block of forest where I had encountered RLUing wolves. Meier had followed his squat-urinating group in the same block of forested land as Manthei's RLUing pair. Meier's pair had crossed east of Highway E into the forest from which my group had emerged.

As I headed south toward home that Friday afternoon, I sorted through the evidence. It seemed likely the pack had split temporarily before crossing Highway E at some point before Manthei and Meier encountered their respective subgroups. The alpha pair had followed a different route across the highway. After crossing the highway, these groups had reunited, shuffling members. Eventually, four wolves, including the alphas, had headed north along the Averill Creek drainage area, where I encountered them. The remainder stayed behind, south of the road. This sequence of events fit the one-pack theory.

If Manthei's RLUing pair did *not* cross the highway heading east, the area might contain an established alpha pair and some wayward two-year-old offspring eager to go off on their own. If this was the case, the pack was in the process of splitting into two packs, one with four and the other with eight to ten.

Days like these made the job exciting. Wolf tracking was challenging, like being a detective. It had been a hell of an interesting week.

Dust, Mosquitoes, and a Few Collared Wolves

The 1980 winter season came to a soggy halt in early March. Temperatures moderated. Southerly breezes clashing with cool arctic fronts created the unending series of miserable rains typical of spring in Wisconsin. The moisture-laden fronts created chaos in the backcountry. Forest roads became sloppy as the frost began working its way out of the ground. By mid-morning the fire lanes were an impregnable quagmire of muck and ruts.

Backwoods road conditions deteriorated quickly, denying me the opportunity to complete the winter surveys I had planned within the Stateline Flowage Pack's territory. I had also been eager to investigate the Moose Lake block northeast of the Bear Lake area. I suspected another group might be living in that area because of persistent reports of wolf activity there, but scientific protocol demanded that I supply the proof. But further exploration of wolf activity within these two areas would have to await dryer conditions.

Meanwhile, I worked out of the Spooner office, preparing summaries of the winter's activities. The data I had accumulated during the winter, while meaningful, was nowhere near the quantity or quality of data a radio-collaring program could provide. I needed to convince Bob Dreis and others on his staff of the merits of such work.

Dreis had been clear about what he thought of radio collaring. He probably would not agree to rethink the issue. It was time to bring in the big guns. I called Steve Fritts, who was in charge of the U.S. Fish and Wildlife Service's wolf-monitoring program outside the Superior National Forest and the wolf depredation control program, both in Minnesota.[1] He had agreed to serve as an adviser to the Wisconsin wolf project. Would he meet with the Northwest District staff to discuss the pros and cons of telemetry?

Steve thought it was a good idea. Mustering what courage I could, I headed over to the headquarters building, prepared to argue my way into obtaining Dreis's consent for this meeting. Bob put up a good fight, but I remained steadfast. "You owe it to yourself, the resource we're here to protect, and to the project to weigh the pros and cons before making such a decision," I told him.

Again, he brought up the deaths of the three wolves. "Two wolves," I interjected. "You and I know the third wolf disappeared *following* the deer gun season. Fact is, we don't know what happened to it. It may have been killed, the batteries in its radio may have malfunctioned, or it might still be alive, having simply moved out of the area our pilots were searching."

Bob glanced at the bulletin board in front of his desk. A moment later he looked at me and said, "Well, you're right about that. I flew with the pilots the last time we had it, and it was getting out of the area considered wolf range. But that still leaves the other two animals."

"Yes, and the death of one of these could have been the result of a poor decision made while handling it." I was referring to the discovery of the first collared wolf near its release point. It evidently was still groggy from the effects of the tranquilizers used to handle it when the grouse hunter came along and shot it.

"If this was a judgment error, it can be corrected so it won't happen again. And, as for the other wolf—it was killed on the opening day of deer season. You and I both have to admit this shouldn't come as a surprise, given the attitude some hunters have toward predators—especially wolves," I reminded him.

"We're in the business to find out just what is happening to our wolves. Radio telemetry has already given us a glimpse of the dangers wolves are exposed to, whether we'd like to admit it or not. Without telemetry we are short-changing our expectations of what can come out of this project."

Bob leaned back in his chair and placed his hand on his chin, contemplating what I had just said. I knew he knew my argument made sense.

"I still think the collars make them more conspicuous, but I'm willing to sit down and talk it out with you and Fritts," he told me. "However, at this point, it doesn't change a thing. I'm still opposed to collaring." We agreed the meeting should be in two weeks and settled on a location.

On March 27 the group assembled at the Grantsburg DNR Ranger Station. Jim Hale represented the Office of Endangered and Non-Game Species in Madison. Dave Mech and Steve Fritts came over from the Twin Cities, representing the U.S. Fish and Wildlife Service. Bob Dreis, wildlife managers Fred Strand and Don Bublitz, and I drove over from Spooner.

Fritts and Mech described the techniques associated with radio telemetry, from trapping, drugging, and handling wolves to flying and searching for collared animals. Telemetry, they argued, was a far better tool for gaining baseline population data than any other technique at the command of wildlife biologists.

Strand, who had immediate jurisdiction over wildlife programs in the area of the Douglas County wolves, fired off some pointed questions regarding handling of trapped wolves. He was trying to figure out how to avoid a repeat of the grouse hunter's killing of the first wolf.

The report of that wolf's death included the results of the necropsy. Mech explained that the trapper found the wolf in the first set of traps he checked that day. It took him nearly an hour and a half to process the wolf. Because he needed to check his other traps, he placed the wolf in a secluded spot well off the fire lane and left. He had in fact caught another wolf and processed that one as well. "So, you see, he had good reason to be anxious to move on," Mech said. "He did the best he could have done."

Dreis expressed concern about the proper procedures for protecting these highly endangered animals. He questioned the wisdom of capturing wolves when the risks were so high.

"I would tend to agree," Fritts commented, "but there are things that can be done to minimize the risks. For instance, all traps are checked daily regardless of weather or other circumstances. Since the concern here seems to focus on what happened to the wolf after it was left, we could have the trapper wait until it's fully recovered and up. We could also take it to an area farther off the beaten path, where it would be almost impossible for anyone to encounter it while it is still recovering."

I interjected, "And we could confine our trapping campaign to the spring of the year when there are no hunters afield. It seems to me we haven't focused attention on the fact that the season in which this unfortunate incident occurred might have played a role in the wolf's destruction. Fall is clearly not the best season of choice for collaring wolves in a place like Wisconsin."

A few heads shook in agreement. Then the discussion shifted to the public's unfavorable reaction to any information that wolves were living nearby. Dreis felt that any official disclosure of their existence, almost inevitable if the state established a formal radio telemetry program, would make the wolves even more vulnerable.

"Acknowledging the wolves' existence would provide no startling revelation. The people in a position to kill wolves already know they're there," I said. "By coming clean with the public regarding the wolf program, we're sending a message to the public that we know what's going on out there, and such a pronouncement will serve notice that we'll be watching. Without telemetry we won't be able to keep track of what is happening to the wolves."

Mech added, "I'd have to agree. Most people are unfamiliar with telemetry, and with the DNR acknowledging its use, I think citizens would be a bit more hesitant to kill a wolf, knowing the possibility exists the animal in their gun sights is being remotely monitored."

Fritts reiterated, "The advantages of using telemetry are immense. This technique would not only yield information on pack sizes, territories, and spacing but on mortality trends. Information on the causes of death could be shared with the public. This might possibly improve their awareness of the problems confronting this endangered species. It might help change some of the old views toward this predator in time to make a difference."

Then we discussed whether radio collars made their wearers more vulnerable, but this theory was dismissed because the collars are black and blend in with the wolves' fur.

By late morning we had reached a consensus. The DNR would move forward assertively, acknowledging the existence of wolves in Wisconsin because (1) it was only right to acknowledge the study, its purpose, and the reasons for working with this endangered species; (2) we needed to keep the public informed of what we were finding if we were ever to gain public support for wolves; and (3) by publicly acknowledging that the DNR was monitoring Wisconsin's isolated wolf population, we were sending a message that the state would not tolerate the slaughter of wolves.

Bob Dreis and the Northwest District wildlife staff agreed that we should trap and collar five wolves. To avoid problems with hunters we would confine the trapping to the nonhunting seasons, primarily spring and summer. There was one proviso: if any of these wolves were killed by humans and even the slightest suspicion arose that the collars had made the animal more conspicuous, the entire telemetry program would be terminated. Period.

This condition was better than no collaring program. I accepted it, hoping, of course, that no small-minded schmuck would encounter a wolf, kill it, and snuff out the telemetry work. Dreis and his staff were putting their trust in me. I, on the other hand, was putting my trust in the hands of fickle-minded citizens. I would keep my fingers crossed the entire year.

We planned the trapping operation carefully. Mech agreed to supply five radio collars. Fritts lent me one of his premier trappers, Tom Meier.

I had already spent nearly half the annual budget for my project. The remainder had to pay for my lodging and travel during the collaring as well as the weekly flights to locate any wolves we managed to capture and collar. By good fortune, the fire control crew at the Minong Ranger Station offered me the use of their station as a base for the project. I gratefully accepted.

On a warm day in early May 1980 I drove up to the station and introduced myself to the guys who ran it. The building was tucked in among some plump aging spruces on the east side of Minong, about twenty-five miles north of Spooner.

After introductions, Bill Scott, the fire ranger, showed me to my room, a small, dimly lit office on the second floor. A cot was pushed up along the far wall, and a closet and some cabinets adorned one of the side walls. "We don't have much, but you're welcome to use what we have," he said. In another room on the second floor was a small kitchen, complete with a stove, refrigerator, cabinets, and cooking utensils. In another area of the building was a bathroom with an old metal-cased shower stall, paint hanging in shreds amid crusty patches of rust. These arrangements would do just fine. I settled in.

Bright and early the next morning I drove nearly one hour north and west to meet Tom Meier in southwestern Douglas County near the Minnesota border. Dairyland, our rendezvous point, was a little speck on the map along Highway 35 on the southern edge of the Douglas County timber wolf range. Its name seemed strangely out of place in this wild, wooded land. The name reflected the dreams and aspirations of hardy pioneers who sought to transform the cutover country and hard clay soils into the envy of the state's dairy industry. It didn't quite work out that way. I thought it ironic that wolves—bane of farmers and ranchers—were staking claims to the territory around Dairyland now.

Meier was waiting for me. He was about thirty, lean, of medium height, and had sandy brown hair and a beard. Like many people whose passion lies with the outdoors, he was comfortable working alone, tended toward the quiet side, and had a great sense of humor. He was also someone who preferred to operate on his own, a lone wolf, you might say. Tom was to be my instructor, here to assist in the trapping effort and to show me how to do it. He was damned good at it.

We spent the day cruising fire lanes, looking for wolf sign and testing the roads to learn where the potholes were and which ones we could drive. The dense reddish-brown clay soil covering western Douglas County repulses water, and in many places the fire lanes were scarred by early spring freshets that poured forth from the forest, seeking low spots in which to collect. Even where the old woods roads wound through upland stands of aspen and balsam fir, the spring runoff had carved away at the roadbeds, making travel treacherous and tedious.

Once in a while we'd find the disintegrated remains of a scat, full of deer hair, which we supposed had been deposited by a wolf months before. Coming to the end of one lane, we hit the blacktop and headed toward County Trunk M, a seventeen-mile stretch of desolate paved road that connects Highway 35 and Highway 53 (for what reason I know not). Three miles out of Moose Junction, a nearly uninhabited collection of ramshackle buildings in the heart of wolf country, we turned toward the Empire Swamp Trail, headquarters of the Bear Lake Pack.

The trail was rough, but Tom's aged government truck negotiated the ruts and washouts in good shape. The trail meanders for its entire eight miles, keeping as much as possible to the high ground, which in this country is a rare thing. At an old beaver pond, most likely created when fill was placed over a small creek to make the trail, we cut our first good sign—a pair of wolf tracks heading north. The tracks were old, maybe two weeks or more, and they were baked into the hardened mud of the trail. Here and there the spoor faded away, only to reappear around the bend or up a couple tenths of a mile, stamped into the ground on a night when the earth was soft. We followed the intermittent tracks for about 1.5 miles before the tracks vanished without a hint as to where the wolves had left the trail.

The sign we did uncover looked good, and a search of a few more woods trails within their territory assured us that wolves were active in these parts. We were encouraged.

The next day, May 8, we laid steel—no. 4 Newhouse double long springs, the Cadillac of foothold traps. Tom had carefully boiled each in a cauldron of water and tag-alder bark to remove all human scent. We wore rubber gloves as we removed them with a stout stick and packed them carefully in a wooden box lined with freshly trimmed balsam fir boughs. His trapping equipment included a geology pick, a screen box for sifting dirt, a trowel, and a soiled length of muslin. In a separate box was an assortment of little bottles filled with the glands—the musk and scent of various animals—with which he hoped to attract an unsuspecting wolf. Quite an aroma arose each time we opened that box.

After driving perhaps three miles over a rutted and abused fire lane, Tom stopped. He had spied a huge pile of soil that a logging skidder had kicked up some years before. "That'll do nicely," he said. He marched back to the truck, put on his gloves, grabbed two traps and other paraphernalia, and returned to the dirt clump. Tom laid down the muslin and knelt upon it. Then he used the pick to quickly dig a hole shaped exactly like the trap he had just set.

A quarter-inch beneath the soil lurked two traps with eight-inch jaw spreads. The weight of a paw on the pan between the jaws would instantly trip the mechanism, securing a grip on a naive canid's paw. When caught, the animal pulls the contraption out of the hole. As it does this, the trap unfolds a chain with a drag. The animal runs off but the chain and drag snag on a small tree or shrub, which absorbs the shock of the animal's lunges and minimizes the likelihood the animal will be injured. Because wolves are so wary and cannot be enticed into enclosed quarters, we could not use a box trap.

He threw a handful of dirt on top of the trap, "to muffle any sound of metal on metal as the animal puts weight down," he told me. As he lowered the trap into the hole, he shifted it back and forth to make sure it wouldn't rock, taking care to keep his fingers away from the interior portions of the spread jaws. As one of the final steps in setting the trap, he tucked a small plastic bag into the dirt around the jaw; springing the trap sent the Baggie flying. When we checked our trapline, seeing the Baggie atop disturbed soil near the trap site was often our first clue that we had caught something.

When he finished, the trap was completely hidden with dirt, although it looked rough compared to the surface around the site. To remedy this Tom fetched from the truck a spray bottle filled with creek water. After a few pumps the moistened soil melted; when it dried, it was impossible to tell the site had ever been disturbed.

Twenty-five minutes later both of his traps were ready.

He had placed a trap on either side of the clump so as to catch a wolf approaching from either direction on the trail. He quickly punched two holes in the clump that were the size of his finger, then put scent from his scent box in one hole to "bring 'em in." In the other hole he put a bit of bait—a portion, no bigger than a kidney bean, of his favorite recipe of dead animal parts— and covered it with a rock "to tease 'em a bit," he said.

"That ought to do it," he exclaimed as he tidied up the sets with a back-handed brush of his glove. "Wolves have real sensitive feet. They can feel the slightest inconsistency in the surface. You don't want to give 'em the advantage. There's enough expense taken to put these things in. You don't want to muff it once you get 'em to come in on your bait."

He was right. Trapping is a blend of art and science. It turns on the ability to lure a wolf into placing its paw within a bit of turf sixty-four inches square within a territory that covers more than a hundred square miles. Still, this was exactly how the old-time trappers had eliminated Wisconsin's wolves.

We worked hard and laid out fifteen sets of traps that day. With expert coaching from Tom, I was able to sink four Newhouse traps. We called it quits at about seven that evening. Tom dropped me off and I headed home to the Minong Ranger Station to snuggle into my sleeping bag. Before turning in, I called Bob Dreis to invite him to run the line with us the next morning. He eagerly agreed.

Bob and I met at the ranger station at 5:45 A.M. and met up with Tom about forty-five minutes later. Soon we were banging our way into wolf country.

About a mile out we spotted the faint fresh skiff of a wolf's paw in the dust on the trail. It was headed north toward our traps. As we neared our first set, my heart began to pound. The sluggish pace of our truck was torture as we neared the site.

The trap was gone. All we found was a gaping hole in the ground.

Tom jumped from the truck and peered into the hole just as I spotted some brush moving beneath an old yellow birch tree alongside the trail. A red fox peered passively from behind the trunk of the great tree. I alerted Tom, who reached into the box in the bed of the truck and withdrew an aluminum choke-snare pole with which to handle the little fellow.

The fox lay perfectly still as we approached it. Tom delicately slipped the snare beneath its chin, wriggled the loop behind its ears, and cinched down on the cable that ran through the pole. The fox jumped, but Tom pushed the pole down, pinning it to the ground. With the fox thus subdued, I was able to reach down, depress the springs of the trap, and lift its foot from the jaws. We quickly made sure it hadn't been injured. A few seconds later the fox was running through the glade beneath the maple trees, looking miffed at its encounter with us.

Another set lay up the trail, not another fifth of a mile away.

The great wolf's paw prints still headed north. Again, my heart pounded with anticipation. After an eternity of bends, hills, and low spots we came to the second set.

"Trap's gone!" Tom exclaimed.

"Coyote!" Bob cried as our eyes fell upon the gray figure of a canid hunched up along the trunk of a gigantic maple tree.

"We're working our way up the canine scale," I joked. "First, a red fox, second trap a coyote, next trap maybe we'll get our wolf." That was wishful thinking, and I knew it. I'm sure Tom had the same thought.

We gave the coyote a pair of shiny ear tags bearing identification numbers and an address, should a human find it again for whatever reason. This might give me some rudimentary information on the movements of coyote in and near wolf range.

The third trap held a skunk. We had to shoot it with our .22 rifle. It got the parting shot. It so stank up our trap that it was worthless for use on wolves.

As we left, Tom commented that he rarely encountered so much action on a trapline. I knew he was preparing me psychologically for the inevitable letdown. After all, it was hardly likely we'd capture a wolf on the first night after the line had been established.

Still, the wolf's tracks dogged on ahead, tormenting us. I could sense that Bob was excited too.

After another mile the truck climbed to the top of a prominent hill. I noticed an old logging tote trail that forked off the lane. Something was wrong. "Tom, wasn't our fourth set *below* the hill?" I asked. He stopped and consulted our trap notes. "Yep, we've overshot it."

He backed the truck up to the spot where our fourth and fifth traps had been. "Wolf!" Tom exclaimed, and I spied a stoic figure beneath several pole-sized birch and maples. The animal was hung up (the trap was snagged on one of the trees) about fifty feet off the trail, peering intently at us. We'd passed right by without seeing it.

I couldn't believe it. Finally, face to face with an actual live Wisconsin timber wolf. I'd dreamed of a day like this, never quite believing it would ever really happen. Who would have believed ten years earlier that anyone would be trapping and collaring timber wolves in Wisconsin? Yet here we were, and there was our wolf.

It stood rather dejectedly, ears flattened back, tail tucked beneath an arched back supported by long, lanky legs. It looked scrawny—not at all like those picturesque paintings that make the wolf appear so regal.

Its penetrating dusky yellow eyes never left us. Skinny, awful skinny, I thought, but a beaut just the same. It was dressed in its short summer coat, making its massive head look all the more impressive.

Tom went to work. I simply stared, admiring this creature. In a flash, Tom prepared the tranquilizer dart by pouring about three cc's of a muscle relaxant into a hollow cylinder, then twisted the hollow needle tip securely in place. He dropped the dart in the chamber of the air pistol as he slowly approached the wolf, motioning me to circle around to its other side.

The wolf's hind end slunk lower as its eyes swept nervously back and forth between the two of us. Tom needed a good shot at its butt, but the wolf was not cooperating. I made several swift movements with my hands that momentarily caught the wolf's attention, exposing its vulnerable spot. Tom aimed and fired. The wolf didn't flinch when the dart smacked into its left ham. Glancing at his watch, Tom softly said to himself, "Oh-eight, oh-one" and retreated to the truck.

In hushed voices Tom, Bob, and I discussed the pros and cons of moving our wolf-processing deeper into the woods. Our concern was that some wolf hater might happen upon us while we were engrossed in our work.

This seemed the best course of action. Bob agreed to stay behind and watch the wolf as the drugs took effect. Tom and I drove up the hill and down the trail about two hundred yards. I helped him unload the processing gear, scale, tarp, and radio equipment. We hastily set up a work area, then raced back to the trap site.

The wolf was still standing—but just barely. With glassy eyes and massive head bobbing up and down, it was trying to maintain an alert stance in front of its human enemies. It succumbed slowly, slipping to the ground, head still bobbing. Ten minutes after it had been darted, the wolf appeared to be out cold.

We approached the wolf cautiously, taking care not to step within the circle, the area within the radius of the trap anchor. Tom extended the choke-snare pole and pushed the wolf at the shoulders and base of the head. No reaction. It was safe to move in.

The wolf had been caught on its right front and left hind feet. This was a bit unusual, as wolves are usually caught by only one foot. Tom had placed two sets next to each other so the wolf could not avoid capture by approaching the lure from behind.

I picked the wolf up, and Tom and Bob worked together to remove the traps from its feet. We first inspected its feet to make sure they were not injured and found that the trap had amputated one of its toes. We treated it with disinfectant, then placed the wolf gently in the bed of the truck for the quick ride down the woods trail. We felt awful that the wolf had lost a toe, but the telltale paw print from then on would prove invaluable in helping us track this wolf.

Our wolf was a handsome male, probably two or three years old. It stood about thirty inches at the shoulder and weighed sixty-seven pounds—light for it size. I was surprised to see that its fur was loaded with ticks, especially around its eyes and ears. Then I remembered that dogs aren't exactly fastidious. And the ticks sure didn't seem to be bothering this wolf. Still, we removed as many as we could.

Bob used a rectal thermometer to monitor the wolf's body temperature. Its temperature registered 101.4 degrees Fahrenheit, normal for wolves. In the trauma and excitement of the moment, and because the drugs reduce the panting reflex, wolves frequently become overheated. Tom related that he had once lost a Minnesota wolf to heat stress despite his efforts to counter the effect. Just to be safe, he instructed Bob to cool our wolf by alternately sloshing cold water on its abdomen and fanning the area with a spare clipboard. Its temperature remained steady throughout the processing.

After weighing the wolf, we tagged the bases of its ears near the forehead. These numbered tags provided the means of identifying this wolf as an individual. I filled out DNR's ear tag form: Ear Tag no. 1187 R, 1186 L. Inside the tags was an address, WI DNR, Mdsn WI 53707. If its collar slipped off and the wolf was ever recovered, these tags would identify the wolf. This wolf would be known as 1187.

We also drew about fifty cc's of blood from a large vein in its foreleg. The blood work would tell us the relative health and condition of the animals we had captured. We might also get an idea of the prevalence of various diseases by searching for antibodies to common canid diseases.

Wolf 1187 finally received a radio collar. The black collar consisted of two heavy-duty machine belt straps riveted together to conceal the twelve-inch antenna. At the base of the collar was an aluminum canister, about half the size of a soda can, that held the battery and radio package. We adjusted the collar according to the diameter of the wolf's neck (adult males average eighteen inches), cut off the excess strap, and bolted the two pieces together.

The radio tested perfectly. 1187's radio sent out a sharp, clear, beeping pulse. Within the dense forest its signal strength would be affected by foliage and topography, reducing its range in most cases to less than half a mile. We would rely primarily on airplanes in locating our radioed wolves.

We released wolf 1187 at 9:56 on the morning of May 9, 1980. It had taken almost two hours to process him. We carried him to a shady spot beneath some balsam firs near the processing point and slowly retreated. Bob stayed behind to monitor 1187's recovery, while Tom and I returned to the truck and gathered up all our equipment. About five minutes later Bob emerged from the brush. 1187's head was up and bobbing. He'd be okay.

The weather turned cool that evening, and light rain fell until midmorning, making our trap-checking routine challenging as our truck slid over the back roads. The morning after that—Sunday—the weather moderated. The rain had added an essential ingredient to the forest floor, and the pleasingly dank smell of rotting vegetation rose up in harmonious contrast to the sweet scent of hepaticas, spring beauties, and other delicate spring wildflowers. The rain also brought out stinging hordes of blackflies, providing us with an unpleasant reminder of what the coming months would be like.

That Sunday we found the tracks of two wolves along our route. This evoked some initial excitement. They evidently had taken an evening stroll past several of our sets, ignoring them all. We finished checking the trapline by midmorning and decided to spend the rest of the day scouting other areas.

I was especially interested in the Moose Lake country to the north and east of the Bear Lake range. Two winters earlier a trapper had trapped and shot a large male timber wolf there. Shortly thereafter a DNR forester cut tracks of three wolves in the snow. Wolf reports had trickled in ever since. The only physical feature separating the two areas was a barren stretch of blacktop—Highway A.

We searched the Moose Lake country until seven in the evening and found plenty of wolf sign along the various woods trails. This contrasted with an almost complete absence of fresh sign in the Bear Lake territory. Could this actually be a part of the Bear Lake Pack's territory? Perhaps wolf 1187 could be relied on to help answer this question.

In the first few days after his capture, wolf 1187's signal emanated from the area of the release site. If he was going to help us identify the wolves responsible for making the sign in Moose Lake, he'd have to start moving—and in the right direction. The only other way to solve the mystery was to catch a wolf in the act of making all that sign. We decided to set some more traps.

The Moose Lake country was different than the Bear Lake area. Glacial eskers and other moraine structures gave the landscape a more rugged texture. This was another forgotten corner of the Douglas County forest lands that sprawl across most of the southwestern portion of the county. Spires of majestic balsam fir stretched skyward, their heavily foliated branches mingling with the still bare limbs of the aspen with which they compete for sunlight.

We feverishly laid out a trapline in the Moose Lake block. Now we were babysitting twenty-six traps.

Daytime temperatures were steadily increasing. Warm weather added to the stress wolves experienced when in traps, thereby increasing the risk they might overheat while we were processing them. So we adjusted our schedule and started arriving on the trapline by 6 A.M. Our daily routine included a brief stop to search for wolf 1187's radio signal on the big hill where he had been captured. The day after we laid the trapline in the Moose Lake block, we were unable to locate his signal.

If he went north into Moose Lake country, he would help us identify the wolf pack sign there. But there was no point in trying to find his signal from the ground by driving the few fire lanes that transected that country. Our telemetry equipment was severely limited on the ground. We could reliably pick up a signal no more than a half-mile from the transmitter. In the air, however, our ability improved considerably, to about ten miles.

We decided to scrap the afternoon's scouting plans, return to civilization, and arrange a search flight for the wolf, if that could be done on such short notice. We got lucky. Jim Dienstl, a DNR pilot, was able to book us that morning. We met at the Solon Springs airport, a beat-up swath of a runway cut through the jack pine forest south of town.

Jim was the Northwest District's chief pilot. The thin, brown-haired ex-navy fighter pilot was in his midthirties and was responsible for supervising the activities of two other pilots and a host of LTE pilots who worked seasonally as needed for spotting forest fires.

The fleet consisted of several planes. The plane we flew was a two-seat Piper Cub. Jim sat forward, I sat aft. At six foot-three, I was forced to cross my legs and tuck them beneath my seat to fit myself into the plane. Jim wasn't any more petite. Between the two of us and the equipment we carried, the plane was quite cramped.

I quickly learned that as the sun beats down on the Plexiglass bubble of the cabin, the temperatures begin to soar, especially on hot summer days like this one.

Jim taxied to the far end of the runway, spun the little plane around, and hollered over the roar of the engine that we were taking off. My eyes were fixed on the rapidly approaching jack pines that wrapped around the far end of the field, but the red-and-white Cub lifted safely into the sky with plenty of clearance. In a few moments the landscape beneath us changed from one dotted with the trappings of humans—trailer homes, junked cars, old washing machines, and dirt roads—to an uninterrupted vista carpeted with forests of aspen, maple, balsam fir, and spruce. The deciduous trees did not yet have their new leaves. Here and there I could make out the soft white and purple hues of the spring beauties that carpeted the forest floor. We were headed west toward the desolate surroundings of 1187 and his buddies.

Being the rookie that I was, I had no idea where to start searching for the wolf. We decided to fly over the release area in the hope that we might locate his signal.

Bad choice. I could hear nothing. Worse, I was getting a particularly loud and obnoxious crackling noise from wolf 1187's frequency. I realized it would either completely mask 1187's signal or substantially reduce the distance within which we could pick up the signal. We'd probably have to be nearly on top of him before we could detect the signal.

About two miles south of his release site I suddenly heard a faint "blip-blip" over the staticky din. I thought the wolf was slightly off our starboard wing, so I signaled Jim to turn 30 degrees to the right. As soon as he began the turn, static overwhelmed the signal. We quickly turned back to our original heading, and the signal came through just fine—still to starboard. We decided to stay on this course. The signal gradually grew weaker and faded into the static. We headed two miles west, then turned north and conducted a reverse sweep paralleling our original heading. The signal returned—off our port wing. The wolf was still west of our position.

After repeating this procedure several times, we managed to hold on to its signal. Then we turned and approached the signal head-on.

Within a minute we found 1187 about 3.5 miles southwest of his release point. Although the foliage prevented us from seeing him, we pinpointed his location in a partially drowned ash forest, close to the place on the fire lane where Tom and I had lost the tracks of two wolves the week before. Could this be the pack's homesite? If wolf 1187 was related to the wolves leaving sign up in the Moose Lake block, why had he moved farther away from that area?

As we headed out in the truck to check the trapline the next morning, we discussed whether the activity in the Moose Lake block and that in the Bear Lake territory were from different groups of wolves. "Too bad 1187 didn't head north from his release site. That woulda cinched it for us," I lamented. Tom chuckled as he replied, "Nothing comes that easy in field biology. It's as if the wolves have a mind to make a person sweat a little from the anticipation." I wondered how long it would take to establish whether we were dealing with one or two wolf packs.

About a week after we started, we struck the trapping doldrums. One evening a fast-moving cold front swept down out of Canada, dropping temperatures to the point where it actually spit snow, but by ten the next morning the black-flies had erupted with a fury. We scouted far and wide. Nothing had moved on our lines in the Bear Lake or Moose Lake blocks in seven days. It seemed as if the wolves had simply disappeared.

When I returned to the Minong Ranger Station, I found a message from Bob Dreis. He wanted a report on our progress. He was surprised to learn nothing of significance had happened since the day we caught 1187 and suggested that maybe we needed a little good luck. Because he had been along when we caught 1187, maybe he ought to come up the next morning and change our luck. I chuckled and told him to meet me at the ranger station at five.

That night another cold front swept through, clearing the skies and dropping temperatures below freezing. The sunrise revealed a world blanketed in a delicate layer of hoarfrost. "It was a good night for animal movements, Dick. I feel lucky today," Bob remarked as I greeted him at the door of the ranger station.

In a few moments we were headed down Highway 53 to meet Tom. The three of us soon were clanking our way up the dusty trails that penetrated the heart of Wisconsin's wolf country.

The first ten sets were empty, but we were still optimistic. The next trap held a skunk. Tom decided not to kill it. Instead, he got out a syringe, filled it with tranquilizer, and fastened the apparatus to an aspen pole about eight feet long.

Fully armed (and very vulnerable) he delicately approached the skunk, seducing it with a soothing voice. "Poor kitty, what did you get into? . . . Poor kitty, I'll help you!" Bob and I gave him (and the skunk) a wide berth, peering from behind the truck in amazement as he slowly faced the skunk and gently lowered the syringe until it was just beneath its chin. To our surprise the skunk sidled forward and actually leaned into the needle as Tom inserted it in the skunk's neck. As soon as the drug was delivered, Tom retreated. A minute later Mr. Skunk was asleep. Tom had figured a way to save a skunk and our trap.[2]

An hour later we still had three sets to check. The sun was already high in the sky, the temperature was climbing, and our spirits were sinking. By that point we had all privately concluded that we didn't have much to look forward to.

At the next junction Tom turned the truck west, heading down the lane that led to the Moose River and the remainder of our line. One set—empty. We continued on.

As we came over a small rise, we could see the broad, heavily timbered slopes on the opposite side of the Moose River. The second set lay just over the next knoll on the east rim of the valley. As was his custom, Tom took his foot off the gas as we approached the site and let the truck coast slowly past the set.

Suddenly, he stopped the truck.

"Trap's gone," Tom shouted as the brakes screeched.

We jumped out and heard the chinking of chain in the woods on the opposite side of the trail. The animal had been startled by the sudden appearance of our truck. It danced about, winding round and round a small balsam fir to which the trap drag was firmly anchored. Bob's luck had held. And this wolf was a gorgeous male.

We went to work. He received ear tag numbers 1188 and 1189. At seventy-four pounds this wolf was heavier than 1187, but he wasn't as tall and had a more stout appearance. He was older too, judging from the amount of wear on his incisors. An hour and fifteen minutes later we were ready to release him.

Tom and I carried the critter into a cutover aspen thicket as Bob followed. Wolf 1189's tongue was hanging out and felt dry to the touch. Tom mentioned in passing that he'd sometimes allowed partially drugged wolves to drink, and he thought maybe this guy could handle it. We found a puddle in the tote trail. We strained under the dead weight of the wolf as we leaned it toward the ground, and Tom managed to push its nose down toward the water. It lapped up several mouthfuls before it started fussing over its predicament. Concerned that it might hurt us in this excited and semidrugged state, we decided to hurry to a shaded spot before it became fully conscious. As we put him down, 1189 lifted his head, a sign that he would soon be fully recovered.

Back at the truck, Tom and I decided to remove our traps and head home for four days of vacation. As we worked we speculated whether wolves 1187 and 1189 — caught six miles apart — were pack mates or belonged to two different packs.

By early afternoon the temperature was approaching 75 degrees. Tom pulled up to one of the last sets left in the Moose Lake block. We'd checked it about an hour before we encountered 1189. Tom hollered, "Trap's gone — wolf!"

In a swale carpeted with delicate Canada mayflower and speckled corn lily flowers stood a wolf, caught by a hind foot. We weren't prepared for this psychologically. Out came the dart gun. Swiftly, Tom placed a charge in the tailpiece, loaded the canister with drugs, screwed the needle on, and dropped the projectile into the chamber of the handgun. He closed the bolt with a muffled click, and . . . in apparent reaction to the noise and with one desperate lunge, the wolf pulled free. We stood near the trap, stunned, watching silently as the wolf sauntered quietly off through the sun-dappled forest.

I turned to Tom and lamented, "Wolf trappers, one; wolves, one."

We pulled the rest of our sets and headed home.

We returned to the field four days later as planned, refreshed and raring to go another ten to fourteen days. By midafternoon we were headed toward the Stateline Flowage Pack's territory, an especially rugged patch of forest straddling the Minnesota–Wisconsin border.

This area was about as remote as remote got in Wisconsin. The distance between the only north-south blacktop roads, Highway 35 in Wisconsin and Highway 23 in Minnesota, was about twenty-five miles. Between them were about two hundred square miles of forest, three fire lanes, and a railroad grade.

Our search that afternoon did not yield any promising sign, so we returned the following morning, hopeful of encountering wolf activity along some trails we had not checked the day before. Travel on these lanes was especially slow. Though officially recognized as town roads, most were rarely maintained. Inconsiderate four-wheelers had had a fine time early that spring and had carved a profusion of furrows, some two feet deep, along the entire length of fire lane that Bob Welch and I had walked one cold winter day several years earlier.

The trip was made even worse because the population of biting insects had exploded in the last few days. Mosquitoes were everywhere, waiting in force. Because wolves have very sensitive sniffers, we could not use bug spray while working on the trapline. We were at the mercy of the 'skeeters.

Tom studied some old topographic maps and noticed a trail that ran for a mile across the state line from the end of the West Moose Road in Wisconsin to the Belden Truck Trail in Minnesota. We parked at the dead end and searched for evidence of the old logging trail. All that remained was a game trail. It was being well used. Perhaps wolves might use it in traveling from one fire lane to the next. We decided to scout it out.

The trail traversed several alder swamps that separated some low-lying drumlins (hills of glacial drift) cloaked by a forest of big-tooth aspen. Fortunately for us, beaver had constructed massive dams along the old trail, which helped us keep our boots dry as we hopped from ridge to ridge. Eventually, the terrain opened up. Years earlier Minnesota wildlife managers had created several wildlife openings by bulldozing the aspen forest and piling the twisted trunks in huge rows. Each opening was forty or fifty acres. They were now carpeted in grasses, bunchberry, asters, and goldenrod in season and other sun-loving, moist soil vegetation.

Tom led the way. About halfway through the first field I glimpsed tiny things launching off a blade of grass and grabbing on to Tom's pant leg as he brushed by. I alerted Tom, who casually looked down to see fifteen little wood ticks gleefully scurrying to and fro, trying to reach safe haven beneath a cuff or over the top of his pants. He picked them off, one by one, chuckling as he flicked each back into the grass. I noticed a half-dozen on me. Impressed with the number of ticks, we decided to make a game of who, by evening, would have the most. That evening I penned an entry into my notebook: "What a field day for ticks! I removed 134 from my body & Tom—220!"

We returned to our truck and plodded on, reaching the Summit Trail and exploring its length. Luck was with us. We cut fresh tracks and found several droppings just north of the Stateline Flowage, the willow brush–choked water impoundment that was the namesake of this family group of wolves.

This trail followed a serpentine route over aspen islands and across swampy alder thickets. Strangely, the aspens had not leafed out yet.

About eight miles north of the flowage we stopped the truck to check some sign. As soon as we got out, we became aware of an out-of-place sound in the woods. It sounded like raindrops hitting the dry leaves littering the forest floor. Yet it was a perfectly still, sunny day. I grew curious. Looking around, I noticed black specks peppering the ground everywhere. And crumpled leaves lying on the forest floor were fluttering as if alive.

Tom and I knelt down and placed our heads on the ground, eyes flush with the surface. Looking up the sloping surface of the road, we found the reason for the leafless aspens. Army worms! Millions of them. The forest floor was crawling with yellow-and-green striped bodies. All were headed east across the trail. The black specks dotting the leaf litter were caterpillar droppings. The sounds of raindrops were caused by worms jettisoning themselves from the denuded tops of nearby trees, searching for greener pastures.

In some places the trail was so thickly covered by worms that the road actually became slippery as our tires crushed their bodies. We also noticed an abundance of an odd species of horsefly. Though present in great numbers, they didn't bother us. We wondered whether they were focusing instead on the writhing mass of army worms. We carried on, managing to make it through this invertebrate wonderland.

My confidence at setting wolf traps was growing. I was slinging out traps one-for-one with Tom. As evening approached and the light in the forest was fading, I decided to put out one last trap. The site I selected was in an alder-strewn stretch at the top of the Summit Trail near the Black River. I selected a spot that I felt looked especially appealing to a wolf. I carefully dug the hole and placed the trap within.

As I worked, I was at the mercy of a cloud of blood-thirsty mosquitoes for twenty-five excruciating minutes. When I had the bait—wolf scat and urine—in place, I ran back to the truck, slamming the door quickly to get rid of those evil little tormentors. We logged in trap no. 10 and called it quits for the day. It was 8:30 P.M.

Back at the Minong Ranger Station, I had a message from Bob Dreis. He

and another wildlife manager would be coming along with us to tend traps the next morning. Fine by me, I thought, we could always use some luck.

And his luck held. In that last trap I had set was a beautiful timber wolf—my first capture. We admired the critter from a distance while Tom busily loaded the dart gun. It had traveled not fifteen feet from the trail before the drag caught on the roots of an alder, securing it. The wolf lay still, panting but with an unconcerned expression. Very pale colored, this wolf had almost white sides and a light gray back. Once, when it nervously stood up, I thought I saw a flash of red on the leg in the trap. "Its leg couldn't be broken, could it?" I wondered aloud.

Tom approached the wolf slowly. The alder thicket created such a tangle that it was difficult to maneuver into position. The wolf, skittish on our approach, got up and slowly weaved to and fro, keeping its back end away from

Tom. I managed to work behind the wolf and get its attention. It turned to face me, giving Tom his chance. I also got a closer look at its leg. It was bleeding. I felt sick.

Tom delivered the payload perfectly, high on the inside of its ham. Within ten minutes the wolf was down. We were perplexed by what we found on her left front leg. An open lesion, roughly one inch wide and three or four inches long, ran the length of her foreleg. Below, a similar lesion ran diagonally across her paw and was surrounded by a rim of dark scar tissue. The lesions were bright red, and a clear liquid was slowly draining from their surfaces. Our trap had merely creased the hair on her paw below the lower lesion. The limb was solid; no breaks were evident. Whatever had happened to this wolf had occurred long before she encountered our trap. Hastily, we scribbled, "radius left leg recent fracture (healed)—festered" into the capture log.

She was lovely. Her teeth were well worn, which meant she was older than 1187 and 1189. She sported six well-developed black nipples, so she had probably bred at least once in her life (although not necessarily so).[3] She weighed a petite sixty-two pounds and became known to us as wolf 1191. We felt certain this was the matriarch of the Stateline Flowage Pack.

By this time Bob Dreis had quite a head count to his credit. His score was three trap runs, three wolves. Tom and I laughed. Maybe he was bringing us luck. And, because it was my first timber wolf capture, we decided to quit early and celebrate. We finished the run and headed to the nearest watering hole—one of two taverns that constituted the community of Dairyland. When I left an hour and a half later, I was feeling no pain.

The weather had turned hot over the past several days. Daytime temperatures had soared into the upper 80s and low 90s, unseasonably warm for May. Fire danger reached high levels in the jack pine barrens stretching through portions of Burnett, Washburn, Douglas, and Bayfield Counties, putting DNR fire crews on full alert. A helicopter with a twelve-hundred-gallon bucket was flown in from the Twin Cities and placed on standby at the baseball diamond across from the Minong Ranger Station.

Even the aspen and maple forests in wolf country were hot and dry. Our pilots were able to squeeze in only a single flight the day after we captured 1191. They were concentrating on patrolling for fires. Jim Dienstl and I couldn't locate wolf 1187. His frequency had simply too much static interference, a technological glitch that began to concern me.

We easily located the other two wolves. We found our Moose Lake wolf about a mile north of his capture site near the edge of a beaver pond complex

within an ash and fir forest. Wolf 1191 was three miles west of her capture site on an aspen-cloaked esker in the middle of a sphagnum-spruce bog that measured five square miles.

Four days later Tom connected with a whopper of a wolf. We caught him on the Summit Trail. From his size and where we found him, we concluded he was the mate of 1191, a suspicion subsequently borne out by telemetry monitoring. This wolf, christened 1193, weighed ninety-four pounds—"Second biggest wolf I ever caught," Tom exclaimed. This time Bob Dreis was not along, but my wife, Debbie, was. With two wolves caught and collared in the Stateline Flowage area, we pulled up stakes and moved our line to the Namekagon Barrens region near the famous St. Croix River.

It was 92 degrees on May 27. The dust on the lanes was thick. Our tires kicked up choking clouds of powder that covered the surrounding shrubbery, the

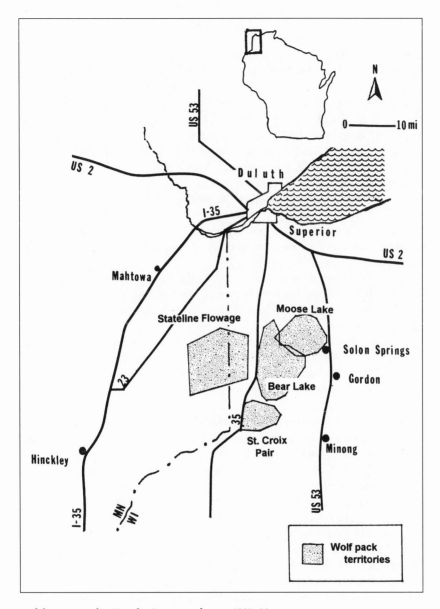

Pack locations within Douglas County study area, 1980–82

truck's interior, our clothing, our bodies, and our lungs. We completed checking our line of ten sets by midmorning, in time to meet Jim Dienstl for a quick flight to locate the four wolves recently radioed. Tom offered to go. I sought the shade of a grove of jack pine near the lone hangar that identified the swath in the forest as a runway.

The two returned around noon, which gave Jim enough time to return to the base at Shell Lake and swap planes for fire patrol work. Tom and I set out again by truck to check on the wolves. Inadequate sleep and searing heat were taking its toll on us. We located an isolated canoe landing along the St. Croix, stripped down to our undershorts, and dived into the cool, dark waters. Our dip provided instant relief from the heat.

The effect was fleeting. Back in the pickup we were sweating profusely within half an hour and were already covered with dust again as we bounced along isolated stretches of fire lane in search of wolf sign. All sign of our quarry had evaporated, as had the many puddles and freshets that had impeded our travel earlier that spring.

Late in the afternoon we went back to the ranger station and met Bob Welch, who had come up to help out on the trapline. We stowed his gear and decided to return to the Namekagon to sink some additional sets before sunset.

Like me, Bob had no previous experience in trapping wolves, but he was willing to try. Under the expert tutelage of Tom and me, Bob sank two sets on a dry, sandy berm along a woods trail near its junction with a town road. Bob had selected the site after spying some week-old wolf tracks only five feet off the trail.

As Bob was applying the finishing touches to his sets, Tom and I returned to the truck and sat in the cab. Tom reached over and turned on the radio, hoping to catch the oldies hour. Above the static on the radio we caught the tail end of a weather report out of Duluth. A dry Canadian cold front was sweeping through the area, dropping temperatures by about 25 degrees. But it was still steaming hot over "the ridge," the area we were in just up and off the Lake Superior basin.

Eventually, Bob returned and stowed the trapping gear in the boxes in the back of the truck. I didn't relish the notion of going back to the ranger station and stewing in the heat of our room, and Tom didn't feel like heading back to his family's cabin for similar reasons. Instead, we headed over to the Dairyland bar for a supper of greasy cheeseburgers and some fries.

On the way over Tom and I told Bob our theories about the Moose Lake and Bear Lake areas. Tom suggested we try howling to the wolves. The technique is relatively simple. Biologists working with wolves use this method to count wolves at night and to determine whether packs have produced pups. Biologists figure out where to howl from the information they glean from the telemetry. Tom explained, "Once a radioed wolf has been on the air long enough, a pattern of locations unfolds. A tight concentration of activity in a tiny area usually reveals a pack homesite—the 'rendezvous site,' as pioneer wolf biologist Adolf Murie coined it." Den sites and rendezvous sites are different. The den, usually earthen and dug by the parents but sometimes a hollow log, is where the pups are born and live for their first six weeks. Once they are too big for the den, the pups occupy a series of rendezvous sites, guarded by a yearling sibling or one parent while the other parent hunts. The pack moves the pups, which are still too young to travel with their parents, to a new site every few weeks because the old one becomes too soiled with feces and the remains of prey. Thus the rendezvous site is like a nursery room without walls.

"Minnesota wolves typically select grassy meadows behind old beaver dams or open stretches along creek bottoms, don't they?" I asked.

"Yeah, up in the remote forested regions of the state. I would expect the wolves' preferences are comparable here because of the similarity in habitat. However, in places where Minnesota wolves are spilling over into farm country, I've seen many rendezvous sites in cow pastures."

Welch jumped in, "How many locations have you gotten on 1187 and 1189?"

"One each, although we've made two flights for 1187 and were only successful locating him once. On the occasion we located him, 1187 was just east of the Empire Swamp Trail. There's one heck of a lot of static on his frequency, and I'm afraid it's affecting our ability to pick him up at any distance."

Bob commented, "Well, if his location was near the Empire Swamp Trail, that would probably make him a Bear Lake wolf. Based on what we've seen from tracking the Bear Lake group these past couple of winters, they sweep down through the Bear Lake deer yard into the Empire Swamp quite regularly. I'd bet 1187 has got to be a Bear Lake wolf."

"Not necessarily," Tom said. "You'll be surprised how much hopping around wolves do. Our friend 1187 was not an old wolf. He may not belong in the Bear Lake area—he may simply be prowling about."

As we pulled into the parking lot of the Dairyland bar, Tom added, "Maybe we should pay 1189 a visit tonight and see what he's up to. The area where we obtained a fix on him this morning was near an old grassed-in beaver pond, which looks for all the world like many of the summer homesites I've seen up in Minnesota. So far, your winter tracking work has revealed more about the wolves living in the Bear Lake area than those responsible for the sign up in Moose Lake. We should check it out. We might just learn something."

As Tom killed the engine, I reminded them both, "Not a word about wolves while in this drinking establishment. I'd like to make it back to the ranger station without the imprints of some lowlife's fists in my forehead."

"Got it," my friends replied, acknowledging the value of that advice.

By the time we left the bar about a half-hour past sundown, it was downright chilly. The temperature had dropped 20 degrees while we were eating supper. A light breeze off Lake Superior from the northeast promised to keep the mosquitoes at bay. Although exhausted, Bob and I decided that howling to wolves was infinitely preferable to sweating it out in the miserably hot upstairs bedroom. The three of us headed north, weaving our way through the forest toward a rendezvous with wolf 1189.

About six miles from the bar we pulled over at a rest area along Highway 35 to consult the topographic maps Tom had used during his flight. From the map we were able to determine that an old woods trail led right up to the banks of the Moose River, within a half-mile of the beaver pond near where we had found 1189 earlier in the day. An hour later we were banging our way down that rickety trail, dodging boulders and mud holes.

The trail ended in a clear-cut on a little knoll. It had evidently been cut five or ten years earlier, judging from the aspen suckers that stood perhaps eight feet high. The knoll sloped east, its base immersed in the cool brown waters of the Moose River. Although we could not see it in the moonlight, we could hear the water, a muffled gurgling over rocks and submerged alder branches. Spreading out, we chose stumps and clumps of brush to sit on.

Light from the full moon illuminated the clear-cut with a soft silvery sheen. The aspen suckers cast dull gray shadows. Here and there the irregular murky silhouettes of young balsams interrupted the suckers. In the distance we could see the jet-black spires of spruces and firs outlining the edge of the tiny clear-cut. No wind. No mosquitoes. No sensation except the soft sound of running water and the sweet smell of aspen flowers and balsam fir. The temperature was now about 60 degrees—perfect howling weather.

We sat in silence for perhaps fifteen minutes, mesmerized by the cool, dry air and the solitude. Eventually, Tom stood, cupped his hands around his mouth, took a deep breath, leaned back, and gave forth with a throaty howl. The eerie sound echoed up and down the little river valley, rebounding from bank to tree-lined bank, suspended in midair like a leaf caught up in an updraft until the shadowy forest swallowed the sound.

He howled again a minute later. Starting high, he dropped quickly to bass, holding there for three or four seconds before ending abruptly. The report was still reverberating down the valley when he got an answer. The reply was a low, ululating utterance that suddenly erupted into a cacophony of high, shrill yips, yipes, and barks. In subdued but excited voices, we exclaimed in unison, "Pups!"

Not two hundred yards to the east, just about where wolf 1189 had been

earlier in the day, were at least three or four pups and an adult wolf. The pups had barely quit when a second adult wolf howled its response, barely discernible in the distance far to the east of the group. Again, the pups and the adult replied. While the group was in midhowl, a third wolf chimed in from the south, not more than a quarter-mile away.

We were surrounded by members of the pack. The group and the two single wolves exchanged songs intermittently for the next fifteen minutes. In awe, we listened intently, fully enjoying the wild symphony.

Shortly after the wolves stopped calling, Tom silently returned to the pickup, extracted the radio receiver, groped around in the trap box for the antenna, and walked quietly over to me.

"Let's see if 1189 is around."

We set the receiver up, fumbled for some time with the dials (which were almost impossible to distinguish in the moonlight), and turned on the power. Tom pointed the antenna in the direction of the wolves and immediately picked up the "beep-beep" pulse characteristic of 1189's radio signal. Bob, who was sitting some distance off in the brush, clearly heard the signal and acknowledged it by signaling thumbs up. Our wolf was babysitting the pups.

Some minutes later we made out a barely audible howl to the northwest. The low, hoarse call snagged on a single note for perhaps ten seconds, wavered briefly, and ended abruptly. The pack evidently had no trouble recognizing the sound and, no doubt, its maker. The wolves replied with exuberance.

"Too bad we didn't bring our sleeping bags," Bob whispered.

"I know," I replied. Tom, who had returned to his perch on top of some log debris, nodded in agreement.

The night was enchanting. Moonlight, the sounds of rushing water, the stillness of the forest at night, and the wolves' songs. What else could a person want? We sat there mesmerized. Another fifteen minutes of silence passed.

Tom was just about to howl one last time when the wolf to our northwest blasted out a coarse howl. It was decidedly closer, moving in toward the pups — and us. From what I could tell, it had been more than a mile away when we first heard it. Now it was less than a third of a mile from us and moving obliquely past us toward the family homesite. Its occasional howls revealed its line of movement as it traveled through the forest. When it last howled, the wolf was no more than a few hundred yards north of the pups.

We sat crouching in the brush in that tiny clear-cut for another half hour before a lone wolf ushered one long, plaintive howl far to the east of the family group's homesite. Apparently no longer in the mood, the family failed to reply.

By now it was well past midnight. We had traps to check early in the morning. It was time to go.

Five-thirty came early, and we groggily threw ourselves out of bed to overcome the urge to slumber on. Bob and I drove out to the Highway T bridge over the St. Croix River to meet Tom. We rolled down the windows so the chilly air would blow over us and keep us awake.

Tom arrived shortly after we did. No one was talkative this morning. Each of us was in a daze, feeling the lack of sleep that had been piling up for some time. Last night was the clincher. We needed R&R. To get that, we needed a wolf.

We checked the trapline stretching through the miles of jack pine barrens that blanketed the landscape south of the St. Croix river bottom. No sign, no action. It was only seven and already 80 degrees. So much for that Canadian cold front. We turned east on the town line road that separated the jack pine forests from the Namekagon Barrens prairie management area.

Two more sets empty. It was going to be another one of those days.

We were down to the last two sets — the sets Bob had laid the previous evening. All of us were gloomy about the prospects.

We were still about one hundred yards away when we saw a drag mark clearly etched in the sand on the lane. It was heading north toward the jack pines. Wolf.

Tom slammed on the brakes and we poured out, quietly following the drag trail through the tangle of brown sweet fern and raspberry brambles beneath the jack pines. One hundred yards off the lane sat a majestic wolf calmly watching our approach. We backed off. Tom and I returned to the truck for our equipment, while Bob remained, watching the wolf from a distance.

With drugging equipment in hand I slowly approached our quarry, trying to get its attention so Tom could slip in and tranquilize it. Sitting on its haunches, the wolf lifted its head and let out a long, deafening, plaintive howl, then a second one. Then the wolf stood up to confront its adversaries.

It watched us both, circling as we moved, keeping its head between our positions and its vulnerable rear out of reach. I moved slowly to one side, clapping and talking loudly to get its attention, but it didn't fall for the ruse. Tom circled in the other direction and the wolf followed, as if it knew that Tom was the one to be concerned about.

I changed directions abruptly and the wolf, momentarily taken off guard, met my movement, giving Tom enough opportunity to deliver the dart. As it hit, the wolf jumped, bit at the dart, and made a feeble attempt to remove it. We withdrew some distance to reduce the wolf's trauma and allow time for the drug to take effect. The wolf laid down, resigned to its fate.

Within ten minutes it was out. Working quickly, we took its paw out of the trap, placed the animal in the bed of the truck, and drove down a woods trail some distance to avoid encountering any passersby. The numerous lakes in this area attract summer vacationers, and we had already seen some on rural roads. We didn't want any trouble for us or our wolf.

We dubbed this wolf 1195. He was a young sixty-five-pound male and in very good shape. In an hour our job was done. Tom and I removed the wolf to a shaded knoll, gently patted him on the shoulders, and wished him well. We returned to the truck, stowed our gear, and immediately set to work pulling up the trapline.

We had set out to capture and collar five wolves by the end of May, and we had met that goal. Our work was now done. With our trapline pulled up, Tom, Bob, and I parted ways. Tom headed northwest to Minnesota and another summer assignment trapping nuisance wolves at farms. Bob and I returned to the ranger station, packed our belongings, and headed south for some rest.

Trying Times

I quickly learned the art of aerial telemetry. It wasn't as complicated as I had been led to believe. The pilot and I both wore headsets. He used his to communicate with any other air traffic in the area and with the DNR's radio dispatchers. My set was plugged into the telemetry receiver.

In one hand I held a switch box. With my thumb I flipped a toggle left or right. This switch brought the signal in from the antennas strapped to each of the wing struts. By comparing the volume of the signal to the left and right, I could tell what direction the signal was coming from. I communicated to Jim Dienstl any adjustments we needed to make in our heading by tapping his left or right shoulder.

As we closed in on a signal, it got louder. To compensate I periodically lowered the volume. This helped discriminate direction by preventing the signal from becoming overwhelming. Once the dial on the gain was below 4.5, I instructed Jim to begin a slow descent. The plane felt like it was coasting, though it was still moving about fifty-five miles per hour.

When the gain dropped below 3.5, we were usually within 1.5 miles of the wolf. At this point our plane was usually cruising about eight hundred to one thousand feet above the ground—close enough to see the world below clearly.

On June 10, 1980, we got our first visual. We were approaching 1189's signal. It was growing very loud and our plane was already in descent. I tapped Jim's shoulder, shouting that we were closing in on the wolf. Nodding, he peered out the right window. I concentrated on the left side, scanning the forest whizzing by beneath us, looking for our quarry.

We had just passed a landmark: the junction of the Gregerson fire lane and Tom Green Road. Next we passed over a small feeder creek that wrapped around the bottom of a gigantic glacial hill carpeted with maple trees. A mantle of mist cloaked the base of the dark blue balsams that choked the stream bank. Here and there a ghoulish wisp reached up to tickle the tips of these stately conifers. Definitely a humid day, going to be a hot one too, I thought, as the brook slipped from sight beneath the tail section of the plane. Jim eased up on the throttle as we followed the feeder creek that paralleled the Gregerson fire lane.

A half-mile north of where the creek tumbled across the fire lane, the signal suddenly pounded in my earphones and Jim shouted, "There they are!"

He deftly cut the engine as the plane glided past two wolves sauntering up the Gregerson, light gray coats sharply contrasting with the deep blue hues of the surrounding fir forest. The lead animal was our wolf. We could clearly see its collar and the radio that sat beneath.

As we passed by them, Jim was busy preparing to turn the plane about. He brought us back to where our subjects had been, but they had disappeared. Evidently, the noise of our plane had startled the wolves, which were still unaccustomed to all this attention.

Thrilled by the encounter, we shouted to talk over the roar of the engine. Jim pulled us up and out, pointing the plane's nose in the direction of other radioed wolves we had to locate. I stared out over the Douglas County forests, marveling at how at ease the two wolves had seemed as they walked up the fire lane in midmorning.

Locating wolf 1187 continued to be a problem because of the interference on his radio frequency. We soon learned that his signal was being overpowered by a much stronger signal of commercial origin from the Duluth area. As time went on, we learned several subtle techniques that enhanced our ability to find him. By swinging the plane around so our antennas stayed out of the direction of Duluth, we were able to minimize the interference. Still, sometimes we simply couldn't get a fix on wolf 1187.

A Russian fable says, "The wolf is kept fed by its feet," and that undoubtedly explains the elusiveness of our quarry. Wolf 1187 performed some interesting and unusual maneuvers that tested our mettle.

One sunny afternoon in early August, I called Jim to see whether we could go out looking for 1187. I had been conducting some night howling surveys in the hope of learning whether the Bear Lake Pack had pups. Because he was wearing a collar, and was the alpha male, wolf 1187 was my ticket to finding the pups. The night before, we had located him along the very southern edge of his territory on the St. Croix River, not far from wolf 1195's haunts. Wolf 1187 was still there around midnight when I tried to get him to howl, with no success.

Jim agreed to fly but warned me he had to be back by seven to attend his son's Little League game. We took off at five and headed toward the St. Croix

River, which was where I expected we'd find 1187. As we neared the area, I began scanning his frequency. No luck.

Jim turned around.

"What do you mean, no luck?"

I shrugged my shoulders, peering intently at the forested landscape below. It was bisected by the majestic St. Croix River as it tumbled over boulders strewn by glaciers ten thousand years ago. I asked him to turn north.

After another five miles had slipped beneath us, Jim turned and again asked, "Anything?"

"No, absolutely nothing. The static is pretty bad, but I'm sure I'd pick it up if he were around."

Jim looked at the clock on the plane's console. A bit concerned, he said, "I'm gonna have to turn around in a few minutes if we don't find anything." I nodded in the affirmative, concentrating on deciphering the noise coming in over the headphones. We were now within four miles of what we felt was the northern edge of his territory.

We crossed the Pioneer Road where Bob Welch had found the injured porcupine several winters earlier. Not much farther and we're at the top of his territory, I thought, feeling discouraged that he'd eluded us once more. As Dienstl turned around to give me the bad news, I heard one, then a second, faint beep. Jim hollered at me, but I impatiently waved him off, fidgeting with the dials in an attempt to clean out the static.

No question about it—1187's signal was coming from straight ahead. I signaled Jim on, shouting, "Straight ahead—within two miles!" He frowned in disbelief. A moment later I had the wolf's location plotted. Our wolf had traveled more than sixteen miles as the proverbial crow flies, from his southern to his northern boundary, in less than twenty-four hours.

Ten minutes later Jim touched down at Solon Springs. The plane barely came to a stop and I jumped out. Jim took off again, headed for his son's Little League game. This trip taught me something about the impressive mobility and large territory sizes of wolves, although not what I had set out to learn (did 1187 have pups somewhere?). Jim and I now had a better understanding of why their territories were so large.[1]

It had become obvious that Douglas County was home to four packs. Wolves 1187 and 1189 ranged different areas and we never observed them together. On several occasions we saw wolf 1189 with other wolves. Wolf 1189 never crossed south of blacktop county Highway A, and wolf 1187 never passed north of it. Wolf 1187, we now knew, belonged to the Bear Lake Pack. The howling in May had confirmed the existence of pups and a rendezvous site where wolf 1189 roamed. I named them the Moose Lake Pack for the tiny bog lake that lay about dead center in the pack's range. And we were convinced that 1191 and 1193 were the alphas of the Stateline Flowage Pack and that 1195 was half of the St. Croix Pair.

We still needed to determine how many packs were living in the New Wood country. Bill Meier, the Lincoln County wildlife manager who had helped me look for wolf sign in New Wood, took an active role in wolf surveys. He and I remained at odds throughout spring and early summer over how many packs roamed the New Wood country, although we agreed to name the known pack the Averill Creek Pack. My experiences with wolves 1187 and 1189 convinced me that the only way to find out how many packs were in the area was to radio-collar some Lincoln County wolves. Besides, we could gain a lot more information on numbers, territory size, and—most important—mortality rates and causes of death if we radioed some of the Lincoln County wolves.

Meier didn't like the idea, but he agreed to call a meeting of warden Don Manthei, the Lincoln County forest administrator, and other members of the North-Central District wildlife staff to discuss whether we should collar some Lincoln County wolves. The meeting was scheduled for early August 1980.

On the appointed date Steve Fritts came over from Minnesota, and Jim Hale came up from Madison. Meier and two tiers of wildlife supervisors attended, as did the Lincoln County forest administrator, Bill's wildlife technician, and several DNR foresters whose areas included the New Wood. Manthei was unable to attend.

The local forestry and wildlife staff were opposed to telemetry work. Meier served as spokesman for the group. "I can't see how collaring these wolves will give us any information we either don't already have or cannot get through conventional means," he said. Fritts responded by providing examples of how efficient and effective Minnesota's radio-collaring program was.

Meier countered: "We don't think it would be a good idea here in Lincoln County. Look at what happened in Douglas County to the two wolves that were killed. We've done a lot of work in convincing the local citizens of the value of having these wolves. How would it look if we, the DNR, accidentally killed them?"

I mentioned that the Northwest District staff had expressed similar concerns. I then reiterated that it wasn't the collars that had killed the wolves.

"At a meeting in Grantsburg we all agreed to a trapping protocol that satisfied the concerns of the Northwest District staff," I added. I went on to explain how trapping was limited to springtime to avoid unnecessary encounters with people, adding that the five radioed wolves captured in the spring were doing fine.

Meier then passed out copies of a memo by Manthei. Bill reminded everyone that Don was widely respected for his concerns and views on wildlife and its management in Lincoln County. It read:

August 6, 1980
To: Dick Thiel
From: Don Manthei
Subject: Radio Collaring—Lincoln County Timber Wolves

I find it very disappointing that I have to write this letter and I am very sorry I cannot be at the meeting today.

. . . The Lincoln County pack established itself by itself. An extensive PR program was started and is continuing in order to gain the support of the public for protection of this endangered species. The Natural Resources Board has supported us by closing Unit 32 to coyote hunting during the deer season. I feel we have the support of the majority of our citizens.

At present, the Lincoln County packs are the only free roaming packs in the state.

I am strongly opposed to radio collaring of the wolves. I feel that an effort of this type will prove nothing that isn't already known. Adequate research has been done in Ontario, Alaska, and Minnesota on timber wolves. Research will show they will expand their territory, which we know they are going to do. The possible detriment to these animals by trapping and collaring isn't worth the only benefit which will be gained, the writing of a research paper. Studies of this type could continue in Douglas County. Why disturb the only free roaming pack in the state?

. . . Your deliberations will decide the fate of the timber wolves. I hope you will consider the wishes of the local citizenry and myself before an effort is made to collar and disrupt this rare and unique animal which has returned to Lincoln County.

Manthei's petition was based on an appeal to keep the Lincoln County wolves "free roaming." In Manthei's view radio telemetry would somehow diminish the mystique of the wolf, which, after all, lay in its secretive ways. But all the telemetry was doing was giving us information; it was in no way impeding the "free-roaming" nature of the wolves.

I shared Don's view that research should not be done for research's sake at the expense of the animal's life or its lifestyle. Our intentions here were legitimate: we needed to gather information to intelligently deal with managing a future for the species in this state. Don's entreaty to keep the wolf wild was spoken from the heart. And although our need for information was (and remains) more compelling than the desire to keep some of the wolf's essence mysterious, his words became, in a sense, a barometer for me. Every time new challenges arose on the wolf project, I would ask the critical question, "Is this necessary and to what end?"

Don's memo had the desired effect on most of those gathered around the conference room table. Unfortunately, Manthei wasn't present, so I couldn't respond to his concerns directly. For the benefit of those present, Fritts and Hale confirmed that I had been hired *after* the problems arose with the three wolves collared in October 1979 in Douglas County.

Among Manthei's complaints was my assurance the previous winter that I had no plans to collar any of the Lincoln County wolves. And that was true. At the time we knew little about the size of the pack inhabiting New Wood. It would have been risky to attempt to collar any wolves in a small pack at least one hundred miles from any wolf neighbors. However, all who participated in the previous winter's surveys, including Meier and Manthei, agreed that at least twelve wolves were living in New Wood. Even if it was only one pack, it was the largest pack of wolves in the state. Therefore, it seemed reasonable to attempt to collar one or two to gather data that we could compare and contrast with the information we were getting from the Douglas County wolves in our effort to learn what factors influenced the survival of these wolves.

In concluding our case, I pointed out that the purpose of our meeting was to decide *whether* to collar some Lincoln County wolves. Had the decision already been made, as Manthei's memo implied, there would have been no point in meeting that day. But the outcome was predictable, a split along party lines. Those representing statewide interests lost to those who represented the local viewpoint. The subject of collaring Lincoln County wolves would not be revisited for several years.[2]

After the meeting in Lincoln County, I returned to Tomah and went on inactive status in order to preserve what was left of my hours allotted for the year. I would be spending the majority of my remaining time monitoring the radioed wolves during the fall hunting seasons.

The telemetry flights in Douglas County were continuing despite my absence because the Northwest District pilots had learned how to locate the wolves. This saved the wolf project some money by keeping me off the road and off the payroll.

Jim Dienstl called me one afternoon in late September. He told me the pilots were unable to find wolf 1195—the St. Croix wolf. "In the past two flights we haven't had any luck. Thought you might like to know."

I replied, "1195's disappearance sounds suspicious to me, Jim. This wolf has been real tight to the area. He hasn't made any journeys out of his range. The fact that he's had close encounters with people in the past few weeks has me worried."

It was bear hunting season. A week before the season started in early September, Dienstl had been patrolling an area of the Namekagon Barrens with wardens on the ground who were searching for illegal bear bait piles in the woods. Jim had spotted a suspicious-looking 4-wheel-drive vehicle in the woods. Although he was working warden patrol, Jim had connected the wolf telemetry antennas to the struts of his plane before he took off. In some idle moments, while the wardens were maneuvering below, he had turned on 1195's frequency to see if anything was up. Ping! Ping! The wolf's signal had nearly blasted him out of his seat. The wolf was near an illegal bear bait site. The wardens found the bait, a hole in the ground, stuffed full of illegal meat scraps.

Jim and I decided that we would conduct a special search for wolf 1195 by executing an outward spiral pattern from the center of the wolf's territory, radiating outward for twenty-five miles. I had the unpleasant task of informing Bob Dreis that we might have lost a wolf.

The next day I walked into Bob's office at 10:30 A.M. We had an enthusiastic discussion about what each of the radioed wolves was up to. Bob was genuinely excited about the information we were gaining through the telemetry work.

"Well, Bob, that brings me to the purpose of my visit. Jim Dienstl believes we lost a wolf—1195."

Dismayed, Bob asked, "Which one is it?"

"It's the radioed member of the St. Croix Pair. I'm having Jim do a search for it, but I thought I'd better let you know the news. We've accumulated quite a few locations on this wolf, and I believe we've got a good handle on the size and shape of its territory. Based on sign this past winter and during the spring trapping effort, I believe it was tight with the other wolf. I doubt it dispersed away."

"I'd like to fly with you the next time you go up."

Two days later, with Dienstl at the pilot's console, Dreis, the district's public information officer, and I crowded into a two-engine plane used primarily to ferry employees to various meetings throughout the state. This plane was much faster than the Piper Cub, and in less than fifteen minutes we were approaching the Namekagon Barrens.

Dienstl briefly explained that his searches had come up with no leads on wolf 1195. I asked him to put us over the spot the wolf had last been located alive.

We crossed the St. Croix River heading west-northwest. Big and Little McGraw Lakes appeared off our port side. Jim edged the plane between and a little south of the two lakes.

"The wolf was last found about a half-mile north of that farm in the woods."

Straining against the G force as Jim banked the plane sharply to the left to keep the area in view, we looked out over a relatively flat expanse of maple forest illuminated by the red and gold fall leaves. To the south was an L-shaped alfalfa field, a white painted barn, some out buildings, and a modest old farmhouse on the south edge at the bend in the L. A driveway led east to a town road that cut a crooked swath through the forest toward the St. Croix.

"No one home today," I commented as we all noted a lack of activity around the farm. Here and there along the road were other dwellings. We saw more fields and farms as we looked south. This, I thought, is definitely the edge of their habitat—they can't go much farther south or they're in trouble.

I listened intently for wolf 1195's signal but heard nothing on the receiver except the usual background static. We searched most of western Burnett and Douglas Counties and adjacent areas of Minnesota for two hours, to no avail. Wolf 1195 had disappeared.

As we rode back to Spooner after landing at the Shell Lake airport, Bob and I discussed the wolf's disappearance. Bob offered, "Bar talk is where we'll learn the fate of that wolf. Whoever killed it will probably tell someone, and it will be the topic of conversation among the locals for some time. The subject will eventually surface in an area tavern." The district's information officer agreed to ask local wardens to be alert for any information that might help us determine what had happened to wolf 1195.

It didn't take long. The following week a warden pulled up alongside my vehicle at the gas pump next to the mechanic's shop at Spooner headquarters. "Got some information for you, Dick, concerning that wolf you lost. Talk around the neighborhood indicates a farmer shot the wolf in late September and quickly disposed of the wolf and its collar."

"Do you know who did it?"

"No. We heard nothing specific other than it was shot on a farm property near McGraw Lake. We're still working on it, but I'm afraid the case doesn't hold much promise. The information is reliable, as far as I'm concerned."

I headed right over to Dreis's office.

"Did you get my message?"

"No, Bob. But I got an update on the missing wolf."

"That's what I wanted to tell you. Two of the wardens heard via the grapevine that it had been shot and disposed of by an area farmer."

Our conversation turned to the decision made at the telemetry program meeting the previous March. I recalled it vividly: If one wolf is killed by a person, the whole project is finished. But Dreis's attitude had changed. "The radioed wolves have survived the whole summer unscathed. I'm less inclined now to believe their collars have anything to do with their deaths. Let's see what happens during the upcoming autumn hunting seasons before we pass judgment." Thank you, God! I thought as Bob uttered those words.

Following the search for wolf 1195, I buried myself in administrative work. Jim Hale, director of the state Office of Endangered and Non-Game Species, had managed to secure a more long-term arrangement for me. I was to be taken off LTE status and hired as a project employee using federal funds. This federal program was initiated at the request of hunters and anglers back in the 1930s at the depth of the Great Depression. It was underwritten by an 11 percent excise tax on the sale of ammunition, firearms, and other hunting equipment. The states sent the money to Washington, D.C., where it was reallocated to the states to support the acquisition of wildlife habitats and wildlife management programs.

The state's project employees were really glorified LTEs who received benefits but could not accrue seniority. Under this system I would be employed under four-year contracts.

There was also a glitch. For some time I had been pushing for an LTE assistant. Jim informed me that the funding for such a position had fallen through. I needed the LTE. Hesitating momentarily, I asked that my time be reduced to ten months per year. That would "save" enough money to pay for an LTE. Hale agreed and gave me permission to hire an LTE.

Before the radio telemetry study began, the state knew more about how Wisconsin's wolves died than how they lived. In addition to the two collared Douglas County wolves and the Lincoln County wolf that had been shot in the fall of 1979, several other carcasses had surfaced. In 1977 the carcass of a Douglas County wolf revealed that it had been shot, perhaps during deer season. Two other Douglas County wolves had been trapped and shot—one in 1978 and the other in 1979.[3] We already knew that deer seasons could be deadly to our state's wolves.

The 1980 deer season was approaching quickly. More than 650,000 hunters would take to the field for nine days. I thought the state's twenty-five timber wolves were probably most vulnerable to death at the hands of humans during this period. And opening weekend probably held the greatest risk of all.

I both looked forward to and dreaded the upcoming deer season. I told myself: This is the reality under which Wisconsin's wolves exist. Deer seasons are simply not going to go away. If wolves are to survive in this state, the species has got to absorb any losses incurred during this annual event and carry on. The scientist in me reasoned: The telemetry work will yield the most unbiased causes of death. Because they're probably being killed by people anyhow, at least this tool will reveal which causes—such as deer season losses—are the most harmful. As a wolf biologist, my role was to sit back and watch what happened. I found this unsettling.

We made our plans weeks in advance. We had to be prepared. In the event of an illegal shooting, I needed to be right on top of things so we could catch the party responsible. As far as I was concerned, illegal shootings had already caused too many deaths. The next time, I vowed, we would make an example of the SOB.

We would need to react quickly, collect the pertinent information, and gain cooperation of the state and federal game wardens (because each had jurisdiction in cases involving the killing of species that were on both the state and federal endangered species lists). I had to be sure that the flight schedules were well coordinated—our window into the wolf's world of life and death depended on the telemetry work.

Normally, wolf telemetry-monitoring flights went out twice weekly, weather permitting. During Wisconsin's deer gun season, Jim Dienstl and I scheduled daily flights. Ordinarily, as we neared a radioed wolf, we dropped in altitude to increase the chance of seeing the individual. Jim was concerned that some crackpot might take a shot at us, and we therefore agreed to forgo sightings and remain about three thousand feet up, too high for a bullet to ruin our day.

Our intent during deer season was simply to make sure the radioed wolves survived. We had to assume that healthy wolves would move every day. So we would treat any disappearances or lack of movement as a potential mishap. In that event, I would conduct an on-the-ground inspection of the animal's last known location to see if I could find out what had happened to the wolf.

The backwoods undergo a pronounced change on the Wednesday before the Saturday deer season. Hunters begin filtering in to the many deer-hunting camps to prepare for the hunt. These dyed-in-the-wool deer hunters have one passion in life—hunting the majestic white-tailed deer.

The typical hunting camp sits on a forty-acre parcel of forested land adjacent to a blacktop highway or, less commonly in western Douglas County, along a fire lane. Except for the camps, though, most of the land beyond the blacktops, including areas through which the fire lanes coursed, is Douglas County forest land where structures are prohibited.

The camps are owned by families or assortments of friends and family and have a long tradition in the upper Great Lakes region. The majority of properties were sold as nearly worthless cutover land by logging and lumber companies from 1900 to 1930. A surprising number are still owned by the descendants of the original camp owners.

With the season bearing down on us, I became increasingly concerned about wolf 1187. I had reason to be. He wasn't your typical wolf, fearful of humans.

On the Wednesday before deer season four men from one of the camps decided to combine some preseason scouting with a little grouse hunting. They spent most of the day exploring the ridges and alder swamps within the Empire Swamp, then climbed in their 4-wheel-drive vehicle and headed back toward camp. As the driver crested a hill on Highway M that overlooks a broad, flat expanse of alder and ash in the Crotte Creek basin, he noticed an animal walking down the middle of the road. It was about three-quarters of a mile ahead. At first he thought it was a deer, but as he got closer, he recognized it as a wolf.

Undistracted, the wolf continued loping toward the oncoming vehicle. The driver expected the animal to become frightened at any moment and jump off the road into the safety of the brush, but on it came. Finally, the driver felt compelled to slow down.

The wolf still made no move to leave the road. Brakes were applied, and the driver slowly brought the vehicle to a halt. The wolf still advanced, bewildering the four men. Its collar was now clearly visible.

The wolf had no intention of exiting into the forest. It was going to pass right by them. The fellows' bird dog, a spaniel, leaped at the window, growling furiously as the timber wolf sauntered past, the men holding their breath in astonishment. Later, the driver remarked to me that the wolf never left the yellow-striped center line and seemed oblivious to their presence. Only when it was about a hundred yards past them did it stop briefly, turn broadside, and gaze at the spectacle of the four grown men and a dog who were having their first encounter with a wild timber wolf.

Needless to say, wolf 1187 didn't meet their preconceived expectations of how a wolf would react in the presence of people. His behavior in this situation was perplexing and disturbingly consistent with his habits.

The previous June, a scant thirty days after he was collared, wolf 1187 paid a twilight visit to a residence along the southern fringe of his 110-square-mile Bear Lake territory. The woman who lived there, Judy Wendgren, had been considerably shaken by his visit; Don Bublitz, the area wildlife manager, referred her to me in the hope that I could offer a scientific explanation for his rather unusual behavior. I couldn't.

She had been finishing the dishes shortly after sunset, when the family's female German shepherd, who was in heat, started barking excitedly. Judy had looked out the kitchen window, past her three small children who were wrestling with each other in the yard. A tall, lanky doglike creature had stepped out of the thicket behind their lot and was approaching the house at a brisk pace. She didn't recognize it as belonging to any of the neighbors, and its posture frightened her.

She ran out the door shouting, scooped the children up in her arms, and quickly ran to the chained dog, fearing the oncoming animal's intentions. By now the family dog was in a frenzy and the creature was still moving toward them, seemingly indifferent to all the excitement. Somehow, Judy managed to drag her kids and the dog into the house, slamming the kitchen door just in time to catch a glimpse of a timber wolf—radio collar and all—as it strolled beneath their window and ambled down their driveway.

She dumped the kids and dog on the floor and ran to the front window in time to see the wolf turn onto the gravel road and vanish behind the row of trees that lined their front yard. It was headed down the town road, bound for some destination known only to it.

After I assured her that wolves do not attack children waiting for school buses or little old ladies in tennis shoes, Judy asked me, "Why would a wolf do something so strange as this?" I had no good answer. Instead, I fumbled around with excuses like, "He was nervous being on the edge of his territory in proximity to people which he's not accustomed to." Privately, I thought, how should I know? I'm not a wolf. They are entitled to have their own ways of doing things, not all of which is or should somehow be understood by us humans. Admittedly, I was a little green at this wolf stuff, having been on the job for only six months. I had a lot of things to learn, not only about wolves but about dealing with people. That would take some time.

"Ma'am, don't worry. Consider yourself lucky," I told her. "Many people

would give their eyeteeth for the chance to see a wild timber wolf. People have lived their entire lives in wolf country and have never personally seen them. I almost guarantee you'll never see one again." That seemed to satisfy her.

I was wrong.

Wolf 1187 struck again about two weeks later. This time, Judy told me, she and her husband had been returning from Duluth on a recent dark, drizzly night when they had spied a pair of eyes illuminated by the headlights of their car. An animal was standing in the ditch along Highway 35, and at first they thought it was a deer. They slowed down so they would not hit it. The wolf, which was wearing a radio collar, remained motionless as they slowly passed it.

"No doubt about it. I'm positive it was the same wolf. Tall and lanky." Rubbing it in, she added, "I thought you said I'd never see another wolf. And here I see the *same one* in two weeks."

She was amazed at the size of its territory. Her house was eight miles south of where they saw the wolf that rainy night, and its range extended eight miles to the north of that location.

Now that the deer season was here, I felt sure that wolf 1187 was a goner. Almost fatalistically, I envisioned having to deliver the news to Bob Dreis. I was also staring at the future of the telemetry program. He'd better make it, I thought, gritting my teeth.

As the opening day of the Wisconsin deer gun season dawned, I found myself toting a rifle in the brush just off the Empire Swamp Trail in the heart of the Bear Lake Pack's territory. I'd driven out to the spot at 4:30 A.M., passing quite a few hunting shacks along the way. Lanterns glowed from within nearly all of them, a sure sign that the occupants were busy preparing breakfast and making final checks of their hunting gear before heading into the woods.

From daybreak to 9:45 I heard the reports of perhaps a half-dozen rifles. This was big country, and despite the number of hunting cabins strung out along blacktopped Highways A and M, hunters easily melted into the remote expanses of western Douglas County.

I had selected this spot from which to hunt deer about two weeks earlier. At that time the bucks were in full rut, the peak of breeding season. One or more bucks had left ample evidence of their presence in this thicket of young aspen. I could see many "rubs," scars in the slick green bark of young trees where bucks had scraped their antlers. I had also found three humongous scrapes, areas where a buck had pawed up the ground and deposited his scent to try to attract does and ward off would-be competitors.

It was an unusually warm day—40 degrees by 8 A.M. I stuck it out as long as I could but left the woods around 10 without seeing a deer. I had to meet a district pilot at the airstrip in Solon Springs.

All radioed wolves were alive and accounted for. Wolf 1187 was along the headwaters of Sheosh Creek, nearly two miles from the nearest road. Was he deep within this secluded portion of his territory by design or chance?

This question tantalized me for the better part of the day while I registered and noted the ages of hunter-killed deer at the Douglas County Forestry Office at Solon Springs. Two hours after dark I headed home to the Gordon Ranger Station for some rest. Although the mercury had reached 50 degrees by 1 P.M., the temperature had dropped sharply after sundown, and a light snow was falling as I pulled into the parking lot of the ranger station.

The following morning's flight was scheduled for 8 A.M., so I slept in, arising shortly after sunrise. As I stumbled into the bathroom from the empty office-turned-living-quarters at the end of the hall on the second floor, I noticed an inordinate amount of light coming in through the tinted glass window. Although the sun was barely up, the light it cast was reflecting off a dusting of snow that covered the ground. The hunters will like that, I thought, as I brushed my teeth. I also knew the snow would enable me to track the wolves if I had to.

I downed a quick breakfast, grabbed my lunch from the refrigerator, and ran out the door. I headed north toward the airstrip, there to await the arrival of the little red-and-white Piper Cub.

We found wolf 1187 had moved about four miles northwest overnight. This morning he was a little more than a mile west of the Empire Swamp Trail. After the pilot brought me back, I decided to cruise the trail to see if I could find out where he had crossed and whether he was with other wolves. So far he'd behaved marvelously, staying far from the fire lanes and roads where he was most likely to encounter humans. As I drove Highway A to the Empire Swamp country, I wondered how long he could contain himself.

I found the tracks of 1187, distinctive because of his missing toe, and those of another wolf about a mile south of Highway A. They had entered the Empire Swamp Trail from the east—the area where I'd located him the day before. The pair had walked south for perhaps three-quarters of a mile, then cut west toward the spot I'd found him in an hour and a half earlier. So far he had managed to stay out of trouble, but I was worried that he'd wander close to the hunting groups scattered up and down Highways A and M.

That afternoon I visited many of the hunting shacks along Highway M, registering deer and getting ages on a number of fine bucks. I met a lot of interesting characters and discussed wolves with a number of people. Most didn't seem concerned about the wolves' presence, and a few actually liked the notion of sharing their hunting grounds with the big critters. A few proffered that the only good wolf was a dead wolf. "Every man's entitled to his opinion," I retorted, "but I hope you all respect the law. As an endangered species, they're off-limits and you know it."

In a number of places I was clearly unwelcome. In some circles the firmly held belief was that what God giveth, the DNR taketh away, and in those camps I stuck to business and went on my way.

Traffic on the back roads and major highways was heavy toward late afternoon as weekend hunters scurried back to homes, families, and Monday morning jobs. I returned to the station around 9:30 P.M. and quickly heated up a turkey pot pie. The drone of traffic whizzing by on Highway 53, a block away, was clearly audible as I turned in, drowsy from a full day in the crisp autumn air.

Our flight the next day was scheduled for 10:30 A.M. We swung northwest toward Moose Lake and followed wolf 1189's signal to its source, then swung west, assuming wolf 1187 would be near his previous day's location. But I couldn't pick up his signal. We began a sweep of the northern edge of his territory above the Pioneer Road because it was only a few miles off our starboard side. Still nothing. I began to worry.

Pilot Ray Marvin pointed the plane south, recrossing first the Pioneer and then the Summit Tower Road. I stared out the window as we neared the southern part of the Empire Swamp, a desolate expanse of tag alder and sphagnum bog from whence sprang the headwaters of a half-dozen creeks that spilled their brown waters into two continental river systems. Suddenly, I heard a sharp ping, followed by another. As I reached forward to alert Ray by tapping his shoulder, the signal vanished.

Wolf 1187's radio was up to its usual tricks.

I informed Ray of the problem. He nodded in acknowledgment and I asked him to continue on course. As I frantically fumbled with the receiver's fine-tuner dial, the wolf's signal reappeared. I could tell we were close.

I glanced away from the equipment for a moment and caught sight of Highway M, one of the few prominent landmarks in this otherwise nondescript forest. He's south of M, I thought, as I turned my attention once again to the gadgets spread out on my lap and clutched in my hands. A minute later we were sailing three thousand feet above our wolf.

To my amazement, wolf 1187 had moved a full seven miles south, crossing at least the Empire Swamp Trail and Highway M in the process. Pretty risky business for a wolf in the middle of deer season.

A bit of snow still remained in the shadows of the trees. I decided to cruise the fire lanes to determine the route of this wolf since the night before. I found his tracks on the Summit Tower Road. He had entered from the south where the old logging railroad grade crossed and had RLU'd there. Then he'd headed east for more than a mile along Highway A, past a year-round residence and two hunting camps, complete with parked cars and sleeping occupants, before turning south where the Empire Swamp Trail left the highway.

Picking up his tracks on the east–west stretch of roads had been fairly easy because the sun hadn't been strong enough the day before to melt the snow in the shadows of the leafless trees. But following his trail on the north–south Empire Swamp Trail was a different story. The snow had evaporated from the right-of-way except for occasional twists and turns in the lane where shadows preserved the snow and thus the wolf's trail. I went three-quarters of a mile between glimpses of his spoor.

Wolf 1187's trail continued south for almost four miles before leaving the grade. He was headed southeast. His little night escapade was bold. Walking past three places where hunters were lodged. What does this wolf think he's doing? He'd had the audacity to saunter down six miles of well-traveled roads before hitting the brush. He was lucky to be alive, and I was growing nervous. Maybe wolf 1187 would survive six more days, but by now I was convinced the suspense would do me in.

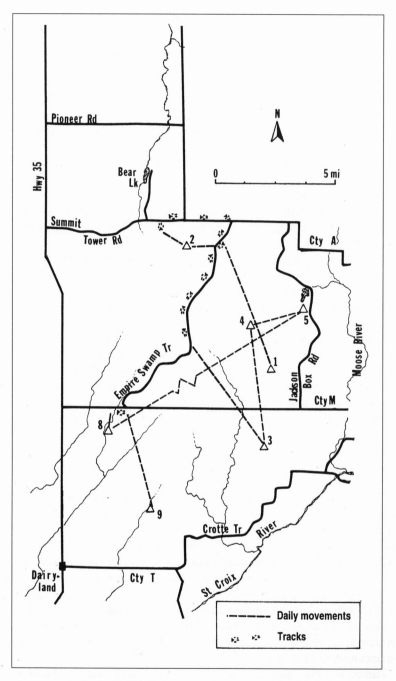

Movements of wolf 1187 during deer season, 1980. No locations were obtained on days six and seven because of foul weather.

The next day we flew bright and early. Hunting pressure was noticeably down. From our vantage point at three thousand feet we could pick out the blaze-orange garments of hunters that they are required by law to wear. We noticed far fewer hunters than on Saturday and Sunday and seldom saw anyone farther than a half mile from a fire lane. Presumably, sometime during the night wolf 1187 had recrossed Highway M, heading north. He was again in the heart of the Empire Swamp.

This was reassuring. The next day was Thanksgiving. In the afternoon I headed south for a brief reprieve from the hunting season and a good turkey dinner. I only hoped he'd stay put.

Early on Friday I headed north again to finish out the deer season. I had scheduled flights for Friday, Saturday, and Sunday. However, a dense fog blanketed the countryside as I drove through Eau Claire and the temperature hovered around 28 degrees. As I suspected, the fog and drizzle grounded us.

I decided to salvage the day by cruising the neighborhood—checking out the Bear Lake area to see what was going on with those wolves. I dropped in at the office at the Spooner Fish Research Building and found my office mate, Greg Sevener, at his desk. Tall and clean shaven, this dark-haired, serious but easy-going chap was a bit shy. He had been in Spooner for several years, and one of his primary responsibilities now was to draft a major report on the water resources of an important watershed in the district. This assignment kept him desk bound and, not infrequently, staring out the dirty window, dreaming about nearly anything but the interminable writing assignment that kept him indoors and away from the biotic world in which he belonged.

I asked if he would like to go with me to see what the wolves were up to. He deliberated for a moment before accepting. We jumped in the car and headed north toward wolf country.

Snow conditions had deteriorated considerably. Little remained on the roads. Although we drove most of the fire lanes within the Bear Lake territory that afternoon, our searches yielded nothing. Toward nightfall we pulled over and chatted with some hunters in a camp along Highway M. They said another hunter had claimed he had seen a collared wolf walking down Highway M between the Jackson Box Road and the Empire Swamp Trail.

"According to this guy, the wolf walked off the road onto the shoulder and let him pass. Then it got back on the road and continued on. He was met by an oncoming car but totally ignored it."

I asked when this happened and he replied, "During broad daylight two or three days ago."

On Saturday Greg and I returned, expecting to find sign because a light dusting of snow had fallen overnight. Indeed, we picked up 1187's tracks in the middle of Highway M in the new-fallen snow. Evidently, he had crossed to the south of Highway M sometime after I had flown on Wednesday. His tracks entered the highway from the south, proceeded eastward along the center line for perhaps a quarter of a mile, and exited back toward the south.

On our flight on Sunday we found wolf 1187 south of Highway M along the Rock Creek watershed, about three miles northeast of Dairyland. Not too far from Judy Wendgren's place. It was as good a place as any for him to finish out the season. He'd made it, the wolf program had made it, and so had I.

On a Monday in early December 1980, I returned to Spooner to complete paperwork and orient the wolf project's new part-time employee, Larry Prenn.

Tall and lanky, Larry Prenn had sandy hair and a beard to match. His straight face was a perfect mask for his wry sense of humor. He had been working for the DNR for more than four years in the district's water quality program. The district's budget did not have enough money to pay him through the winter, although it had plenty of work for him.

Larry was just the person I needed. He knew the bureaucracy and the paperwork routines. He was familiar with the backcountry throughout the Northwest District. He knew little about tracking animals and could be trained to be a good tracker.

Larry and I retrieved a wolf-killed deer Jim Dienstl and I had found in the Stateline Flowage Pack's territory earlier in the day. On the ride back to Spooner I took Larry through the Bear Lake Pack's territory, along the Summit Tower Road, east on Highway A, then right onto the Empire Swamp Trail. Flurries started, and I didn't expect to find any sign. I was wrong. Wolf 1187 and a big-footed wolf had cut across the grade about halfway to Highway M. They were heading east.

"Well, I'll be damned," I said as we stooped to inspect the sign. "1187 is traveling with another wolf. I haven't seen this track before."

I walked a short distance ahead of our truck, which I'd parked awkwardly in the middle of the fire lane and left idling. The tracks of 1187 and his pal went straight down the lane for one hundred yards, then swerved suddenly to the edge of the road. A bright yellow urination adorned the snow bank. The other wolf had squatted to urinate. I showed Larry the sign and explained the difference. "I haven't seen 1187 with another wolf in about a month. This is good news. There's supposed to be a pack here with pups. By the way he's scent marking, I'm convinced he's the owner of the territory. What happened to his pups? Maybe we'll find them later this winter." But we had no chance to do so before Christmas.

On January 3 we returned to work. I was eager to fly out and figure out where the wolves were and what they were up to. Jim Dienstl met me at the Solon Springs airport. The plane lifted effortlessly off the decrepit pavement, and, once clear of the jack pines surrounding the strip, Jim dipped the starboard wing and we slipped off to the northwest under cloudy skies and occasional snow squalls from Lake Superior, twenty miles north.

We picked up the signal from the Moose Lake Pack's 1189 first but could not see him. Next, we headed a bit to the southwest, scanning for 1187. I caught his signal.

"Not too far off, Jim. Let's go down," I shouted out over the roar of the engine.

The Jackson Box Road slid by beneath us. The wolf's signal was leading us toward the Empire Swamp.

"We're closing in on him," I hollered.

Ahead I could see the snakelike contortions of the Empire Swamp Trail as it weaved through the swamp, using what little upland ground there was. Below was one of many recent clear-cuts that flanked the grade. Within these sites the aspen regrowth sent dense shoots eight feet in the air in search of sunlight. From above I could see the traces of loggers' trails as they radiated out from cutting areas.

"Wolves! Two of 'em off the left," Jim barked out as he cut the throttle.

As we dropped down, I caught a brief glimpse of our truck ambling down the Empire Swamp Trail, Larry obviously at the helm, not a half-mile from where the action was unfolding.

Jim was a talented pilot. The plane seemed like an extension of his hands, feet, and mind. Whatever he willed it to do, it did. We slowly glided past the two wolves, which seemed not at all bothered by our sudden appearance. The lead wolf was 1187. Tail arched over his back, he trotted nonchalantly down a logging trail. He stopped briefly on the side of the little lane, sniffed a tuft of grass protruding from the snow, leaned with dramatic effect, lifted a leg, and peed.

The second wolf, fifteen body lengths behind 1187, was darker and a bit smaller. Something seemed wrong. Jim's eagle eyes detected it.

"Dick, that second wolf's not using a hind leg."

The second wolf carried its leg high and only occasionally dropped the paw to the ground. Nonetheless, it had no trouble keeping up with our wonder wolf.

We made repeated dips over the area, observing the pair. On one swing through we noted that Larry was parked nearby and watching the action. The wolves were headed in his general direction. Jim and I doubted they would cross with Larry standing there. We followed them for eight minutes, then peeled off and headed west toward the Stateline pack, dive-bombing Larry just for fun. His reaction—a wide grin and shake of his head.

After finding the Stateline Flowage Pack wolves, Jim and I returned to Solon. Jim dropped me off and gradually disappeared into the blue sky. I walked over to the jack pines, brushed the snow from the base of one, and sat down to wait for Larry.

We went right back out to the Empire Swamp Trail to inspect 1187's trail and found it with no problem. Written in the snow was the confirmation I sought. The second wolf was not using its left hind leg. We trailed the pair for three-quarters of a mile. Not once did the second wolf put down a print from that paw. I was curious: Would we ever know what caused this wolf's injury?

A little later in the day we drove up the Bear Lake Road. Not far from the lake, we encountered a fellow who was loading pulp wood onto a flatbed truck. His rig was parked in the middle of the road, so we waited patiently while he finished. He noticed us only after he was nearly done and speeded up so he could move his rig out of the way. He walked toward us and asked whether we were foresters.

"No, we're wildlife biologists studying timber wolves in the area. We're looking for sign."

"No kidding," the young man responded. "I've seen 'em right on this road. Craziest thing. A few weeks back—before Christmas—I was loading my rig when I looks up and out of the woods up by the bend in the road comes this wolf. It walks to within fifty feet of me. I could see a black collar hangin' down from its neck. He stood there lookin' at me for a few seconds an' turned around. He went right down the center of the road an' walks right out of sight behind that very bend." He paused a moment, then added, "I didn't think they'd do that."

Larry and I traded looks. "Neither did we," we answered in unison.

We thanked him for the information. He jumped into his rig and moved it over. As we passed by him, I remarked, "Our friend 1187 is up to his usual tricks."

Larry started laughing and I asked him why. Looking for a sign, I hadn't been paying attention to the road. Larry was looking at a trail of peculiar human footprints.

We got out and inspected the tracks. We were looking at the trail of a resident of Bear Lake, a short distance ahead. He evidently had some type of defect in the structure of his legs. The toes of his feet were splayed out at an unnatural angle, heels nearly together, giving his tracks the appearance of a wide V as he shuffled along.

"He walks his dog up and down the Bear Lake Road a lot," I told Larry. "Found his tracks here regularly all last winter."

Before we left the area, Larry duly recorded the man's tracks on the tracking data form, the one we used for all predator tracks we encountered.

That January Larry and I spent a lot of time discussing wolf 1187's bold nature as we roamed the area looking for sign. I worried that it would be his undoing. Larry was curious to learn why he was behaving in this manner. I reasoned that as the Bear Lake Pack's alpha male, he evidently took his role seriously.

"Kind of like King of the Mountain," I said. "Think of it from his perspective. He's top dog in the area. Wolves evolved over the millennia as a top predator. Nothing out there was 'higher,' so to speak, than the alpha wolves . . . that is, until the advent of agriculture and modern weaponry. So it seems logical that while alpha wolves have gained some respect for humans and their potential to do real damage to a wolf, they're still a bit big-headed. They've got to be or they'd risk losing their position as the alpha and maybe even their life when another wolf challenges them."

"What's the chance of actually seeing a timber wolf?" Larry asked.

Recalling how my assurances to Judy Wendgren earlier in the year had caused me to eat my words, I was hesitant to give Larry any odds, especially where 1187 was concerned. "I don't know," I told him. "I've put in an awful lot of time and only seen them once since beginning survey work in the winter of 1977–78. Chances are slim, but anything is possible."

We were rewarded sooner than I had imagined, on a cold, snowy morning in early February 1981. The thermometer at the Gordon Ranger Station registered 20 degrees below zero. Larry, who lived thirty miles east of Gordon near Cable, Wisconsin, arrived at the ranger station by 7:45 and we headed out about a half-hour later.

About ten o'clock a furious snow squall struck from Lake Superior, creating nearly white-out conditions. Within fifteen minutes an inch of new snow had fallen.

"Well, that just about shoots it for tracking today," I exclaimed in exasperation.

"You want to head back?" Larry asked.

"Nah, we'd be just sitting on our butts at the ranger station. I'd rather keep driving for a while and stall getting back there as long as possible."

We stopped at the junction of Highway A and the Jackson Box Road. "Let's go west and check out the tower road. Those dense stands of balsam might hold this snow aloft, protecting any tracks laid last night."

I didn't for a moment believe what I'd just said. The snow was driving hard at the windshield as we headed into a stiff northwest wind. We pulled off Highway A and headed west on the Summit Tower Road. Snow was still pelting the windshield, considerably diminishing visibility.

We drove over the first hill, dipping down on the west side in a gradual descent toward the abandoned logging railroad grade. We mounted another rise that presented a panoramic view of an expanse of tag alder, stunted tamarack, and black spruce, right where the grade crossed the fire lane.

As we crested the hillock, a timber wolf stepped out from the alder-strewn edge of the lane. We glanced at each other with a look of astonishment. There he was. 1187's coat was beautiful—creamy white undersides blushed with a hint of rufous that blended into deep gray flanks heavily influenced by the dark salt-and-pepper coloration of nape and back. He was less than 250 yards away and faced us with not a concern in the world. After perhaps six seconds he turned broadside, trotted to the opposite side of the lane, and disappeared along the abandoned railroad grade.

As I jumped out of the truck, I shouted, "The gimpy-legged one will follow soon." I didn't worry that my shout would scare the wolves because we were downwind and several hundred yards away from them.

Sure enough, within fifteen seconds the dark-colored wolf darted across the lane, keeping to the brush rather than exposing itself by traveling down the grade. I jumped back in the truck and drove to the spot.

We got out to inspect their tracks, scratching heads as we stopped to consider what had happened. The blowing snow would soon obscure their prints. Our friend was so confident that he had lifted his leg on a tuft of dirt sticking out of the snow—just out of our sight—and then sauntered off along the old railroad grade. Talk about composure.

"Isn't it strange, the difference in behavior of these two wolves?" I said. I pointed out to Larry that this one pair was a good illustration of the extremes in behavior that complex social creatures can manifest. This complicates matters for wildlife biologists, who are trained to look for patterns in life systems that follow predictable paths. And, in fact, most wild critters are fairly easy to predict: they are born, they eat certain types of food, they mate with any receptive member of their species, they stay put in discrete spaces, their populations respond to certain stimuli, they die. But as very social creatures, wolves are not quite as predictable.

We returned to the Bear Lake area the next day to try to determine whether wolf 1187's companion was a female. Convinced that the Bear Lake Pack had failed to rear any pups in 1980, I wanted to learn the prospects for pups in 1981.

February is the peak of the wolf's breeding season. RLUs from the two would likely tell whether the second wolf was a she-wolf. At this time of year most females in breeding condition spill small quantities of blood in their urine.

We didn't have to look far. I had a hunch the wolves would swing east, crossing the trail about halfway down. Indeed, the pair had crossed the trail in the night. At the edge of the road they had anointed the snow bank. And within this RLU was a tiny drop of blood. Our gimpy-legged wolf was a female.

The wolves' trail headed south toward Highway M, and we found their tracks right where we expected to. Our road walker was up to his usual tricks. Wolf 1187 had crossed the blacktop but returned and, altering his course, walked straight west down the center line of the road, which had been blown clear of snow. We found his prints here and there in patches of snow.

But where was Gimpy? Larry left the road to check out the brush on the north side of Highway M. He emerged a quarter-mile west of where we had parked and hollered to me.

"The gimpy-legged wolf paralleled the highway, walking west," he told me. "Her track is pretty evident. She's not putting much weight down on that left hind leg. Most places, all I could see was a skiff where the leg brushed the surface of the snow, despite the fact that the snow is almost belly deep where they break through the crust."

The trails of these two wolves were different. Gimpy had a reason for refusing to cross Highway M to follow her mate. Wolf 1187 had returned to the road not because he chose to walk down Highway M but because Gimpy had refused to cross it. We returned to the truck in silence.

As we jumped into the truck, I said, "Larry, Gimpy's injury was caused by a car. She was hit by a vehicle. That's why she flashed across the Summit Tower Road the other day, and that explains her behavior here."

Larry peered out the frosted side window at 1187's trail, then turned, and said, "You're probably right. She acts different than he does. Especially when a road is involved." Before we called it quits for the day, we snowshoed in on their trail a ways to confirm they had reunited and headed away from the road.

On Friday, at the end of a very productive week, Jim Dienstl and I located wolf 1187 on the eastern edge of his territory. Peering down between the branches in the area of 1187's radio signal, we spied numerous wolf tracks that marred the snow in a small swale of balsam firs. The pair had spent considerable time here. As we circled the scene from above, it became obvious to me that we were looking at sign of a very intimate nature. Clearly, the Bear Lake Pack would have pups to raise in 1981.

After a few days off, I returned to Spooner on Tuesday, eager to learn where we would find 1187 and Gimpy. Unfortunately, Jim Dienstl and I had mixed our signals, and he flew the wolves without me.

I left a note for him at the hangar asking him to bring the flight data and meet me at the Fish Research Building in Spooner. In the meantime I caught up on some office work.

Jim returned with the flight material shortly after lunch. Though he hadn't seen our pair, he'd picked up 1187's signal from deep within the Empire Swamp. Good, I thought, as I packed up my things and headed back home to Tomah, watchful of my hours.

That night 1187 and Gimpy entered the southern rim of a forest of balsam fir and poplar. This timberland stretched north for eight miles from the tag-alder-strewn Empire Swamp. It was a prime deer-yarding area. Riding high off the Lake Superior basin, the ancient continental glaciers had deposited tons of rock here, molding the topography with pockmarked kettles, hills, and eskers. Poplars cover the ridge tops, whereas balsams blanket their slopes. Swales and low spots are carpeted with white cedar — prized winter deer food. On the more expansive ridges, maples predominate.

It was a foggy night. A warm front had slipped in shortly before sunset, sending pulses of mist across the Empire country. The warm air clashing with the cold snow created a thick blanket of fog that enveloped the surrounding forest.

Wolf 1187 and Gimpy slid like shadows beneath the balsam boughs. Up over one ridge and down into a cedar pocket they moved like death on paws. Over the next ridge top they surprised a doe and two fawns who leaped from their beds, racing off in the fog. The wolves took chase but became confused as the three deer bounded through another group of deer, scattering hooves in all directions. The wolves continued on.

They approached the Summit Tower Road. Gimpy hesitated. Wolf 1187 loped unconcernedly out onto the road and, in seeming defiance of the world of humans, anointed the plow bank. He continued down the lane another twenty-five yards, then crossed over into the shadowy underworld of the conifer swamp, beckoning with a whimper for Gimpy to follow.

She hesitated, pranced nervously back and forth, then sprinted forward headlong, leaping clear of the deep snowbank, landing once in the center of the road, and clearing the other side for the safety of the forest. The two wolves scaled an esker, which meandered through the balsam fir, and ran the length of its spine, then jogged down into a pocket, jumping deer several times but resisting the temptation to give chase. Wolf 1187 headed north, perhaps to reconnoiter the upper boundary of his massive territory.

Ten minutes after crossing the Summit Tower Road, the pair approached the Bear Lake Road where it flanks the eastern shore of the lake. Wolf 1187 stepped brazenly out of the shadows and sauntered across the road, over the side of the esker upon which the road rests, and plunged down toward the lake. Gimpy hesitated momentarily at the road, then crossed, trailing behind.

At the base of the hill 1187 crossed the driveway of the man with the odd V-shaped track and sashayed right through the yard. No lights were on in the cabin. Gimpy followed. The two wolves walked between the cabin and an A-frame cottage the man rented out to anglers each summer. As the two wolves neared the shoreline, their presence aroused the family dog. The pair continued on, ignoring the frenzied barking and plodded through an inch of slush lying on top of lake ice.

They were about sixty yards from shore, when the sound of a screen door slamming shut rocketed out across the lake. Wolf 1187 turned around to see what had caused the disturbance. A flashlight beam caught his eyes. A loud "Cr-a-ack" shattered the silence of the night.

The next morning, just as Deb was heading out the door for work, the phone rang. This was unusual and we exchanged puzzled glances. I picked it up.

"Dick?"

"Yes?"

"This is Pat Savage. I've got some bad news for you. I just got some information that a radio-collared wolf was shot last night on Bear Lake."

"What?" I was shocked at the news from the Spooner wildlife manager. Deb gazed at me with an anxious look.

"Does it have ear tag 1187 on it?"

Pat had no answer but said the carcass was just then being retrieved by Joe

Davidowski, the Superior game warden, and they'd have more information later in the day.

As I drove the 150 miles north to Spooner, I kept thinking of the possibilities. I didn't want it to be 1187. Maybe, I thought, it was Moose Lake's wolf, 1189, out for a little stroll, trespassing into the Bear Lake deer yard. No, he had never crossed Highway A. Some trade-off, mentally dickering one animal's life for another because I *liked* 1187 more. I didn't want to barter for any of their lives. Pat Savage had said the dead wolf had a radio collar. One of Mech's wolves down from Minnesota? Fat chance. I didn't want to acknowledge what I already knew. Wolf 1187 was dead.

The carcass was delivered to the Spooner District headquarters late that afternoon. Nearly the entire DNR staff emptied out of the building to see the wolf, whose body lay on the pavement, as game warden Jim Flannigan briefed me on the situation.

The cabin owner with the V-shaped track claimed people were constantly dumping dogs on the Bear Lake Road that would chase and maim deer. He didn't know wolves lived in the area. The fuzzy image he caught in his flashlight beam looked like a dog to him, so he shot it. It wasn't until his wife went out and checked the critter that they saw its radio collar and realized they'd shot a timber wolf. She got in the car and drove five miles to a tavern and called the conservation warden.

Flannigan explained, "He's admitted his guilt. He was issued a citation for violation of Section 29.415 of Wisconsin State Statutes. He will probably forfeit rather than contest. The amount of cash he'll forfeit will depend on what the D.A. and the judge determine is appropriate. The statute allows for a fine up to but not exceeding a thousand dollars. We are recommending they go easy on him because he voluntarily stepped forward, admitting his guilt." (He ultimately was fined $194.)

I thanked the warden and turned to load the wolf into my state car. A crowd still surrounded his body. Most had never seen a timber wolf, dead or alive. One person in the group looked vaguely familiar. With an air of authority he gruffly commented, "We're gonna have this mounted and put on display in our front office for people to see."

I retorted, "Over my dead body. The DNR has an agreement with the University of Wisconsin–Madison to properly preserve rare and endangered species so that the information can be kept intact for scientific work. This wolf isn't going anywhere but down to Madison."

I was furious that in this day and age resource managers still wanted to put rare animals on display. Such displays send mixed signals to the public. We were making a concerted effort to convince people of the value of these animals as *living* members of our state's fauna. By placing the animal in a glass case, we would be reinforcing the notion that this endangered species somehow still retained value as a trophy. Wisconsin residents may no longer legally keep and display protected species in *their* homes. How, then, is it acceptable for a government official to have one mounted behind his or her desk? Further, valuable information on the sex, age, location, and manner of take is all too often lost because no one bothers to ensure such information is preserved. Thus many rare specimens, like the Canada lynx, are on display in several DNR and U.S. Forest Service facilities and are utterly worthless to the scientific community because the staff who collected them no longer work for the agency or have moved on.

This guy backed off, grumbling aloud that he'd display the next wolf brought in. He stomped off.

Greg Sevener leaned over to me and whispered, "Do you know who that fellow is?"

"Not really."

"He's the district director."

I'd saved the wolf from an ignominious eternity and won the personal enmity of the dreaded "DD," who had the power to make professional lives miserable.

I didn't have to worry about Bob Dreis's reaction to 1187's death. By now he had accepted the telemetry program as a beneficial tool. And, rather than being implicated in the wolf's death, the radio collar had actually caused the shooter to confess. The telemetry program was here to stay.

What's in a Name?

Spring came quickly. By mid-April we had made plans for the upcoming trapping campaign. All we needed was equipment, drugs, and a vehicle that could maneuver the beat-up trails in wolf country. Dave Mech at the U.S. Fish and Wildlife Service generously agreed to lend technical assistance once again. Tom Meier was unavailable, but Steve Fritts agreed to take his place.

I met Steve in downtown Solon Springs at about noon on Monday, May 11, 1981. We headed straight for the brush west of town. Our objective: to trap and collar two wolves in Bear Lake and two in Moose Lake. We set out five traps that afternoon, then headed to Gordon to establish our base camp in the back room of the ranger station.

The next morning we hit the trail bright and early. No luck. We continued scouting. On the Jackson Box Road along the eastern flank of the Bear Lake Pack territory, we found a peculiar set of wolf tracks. The left center toe of the animal's left hind foot registered well forward of the right center toe, producing an asymmetrical track, highly unusual for a canid.

"I'll bet you it's Gimpy," I commented as we squatted in the lane to get a closer look. We worked all day, setting an additional twelve traps, then returned to Gordon for the night.

The next morning a light frost blanketed the ground as we drove down Highway M, past the spot where wolf 1187 had tried to coax Gimpy to cross on a blustery cold February day.

A deer jumped out of the brush alongside the road next to a hunting cabin. Up over the next hill a raccoon scurried for cover.

"Great night for animal movements, Steve."

He nodded. We slowed down to turn onto the Empire Swamp Tail. I reached for the trap data log on the dash.

I found what I was looking for and told Steve, "First trap one-point-one miles up, left side, opposite downed poplar branches. Your trap."

We plodded on up the Empire Swamp Trail. A layer of cirrus clouds had blown in off Lake Superior and momentarily obscured the morning sun. Four sets later, we were still wolf-less. The dust bellowed out from behind the truck as it ambled up the lane. We crested the big hill that slopes down into the

Crotte Creek drainage, said to be a good trout stream farther south where it merges with the St. Croix.

Steve slowed as we approached a set I'd placed on the east side of the lane just beyond the pipe that carries water from one side of the grade to the other.

"Baggie's up," I shouted.

Steve brought the truck to a stop ten yards from the spot. We quickly canvassed the scene. The plastic bag lay in the center of the lane. Dirt from the trap site was thrown over the road, and we could see the hole in which I had set the trap. The two-pronged anchor had etched a trough in the road from the hole to the center of the lane where the Baggie lay, then angled back, leaving the road on the same side where the trap had been. Brush and grass had been disturbed, which told us the animal had left the road. Steve caught some motion beyond a four-foot mound of dirt left by earthmovers when the road had been put through.

"It's a wolf," he hollered.

We jumped out and ran to the back of the truck. Steve grabbed the drug kit. I grabbed the clipboard with the data sheet while Steve loaded the dart. Two minutes later the wolf was darted. We returned the equipment to the truck and looked around. This was too public a place to process a wolf. We decided to take it to a side lane that Gimpy and wolf 1187 had often used.

We quietly returned to the animal. It was lying down, head bobbing, eyes glassy. Using the aluminum choke-snare pole usually used to subdue smaller animals, Steve gingerly approached the wolf from behind and pushed its head down. The wolf did not react.

I moved in as Steve took the slack off the trapped foot, which had been anchored securely to a clump of chokecherry. We removed the animal's foot from the trap. I took the trap and pole back to the truck and spread a tarp across the tailgate. Meanwhile, Steve picked up the wolf and laid it on the tarp, then hopped in back with the wolf. I drove us north to the side trail.

I chose a spot on the side trail where the lane widened. We worked quickly. We had more traps to check.

Steve assessed the external condition of the wolf and recorded it on the Wolf Capture Data form, while I took the wolf's temperature, an elevated 104.6. Steve recorded the information next to the time, 0840, and I began cooling the wolf by lifting her hind leg and pouring cold water over her abdomen. A wolf's normal body temperature is 101.4 degrees Fahrenheit. Wolves are greatly stressed by being trapped, then approached by humans, and their body temperature rises in response. This is a potentially life-threatening situation, which is why I started the cooling procedure so fast. Now I fanned her wet abdomen with a clipboard, noting at the same time that this female was lactating.

Within an hour our job was nearly finished. The wolf, an adult female, weighed sixty-five pounds. She was young, perhaps three years old. She now wore ear tags 001 and 002. Before releasing her, we inspected her left hind foot. The left central toe rode forward of the other one. This was the wolf whose track we had seen the day before, four miles to the east on the Jackson Box Road. We found no obvious sign of injury to the leg. Still, I felt certain this was Gimpy.

We released wolf 001 in the shade of a dense stand of balsam firs north of the trail. It was nearly 10 A.M., and we still had traps to check. We hurriedly checked the remainder of our line and were relieved to find nothing in our sets.

Back at the station Steve and I centrifuged the blood, separating cells from serum and packing vials in a box that we refrigerated until the next morning when the mail went out. Blood samples went to Minneapolis for analysis at the lab of one of Dave Mech's collaborators, Dr. Uley Seal. We also sorted through the equipment, replenishing syringes, needles, drugs, and other paraphernalia in preparation for more action.

It wasn't long in coming. Two days later we caught another wolf, this time on the northern edge of the Empire Swamp Trail. We ear-tagged this one 003 and 004. It was a sixty-seven-pound young adult male. A member of the Bear Lake Pack or a trespasser? Interestingly, we encountered fresh tracks of one or two wolves sauntering down the lower stretches of the grade, investigating spots where Steve and I had pulled up sets after capturing wolf 001. But this wasn't her sign.

The next day was Saturday and my office partner, Greg Sevener, accompanied us on our rounds. Bang, another wolf on the Empire Swamp Trail! This one lacked guard hairs on its coat, giving it an unkempt appearance. Dubbed wolf 005, we figured this scruffy sixty-seven-pound male was a yearling, because of his intermediate weight and the lack of wear on his teeth. Greg volunteered to monitor temps. While I prepared to tag the wolf's ears, I taught Greg how to take its temperature.

Greg did exactly as I said but declared he could not insert the thermometer. Nonsense, I thought. I went over the procedure again for Greg as I placed an ear tag in the wolf's right ear.

"Still no go," Greg told me.

I suggested another technique, but Greg told me, "It seems like there's something in there blocking the thermometer."

Ridiculous, I thought. "Its only a turd, Greg. They're soft enough that you can push the thermometer through it. Try again."

Leaning back, Greg replied, "No go. Something's coming out and its very hard."

I dropped what I was doing, noticing that Steve, busy adjusting the collar, was chuckling. There *was* something protruding from the animal's anus.

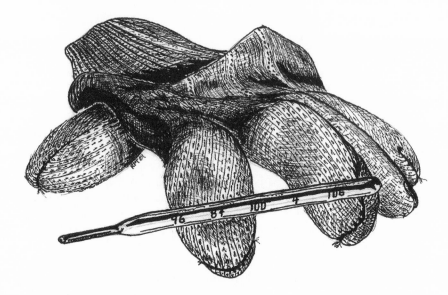

Grabbing two sticks from the limb of a nearby tree, I pinched the object and pulled it out.

"Well, I'll be . . . !" I exclaimed as Greg sat back on his haunches with a perplexed look on his face. "It's a cloth glove."

Steve looked up.

"This proves it. Wolves *do* eat people after all. Steve, we've got a scientific paper here. The poor old sot who got eaten will be immortalized."[1]

Steve, Greg, and I were laughing as I unraveled the remains—three fingers of a Wells Lamont cloth glove. "Wolves sure have an incredible digestive tract," I joked. "For some unexplained reason the cloth glove is intact, but the fingers of the human have been completely digested—bones and all. We're damned lucky to be alive to tell of it. This wolf could have killed us!"[2]

As we settled back to our routines, Greg had no further problems.

We pulled all remaining sets after releasing wolf 005. Steve headed home to Grand Rapids, Minnesota, for a twenty-four-hour break. After preparing its blood to send to Seal, Greg and I retreated to Spooner for some fishing. On Sunday afternoon we headed up to the Moose Lake Pack's territory and put out seven sets.

Steve rejoined me the next morning. The weather was warming up. So were the mosquitoes. We decided to get up and out a bit earlier to get a jump on the heat and the bugs. We were finished checking the line by 9:15. While we were inspecting an old logging road that ran east off the Gregerson fire lane, we ran into Russ Hoag, assistant forest administrator for Douglas County. We chatted a while about wolves before Russ left.

About ten minutes later, just as Steve started sinking a trap in the ground, we heard a vehicle come roaring down the old trail. Because we didn't want to be spotted by anyone who might want to molest our sets or harm a trapped wolf, Steve threw the trap in the woods and gathered up his equipment, pitching it in the bed of the truck. It was Russ.

"You got a wolf in a trap," Russ reported as he jumped out of the truck.

"It's down where the water's spilling over the Gregerson Road. Awful ratty looking. Like something's wrong with it. Must'a just got caught, too, 'cuz it was standing in the road wondering what to do when I rounded the bend."

We quickly drugged the wolf and processed it in a nearby thicket of balsams. It was a sixty-three-pound yearling female that we ear-tagged 007 and 008. Like wolf 005, she was shedding and lacked guard hairs, which made her look ratty. We collared and released her about a quarter-mile off the Gregerson lane. After we put out some additional sets, we returned to Gordon.

The next day, May 20, we caught our fifth wolf, a lactating adult female, which made her the alpha of the Moose Lake Pack. We collared her and gave her ear tags 009 and 010. We had reached our goal in a record ten days. Content, Steve and I packed up, said good-bye, and headed to our respective homes.

The pilots would have their work cut out for them. We were still following three wolves from the previous year, and now we had five new ones.

On a warm day in mid-June I stopped by to fill Bob Dreis in on what was happening with our collared wolves.

"1191 and 1193 are still roaming the Stateline area. She holed up in a spot out in Minnesota but began cruising again by mid-May. Wolf 001 remains in Bear Lake, and wolves 1189, 007, and 009 are holding tight to the Moose Lake country. We still haven't ascertained the pack affiliations of either wolves 003 or 005." (We eventually determined that both 003 and 005 belonged to the Moose Lake Pack.)

"Hold on a minute," Bob interrupted. "I'm all confused by these numbers. You named one of them Gimpy."

"Yeah, but that was before she was collared. She's 001 now."

"Wouldn't it be a lot easier on everybody if you just named them?"

I agreed, but it wasn't good scientific protocol. Researchers had long argued that naming wild animals marked for study might lead the investigator to become emotionally attached to them. The scientific community abhorred any hint of anthropomorphism. Besides, emotional attachment might bias conclusions and their interpretation.

Bob understood. Still, he thought it might be easier. I too had some misgivings about the logic of this so-called scientific protocol. Hadn't I been especially fond of wolf 1187, although I'd followed protocol and given him a number? Somehow the number had made no difference as I had responded to wolf 1187's quirky individuality. Yet nothing I had done in my so-called attachment to 1187 had altered this individual's outcome—he was dead and wolf 001 was evidently raising their pups alone.

For the time being, I stood my ground, trying to do what was best in the name of science. We would stick to the ear-tag numbers.

The policy against naming wolves didn't last long. Jim Dienstl had been flying the wolves solo while I vacationed at home, eating up the overtime I'd accumulated while trapping. I returned to join Jim in locating the wolves one day in late June. We found the Moose Lake wolves, male 1189 and females 007 and 009. Wolves 001 and 003 were in Bear Lake, but so far we had not observed them together. Yearling male wolf 005 was another matter. He had been wandering all over the place.

Pulling out of our low-level circling pattern after locating wolf 001, Dienstl matter-of-factly announced, "Mailrunner is next."

"What?" I asked.

"Mailrunner."

Dienstl could tell I didn't know what he was talking about. He scrambled through the data sheets and map on his lap, then produced a number.

"Wolf 005. He's been all over the place. First, he's in Bear Lake. Next, he's in Moose Lake. Then he's out in the Stateline Flowage area. Last Friday I found him near the edge of a cow pasture on a beef cattle operation near Marksville, way out in Minnesota. I think he's delivering the mail to all the wolf packs out here."

Mailrunner—somehow I liked the name. Bob Dreis did too.

The temptation was too much. I tried to convince myself I was allowing this compromise to make things easier on my coworkers. It was the first step in my total conversion. Wolf 007 was next. She became known as Jamie Bond. But I held fast with the others. For the time being at least, they would remain numbers.

A problem suddenly developed in late summer. In the space of a week we found the chewed-off collars of two Stateline Flowage Pack members, 1191

and 1193, and three collars from the Moose Lake Pack—the ones that had been on 1189, 009, and Mailrunner. Members of their respective packs probably did the deed, but that it was happening simultaneously in two different packs was highly unusual. Jim Dienstl wryly remarked: "Mailrunner spread the news."

This development forced me to resume a trapping campaign in late August 1981. I managed to recapture wolf 1193, but within a week his new collar was chewed off. Clearly, I needed to modify our collars, which were made out of two straps of machine belting. Dave Mech suggested coating the collar with dental acrylic. It was worth a try.[3]

In early October I returned to Moose Lake. Trapping in a Chevette, a small hatchback made by GM for the economy market, was not wonderful, but such was the state of the wolf program. At least I was now a full-time employee of DNR.

Administrators in the DNR's Resource Management Division could not justify assigning a truck to the wolf project. They reasoned the project would last only two years, and the budget simply did not have enough money to buy and operate such a vehicle. This was standard operating procedure for a government agency, not a decision peculiar to the wolf project.

Within four days I caught a wolf. I had been checking traps very early each morning because grouse hunters were using the fire lanes. I couldn't take the chance that a disreputable person would find a trapped wolf before I did and kill the animal. Still, chances were good that my early morning presence could chase wolves off the lane and away from my sets.

I had placed a set deep in the shadows of a balsam thicket along the Tom Green Road. The gravel on the road was disturbed; the Baggie up. As I pulled up next to the site, I glanced quickly into the undergrowth and saw a half-grown wolf pup.

I decided to restrain it with the choke-snare pole rather than drug it. I brazenly walked up to the little bugger. It reared up and lunged, snapping its jaws and growling fiercely. Its reaction surprised and startled me. I then noticed that the trap drag wasn't anchored well and quickly retreated. The pup had defiantly and successfully rebuffed my approach. I slunk back to the car, popped the hatch, and dived for the drug kit, thankful no one had witnessed this embarrassing scene.

I'll teach this sucker a thing or two, my bruised ego proclaimed, as I prepared the dart and dropped it into the chamber of the air pistol. After ten minutes of dancing, I finally got off a shot in the direction of the pup's butt. In three minutes my snappy adversary was down.

It wasn't safe to process the little wolf on such a busy fire lane. Within two miles was a little trail that led to an old farm field. It would be the perfect place to do my work. Because I had no other alternative, I covered the front passenger seat with the tarp and placed my little friend in the car. Chuckling as I carefully laid the wolf on the front seat, I thought, this is probably the only wild timber wolf to have ridden in the front seat of a Chevette—GM could get some mileage with a TV ad like this.

I turned the car around and headed for the Gregerson fields. During the trip I twice had to place my right hand on the wolf's head and force it back to a prone position. We made it to the fields and I quickly processed the little female.

She weighed twenty-seven pounds, and I gave her ear tags 013 and 014.

Right then and there I put an end to the scientific protocol facade. I defiantly declared this wolf's name to be Lucky 13.

Bob Dreis was elated. Lucky 13 heralded the beginning of a new policy. We would henceforth name the wolves. Further, the person who caught the wolf had first dibs on naming it.

Naming wolves involved complex reasoning. Sometimes we named a wolf months before we trapped it. For example, in late 1981 we learned of the existence of a lone male wolf that lived in northeastern Wisconsin, but we did not collar him until 1983.

In early December 1981 I received a call from a fisheries technician out of Sturgeon Bay. He had seen a big timber wolf while deer hunting in the Woods Creek drainage in Florence County. The report intrigued me. The Woods Creek drainage had been the home of one of the last timber wolf family groups in Wisconsin before the species was extirpated in the late 1950s. It was wild country, tucked on the border of the Nicolet National Forest and the Goodman Timber industrial forest lands in northeastern Wisconsin.

Larry and I made plans to check the area and coordinated our activity with Tony Rinaldi, biologist for the Nicolet National Forest, and Ed Wenger, the ranger for the Florence Ranger District of the U.S. Forest Service. Ed kindly allowed us to use a forest service cabin on the south shore of Lost Lake, warning that the long trail off the fire lane—two-thirds of a mile—might not be plowed and that we would probably have to cut wood for heat (ironically, the cabin did have electricity).

We planned to arrive on January 12, 1982. My brother Scott went with me and Larry, and we ended up snowshoeing and skiing all our provisions to the cabin along the trail, which was covered with fourteen inches of snow. By nightfall we were all settled in.

The next morning Larry found our milk frozen nearly solid. It had been sitting on the table, not four feet from the wood stove. In no time Larry had a roaring fire built, and soon we were able thaw out enough milk for breakfast.

By 8:30 A.M. we were ready to go. Larry stuffed the little wood stove full of split wood, turned off the lights, closed the door, and joined us as we skied back to the fire lane. Although it was 20 degrees below zero, our trucks started.

We decided to check out a little lane that ran east along the north end of Lost Lake. It provided access to a campground in summer and now was plowed for a short distance because of an active tree-cutting operation. As we slowed down to turn, I spotted a faded yellow spot on the snowbank opposite the lane.

Must be a fisherman's or logger's urination, I thought, because it never occurred to me that finding wolf sign could be so simple.

We got out. It hadn't snowed for nearly a week. Beneath the snowbank was the faded imprint of a large canid. The track had been dusted in by snow, but its outline remained firmly etched in the crusty substrate. Its front paw measured 4.25 by 5 inches.

Larry found another yellow-stained bank on the south side of the lane, not twenty yards in from the main road. Tracks were not evident here; the tires of logging trucks had pulverized the snow into a glazed surface as smooth and hard as glass.

The canid had left the campground lane and headed south, so we followed. A mile farther on we found another raised-leg urination. Tracks in this area were better preserved. The creature was still heading south. Generally, it walked within the tire tracks, avoiding the center of the lane, which had about an inch of snow, and so left no evidence of its presence. Only now and then did it stray, leaving imprints on the snow between tire treads. We found still more RLUs.

We followed the animal for six miles on the first day, and we managed to find his sign each day we were there and follow him. We gained a surprising amount of information on his movement patterns and the size and shape of his territory in four days of work.

In mid-February we returned to Lost Lake. Our luck held despite poor tracking conditions. Daytime temperatures hovered around 30 degrees, warm enough to melt the surface of the snow, which quickly glazed over as nighttime temperatures plummeted to nearly zero. Finding tracks is a matter of luck under these conditions, because animals moving at night leave few, if any, traces of their presence. Still, we managed to find wolf sign.

At the end of the week we closed down the cabin and stowed our gear in the back of the truck. We headed down the Lost Lake fire lane through the center of the lone wolf's territory just one last time, aware that we would not return until the following winter.

The sky was clear and the sun's glare on the bright, glassy covering of snow burned the retinas of our eyes as the truck slowly negotiated the hill south of

Lost Lake. As we crested the hill, our eyes locked on a huge, dark object in the middle of the road.

"Cripes . . . look at that," Larry muttered incredulously. "It's as big as a loaf of bread."

We stopped and got out to inspect it. This was a truly massive dropping—nearly the diameter of a stick of summer sausage. Nearby, etched in a thin veneer of unglazed snow, was the faint outline of a timber wolf's paw. It measured 4.25 by 5 inches.

As I stepped back to examine this exquisite piece of work, I chuckled and said, "Larry, you just found us a name for this wolf—Loafer!" We laughed deviously, because most people would assume that a wolf named Loafer would be a large, laid-back, lazy animal. None would suspect the name was a scatological reference.

During the winter of 1981–82 we also learned of the Bootjack Lake Pack, which made its home along the wild border between Price and Oneida Counties in north-central Wisconsin. We had been working on several tips.

On a frosty morning in March 1980 Chet Botwinski, the wildlife manager in the area, got a call from a Squaw Lake resident who claimed to have seen a timber wolf feeding on a deer carcass on the lake ice. Chet checked it out and determined that a single timber wolf had indeed killed a buck fawn there. The next spring a memo landed on my desk. Several fish management technicians working along the Buck Creek drainage in eastern Price County in February had reported seeing two very large canid tracks on several trips to that stream. In December 1981 Botwinski again encountered sign while hunting coyotes with his hounds, this time the tracks of two to four wolves.

In February 1982 Larry and I hit the trail, searching for sign of the pack we now felt certain was living there. Chet accompanied us on our first check of the area. As we pulled off the blacktop onto the Sheep Ranch Road, a fairly remote fire lane named in the 1930s for a sheep-raising operation deep within the woods and now long defunct, our truck began sputtering and coughing, jerking violently as it chugged up a small rise. Chet laughed nervously, "Oh, boy, you guys got some truck here."

As he coaxed it along, Larry replied with confidence, "Yeah, it's a little fussy, but she gets us where we need to go." A final deafening belch signified the end of our truck's antics, and we lurched forward without further problems.

Despite a fresh snow to work with, we found no sign of wolves. Late in the afternoon we stopped for a potty break, each of us selecting a spot along the plowed snowbanks to leave our marks.

The next morning we re-ran our survey. I reminded Larry not to pay attention to the yellow-stained snow as we approached the spot where we had urinated the previous afternoon. They would be ours, I assured him, and not the markings of some wolves. But as we passed the spot, we both saw the unmistakable outline of four timber wolf paw prints crossing the lane.

We hit the brakes and jumped out to inspect the area—and found that we had peed within a hundred yards of a deer freshly killed by timber wolves. Judging from what was left of the fawn, the wolves had finished feeding and headed north, crossing the lane precisely where we had relieved ourselves to enter a block of forest filled with cedar swamps and plenty of yarding deer. We'd found a whole pack.

As we looked over the kill site, which was not one hundred yards south of the lane where we had stopped, I realized we had participated in a Far Side moment the day before. "Larry, these wolves were probably sitting here watching us as we anointed the snowbanks."

Naming this pack was not difficult. In the vicinity was a small lake with an unusual name—a name with a bit of wolf history. On a weekend in late January 1947 a crew of Wisconsin Conservation Department biologists working for Bill Feeney had followed the trail of four timber wolves along the Pine Lake Road north of Pier Lake. Their field notes recorded the event:

> They traveled up the road for over five miles. We followed by car to the end of the plowed road where the Nekoosa Paper Mill gate was. We left by snowshoe from here at 9:30 A.M. The wolves went west and continued across the north portion of Bootjack Lake and kept on going west into Price County.

The Nekoosa gate on the fire lane leading to Bootjack Lake was still there. Nekoosa-Edwards still owned the land.[4] And Bootjack Lake was still undeveloped, a natural place for wolves. Biologists from a bygone era had once followed them in these haunts, and it seemed fitting to name this pack after the little body of water called Bootjack Lake.

In July 1982, I returned to collar one or two of the Bootjack Lake Pack wolves. I was primarily interested in trapping within the Nekoosa timberlands south of Squaw Lake. This paper mill company's land holdings were extensive, encompassing about thirty-six square miles of forest. The area had a well-manicured system of logging trails that were cordoned off by impressive gates, effectively eliminating public access to the property. The company gave me permission—and the keys to the gates—to look for wolves there.

Wolf sign was abundant in the area. I set about twelve traps out on a series of logging trails that transected the headwaters of Squaw Creek. On the tenth day I finally connected. With me were Ron Schultz, a local volunteer with the Chequamegon National Forest, and Ron Eckstein, the wildlife manager.

At 8 A.M. it was already hot and humid. As we rounded a curve on the lane leading to our sets, we disturbed a red-tailed hawk perched atop a massive white pine that held its nest. We entered a dense stand of balsam fir whose shade offered escape from the glaring sun. It also provided ideal habitat for mosquitoes. The Baggie was up.

Ron hollered, "Coyote . . . or . . . some kind of pup," as he spied something moving in the grass on the edge of the forest.

I walked over to the animal and looked at its paws. It was a tiny tyke, only fifteen inches tall, but already its paws were three inches wide.

"Timber wolf," I declared and ran back to the truck. I grabbed the choke-snare pole and barked to Ron to get the tarp and processing equipment. He found a shady area and helped me subdue the pup. I slowly circled the animal, gradually extending the rubber-coated cable until it dangled right in front of its nose. I pulled sharply and the noose passed over its ears and around its neck. I gave a jerk and the noose tightened around the little warrior, who was growling fiercely. I gently coaxed the wolfette to the ground, where she gave up without a struggle.

Ron Schultz reached out and grasped the pup by the nape of its neck, hoisting it aloft. The fifteen-pound wolf lay in his arms in a stupor. The effect is not clearly understood, but wolf pups and even some adult female coyotes will not resist and will go into some kind of a trance when handled by humans. We forcefully knock them off their feet, being careful not to present an opportunity to bite us, then pick them up by their nape and rump.

"Whatcha gonna name it, Dick?" Schultz asked me.

I thought for a few seconds. It had been born in late April, by coincidence the same month and year that our first child had been born. I decided to name it in honor of our daughter, Allison.

"I'm gonna name it 'Big Al, the Little Gal,' after Allison."

Forty-five minutes later Big Al sported a radio collar and shiny ear-tag numbers 098 and 099. I picked her up by the scruff of her neck and the fur lining of her rump and gently placed her back on her paws. As soon as they touched the ground, I let go. The little wolf sailed off through the dense undergrowth in a flash. We lost sight of her almost immediately, and the sound of her crashing through the brush gradually diminished until the chirping of the birds and the buzzing of the mosquitoes drowned out the sound of her retreat.

Two days later I caught an adult wolf. Judging from her big, black nipples, she was the pack's alpha female, which meant she was the mother of Big Al. Isn't Deb an alpha female, and didn't she give birth in the same month as

this wolf did? I thought. And weren't their daughters' names the same? The decision was easy. This wolf would be Deborah.

A few months earlier, in May, John Archer, a graduate student researcher, tagged along with Larry and me as we tended our trapline. That spring we caught quite a slew of yearling wolves in Douglas County's Moose Lake Pack. One was a small male. He was nondescript in coloration, and the tranquilizer dart knocked him out fast.

Outward appearances can be deceiving, however. John suffered immensely while processing the wolf. He had the duty of taking rectal temperatures. This wolf had a bad case of flatulence. Each time John inserted the thermometer, an audible whoosh of gas belched forth, wilting every living thing within yards of the animal (afterward we agreed that dog farts weren't nearly as bad). Thus this wolf was known as Flattus.

After watching me and Larry set traps, John asked if he could sink one. We readily consented because the recent mosquito hatch had made trapping disagreeable work. While John set his trap, we sat in the pickup truck, windows rolled up. Two days later the rookie caught a timber wolf.

John was dating a girl named Sharon at the time, so he decided to name the wolf after her. Nearly ten months later Sharon the wolf turned up dead.

I called John to give him the news, adding, "I don't know what you're going to tell your girlfriend."

"That's okay," John replied nonchalantly, "I dumped her a while ago, so it doesn't really matter."

Luck seemed to follow John. We chided him about his apparent skill at capturing wolves. Larry, on the other hand, was in a rut. He too was a rookie. He assisted throughout the 1982 trapping season without capturing a single wolf. His unlucky streak finally broke in May 1983. He named his first wolf Jinx.

The names of a few wolves reflected the reverence we held for them as individuals.

In November 1982, during Wisconsin's first major snowstorm of the season, I captured a female timber wolf within the Stateline Flowage Pack territory. Larry and I were pulling up our sets as we checked them, concerned we would be unable to access our trapline with the predicted snowfall. Over the crest of the lane we saw a lone raven standing in the road, picking at a fresh timber wolf scat.

"You got one, Dick," Larry said. It wasn't until we had drugged the wolf and brought her back to the warmth of the truck to process her that Larry spotted the ear tag. It was 1191, the first wolf I'd ever captured. Her collar had been chewed off in 1981.

She had turned white with age. Because she was the Stateline Flowage Pack's matriarch, I decided to name her Babushka, Russian for grandmother.

The last timber wolf I caught was on the Empire Swamp Trail in the early part of June 1989. Sign had indicated two or three wolves were present in the old Bear Lake area, and I was intent on capturing one of them. It took more than thirty days.

I am convinced that I never would have trapped that wolf if not for a trick I had learned early in my wolf-trapping career. About every three or four days the wolves would walk past our sets, ignoring them completely. I knew these animals were experienced. Two or three days before I caught this wolf, a coyote got caught in one of the traps. I immediately sank a fresh trap at the site, hoping the coyote's "fear scent" would mask our scent and reel the wolves in, by appealing to their curiosity and overriding their caution.

It worked. The old duffer looked thoroughly humiliated when we approached it (Bob Welch and my brother Scott were with me). As we carried the wolf deep into the forest where it could safely sleep off the tranquilizer, Bob referred to my long dry spell by joking, "The Empire strikes back." I immediately named this wolf Darth Vader.

Deer, the Wolf's Bread
(and Bane) of Life

It is no secret, of course, that the timber wolf is a deer predator
and that they are able to and do kill deer.

Letter to Aldo Leopold from Bill Feeney, December 18, 1944

It was the Monday after the opening weekend of the 1980
deer season, and we were looking for wolves from the air. The Stateline Flowage Pack's territory was largely roadless. When I was certain we were on top
of the pair, I hollered to Jim Dienstl to begin circling, and I started fiddling
with the equipment to pinpoint their location within the last circle. Suddenly,
I felt the plane lurch. Looking up, I noticed Jim was peering intently out the
port side as he deftly maneuvered the plane into a rapid descent.

"There's a patch of red down there. Lots of ravens too," Jim shouted over
the roar of the engine. I gazed at the spot as he described it, but the land was
so nondescript that it was difficult to determine where he was looking.

"See the two spruces on the edge of that narrow marsh? There's a patch of
red and lots of—there's a dead deer down there." We were still twelve hundred feet up and descending fast, but I could not locate the spot. Hundreds
of spruce were scattered across the landscape down there, and the low-lying
ground was seething in marsh grass. "There's a wolf! Standing next to the
deer . . . don't you see? Next to the spruce!"

"What spruce?"

Jim flipped me a look of incredulity. I didn't see the site until we were so
low that flushed the ravens. They erupted out of a little crescent-shaped
marsh pocket and alighted in the branches of the surrounding stand of dormant quaking aspen. The deer lay on its side. Red blood bathed the grass for
a radius of perhaps five yards. Evidently, the wolf had disappeared about the
time the ravens flushed. I didn't see it, but I could tell by their signals that
both 1191 and 1193 were nearby.

Jim hollered back, "Seen enough?"

I asked him to fly higher by pointing upward with my index finger. As he
opened the throttle and pulled the nose skyward, I contorted my hulk sideways, straining to reach a roll of topographical maps stashed in the cubby behind my seat. When we got to about twenty-five hundred feet, we were able to
determine the approximate location by estimating the distance and bearing
from the T intersection of two fire lanes to the south.

The kill was located about 23 degrees northeast and about 1.5 miles from the junction of the fire lanes. Smoke curling out of stovepipes told us that several hunting shacks just east of the junction were occupied. As the plane bounced eastward, I placed a dot on the map and scribbled the notation "11/25/80—1191&93 DK" next to the spot.

Jim dropped me off at the Solon Springs airstrip. I headed down to Spooner to check for messages and give Bob Dreis an update on the doings of our wolves over the previous weekend.

Bob wasn't in. I left him a note and headed over to the Fish Research Building to check in with the gang and catch up on what had happened since the last time I'd seen everyone. Nearly everybody was out, on annual leave so they could hunt deer. The only two around were Greg Sevener and Larry Prenn. Neither hunted deer.

I told Larry and Greg about the kill we'd seen from the plane and mentioned that I was thinking about going out to look at it. Greg asked what that would entail.

"Well, first we have to find it. The deer was fairly intact a few hours ago, which means the wolves are likely to be working it over. I'll start from the road junction, walking in on the bearing we got until I can pick them up. I should be able to locate the kill by following the wolves' signals. Once there, I'd like to determine the age, sex, and condition of the deer."

Greg wanted to go, and despite some intensive coaxing, Larry remained behind to catch up on some lab work. We headed out immediately. About two hours later we pulled over at the junction of the two fire lanes, ironically named the Swedish Highway and the West Moose Road after the settlers who had tried, apparently unsuccessfully, to wrest the land from one of its native inhabitants.

"We gotta move fast, Greg. The sun will set in another two and a half hours, and we have a three-mile walk ahead of us through the brush." As we donned our pullover blaze-orange sweatshirts, I wondered aloud, "Should I take my gun in case we see a deer?" Greg was a big help, answering, "I don't know." I decided that carrying the firearm would just be more weight to carry. Besides, what were the chances we'd really see a buck?

I stuffed the radio receiver and portable antenna into my backpack and I double-checked my pockets for my compass. Pulling it out, I set it to 23 degrees. I stood in the middle of the intersection, lined up the bearing on the compass against magnetic north, peered down the line-of-travel arrow, and motioned Greg toward the route we had to take. We set off on our jaunt through the woods, skirting to the west of an occupied hunting cabin on the east side of a small creek.

We hiked into the woods for perhaps five minutes before I thought it safe to pull out the radio equipment. I didn't want to alert nearby hunters that a wolf pack was in the neighborhood lest it increase the wolves' vulnerability. Hunters who saw our equipment might put two and two together. To save time I hooked up the equipment while we walked. The signals were coming in weakly, but they were in line with the direction of our compass bearing. We continued on.

After walking for perhaps forty-five minutes through a low-lying mixture of balsam fir, white spruce, and overmature aspen, we found ourselves on a large sloping ridge that rose imperceptibly from the surrounding lowlands. The forest composition had changed. Towering big-tooth aspen, with their yellowish bark, shot gracefully skyward, and here and there were clusters of stately northern red oak. The canopy was twice as high on this ridge as on the adjoining swampy ground through which we'd been trudging. The understory was composed of ironwood, with their double-tiered, serrated, teardrop leaves still clinging to branches in yellow streaks. Interspersed were occasional clumps of hazel. Both species reached the northern edge of their ranges in these environs.

The ground was littered with leaves, which crunched noisily beneath our feet as we weaved between the trunks of the majestic trees. Greg, a few feet behind and to my left, motioned to me, pointing carefully to our left. About thirty yards away stood a hefty six-point buck, standing broadside and unaware of our presence. It would have been a perfect shot through this open hardwood stand, and I, of course, had elected to leave my gun in the trunk of the car. As I noted the smirk on Greg's face, I slowly raised my arms in the direction of the deer and barked out, "Bang!"

Startled, the deer turned its head to confront the noise, raised its tail in a stiff arch, and trotted in a calculated fashion off to the southwest. We could see it clearly until it disappeared over a rise about two hundred yards away.

By now the sun was well along on its dive toward the western horizon. Light was fading on the leeward side of the great hill, and I estimated we were three-quarters of a mile from the kill. The countryside sure looks puny from the air, I thought, as we trudged on. Greg asked if I'd seen the aspen and oak ridge from the plane because it was such a massive feature from our perspective. I hadn't.

I checked the signals. They were coming in clearly but from a slightly different angle than our compass bearing. We abandoned the bearing and began homing in on the signals. "I only hope the wolves haven't left the kill site, or we will be walking around here forever." Greg let out a little chuckle, acknowledging that he was thinking that very thing.

After fifteen minutes we lost our hill and were plunged into a morass of loosely matted marsh grass that kept grabbing our feet. The aspens in this section were stunted, and the trunks were heavily infested with blackened cankers, an indication of the poor growing conditions in the moist soils underfoot. The going got rough. Dense undergrowth of alder brush and marsh grass slowed our progress, eating precious time.

After what seemed to be an eternity, I turned to Greg and declared that we were closing in. "I have the gain down to three. The wolves have got to be close."

"Recognize any of the local features here?" Greg asked.

"No. Everything looks the same. Jim kept pointing out two spruce, but I saw countless clusters of spruce. This stand of timber is just as featureless."

We had been walking slightly north of northeast for quite some time. I rechecked the bearing by sweeping the hand-held antenna and noticed that the direction had shifted slightly to our right across a small pocket of marsh grass.

At that very moment raucous crows and ravens exploded from the trees, fleeing that very area. The signals on my receiver suddenly went ballistic. *Beep* . . . beep, beep . . . *BEEP* . . . beep, beep, *BEEP.*

"We jumped the wolves, Greg!" I exclaimed. Poor Greg was left in my dust as I sprinted across the swale of grass and splotched through ankle-deep water.

Greg caught up with me on the far side of the opening. Sentinel crows, perched atop nearby spruces, voiced their indignation at the intrusion on their feast, but we still hadn't located the dinner fare.

"Anything look familiar here?"

"Yeah. The spruce Jim identified are over there," I said, pointing to the east where several crows sat, busily giving us a piece of their mind. We decided to work in opposite directions, moving out from a clump of alders in a spiral that encompassed the eastern half of the marsh.

Within a few seconds Greg hollered, "Over here—I got blood and hair. Over here!"

By the time I reached him, he'd located the kill. It was a skeleton. Evidently, the wolves had not been aware of our approach until we were on the opposite side of the marsh. Startled, the wolves darted off, flushing the crows and ravens and revealing the presence of the kill site.

The buck's head was attached to a thoroughly mauled vertebral column. Hidden at the base of another clump of alder brush a short distance away were the femur and tibia-fibula of one hind leg. This was all that remained. Blood bathed the surrounding marsh grass for some distance. Thick patches of hair and pieces of hide lay scattered within a ten-yard area of matted marsh grass. Anchored to the ribs, which had been cracked off close to the backbone, were tiny shreds of rosy red flesh. The buck's eyes were glazed, blue-brown pupils gazing eerily into eternity.

By now the sun was nearly down. We went to work, taking photographs and cracking open the femur to inspect the marrow. Deer in advanced stages of

starvation have depleted fat reserves, including marrow fat, which normally gives marrow a creamy appearance. Depleted marrow is typically red and runny. This buck had plenty of marrow fat.

I wanted to age the deer, which is a matter of checking the wear of the teeth in the lower jaw. To save time Greg and I chopped the buck's head off and stuffed it in my backpack, its eight-point rack sticking out. I could age it later.

Fortuitously, one of the few useful lessons I'd learned in tenth-grade geometry came streaming back to me as we stood in the darkening forest. *The shortest distance between two points is a straight line.* Ahh, yes!

"Greg, let's set our course for 180 degrees—due south. Rather than groping back on the course we took, we head straight south to the West Moose Road. According to my estimate, we should come out east of where we parked the car. When we reach the road, we turn right and head west."

"Sounds good to me. But aren't we cutting it close to those cabins? What'll we tell the hunters if we bump into them?"

"We won't bump into them. Don't worry."

We headed out at a quick pace, unencumbered by the need to stop periodically and check signals. We made time.

At one point we heard water gurgling as it rushed over rocks, so we diverted around the rivulet hidden in a dense maze of marsh grass. The tiny creek swept in from the left and bent back to the east. It was soon lost in the twilight haze.

Roughly a half hour had elapsed since we had left the kill site. The horizon was awash with the colors of sunset. We mounted a rise covered by red oak, and suddenly right in front of me appeared a fellow dressed in blaze orange. We had no time to duck out of sight. He'd already spotted us.

I thought, for chrissake, he's coming out of an outhouse!

Greg chuckled nervously, mouth dropped ever so slightly in a look that said uh-oh.

What's a cabin doing so far from the road? I thought, as the guy shouted out a greeting.

As we walked toward him, I uttered a reply. The buck's rack in my backpack towered above my six-foot, three-inch frame, and I could tell the fellow's eyes were bugging out at its magnitude. Shit!

"Howdy," I said as we got closer. The fellow was dressed in a slightly faded and smudged blaze-orange pullover, unzipped from neck to waist. He was about thirty and sported three days' worth of stubble on his rotund face. Behind him was the cabin, smoke curling cozily from its stovepipe chimney. Two other gents stood near the front of the tarpaper structure, warming their hands next to a bonfire. This is going to be fun, I thought.

"Whatcha guys got there?"

I was thinking, don't offer any information—"It's a buck we found."

"Whatcha guys doing back here?" another fellow asked as they stared at the rack. They could also see the stem of the folded antenna sticking up through the backpack. It was resting against the tines of the buck's rack.

Here goes nothing. "We're from the DNR. We're studying timber wolves and got a bunch with radios out here. A warden pilot reported a dead deer near the West Moose Road this morning and asked us to bring it in."

"Goddamn wolves!" one man proclaimed in disgust as he eyed the rack.

"We been hearing 'em the past two nights howling up to the north. I think they're pretty neat," another proffered.

"I'll shoot the sonsabitches if I see one," the first retorted.

"You'll do no such thing—or that's it between us, Cousin," the third replied.

Now here's an interesting twist, I thought. Things don't always turn out the way you think. Of the three men, two didn't seem to mind that wolves were living in their hunting area. I sensed they wished the wolves weren't around but got the distinct impression they wouldn't harm them. One felt so strongly that he even threatened to break family ties if the other one misbehaved. Clearly, this would not have been the case twenty or thirty years earlier. Times were a-changing, even up here in the brush.

"You didn't answer my question. Did the wolves kill that buck?"

"No." *Of course they killed it. But I don't think you want to hear that.* "Looks like it was shot and wounded, probably on opening day," I told them. "The wolves found it after it was dead and devoured most of it. I'm taking the head out and will age it later back at our office."

"That's funny," the supportive one said. "We didn't hear any shooting from up in that direction all week."

I got the distinct impression that none of them bought my little lie. We chatted some more, then bid adieu and walked down the drive to the West Moose Road. Our car was a short distance away. Silently, we loaded the equipment into the backseat, got in, and headed south, returning to Spooner for the night.

I was disturbed by my less-than-honest behavior with these hunters. I hadn't come clean with them or myself. And I hadn't done the wolf project any favors. I'd been afraid of the fallout. A lame excuse. I'd failed myself.

But it was over and done with. However, I resolved from that moment on to tell the truth in discussing wolves with the public, however uncomfortable that might be. What was at stake was integrity—my own personal integrity and the integrity of the wolf program. Coming clean with the public was vital to ultimately restoring a place for the wolf in a place called Wisconsin. This experience was a good lesson for an overanxious, neophyte wolf biologist.

Deer are the center of the wolf's being in Wisconsin. Dan Thompson's pioneering study of wolves' food habits, conducted as Wisconsin wolves were becoming extinct at midcentury, showed the extent of their reliance on deer—nearly 95 percent of their diet.

Food habits studies conducted in the 1960s and 1970s in neighboring Minnesota, at Isle Royale National Park in Lake Superior, and in Ontario, Canada, revealed that wolves supplement their diets extensively with beaver, especially in the snow-free months. Beaver, which were exceedingly rare in Thompson's day, have since rebounded and are abundant. They are Wisconsin's largest rodent, weighing thirty to sixty pounds. With the reappearance of wolves in Wisconsin, I felt it would be valuable to determine just how important deer and beaver were in the diets of wolves.

We set up a food habits study, enlisting a graduate student from the University of Wisconsin–Eau Claire to perform the analyses. I usually drove through Eau Claire as I returned home after a week afield, so it would be convenient for me to drop off scat samples periodically.

For our part, in the field all we had to do was collect the scats. I kept the Wolfmobile stocked with brown-paper sandwich sacks and a clipboard that held a data sheet and a pen. Each time Larry Prenn, Ron Schultz, or I encountered a dropping, we would use twigs chopstick-fashion to pick up the scat and deposit it in a bag. On the bag we recorded the date, location, wolf pack name, and the name of the person who collected the sample. We recorded the same information on the data sheet attached to the clipboard.

While picking up and bagging an animal's droppings may sound disgusting, the task was usually not all that unpleasant. Biologists, after all, are trained to search for clues by poking around in the byproducts of living things.

However, on occasion, shit happens. Take, for instance, the time Larry and I were driving down a logging road in Lincoln County's New Wood country. The Averill Creek Pack had been working the vicinity of a lumbering area for several days, and we were interested in looking for droppings. As we came up over a small rise in the ice-covered trail, we spied a big, black, greasy pile of dung in a swale in the middle of the trail. Larry stopped the truck and we walked over to inspect the pile.

It was perhaps 10 degrees that day. The feces appeared to be frozen, probably deposited the day before. We peered at it without stooping to inspect it closely. It was rather large. Unusually large, in fact, but Averill Creek Pack wolves are large, I thought.

Mechanically, I said, "I'll collect it." I turned and walked back to the truck to retrieve a bag and pen. While I did this, Larry walked up the trail, searching for a track to verify its depositor as a wolf. In a crevasse in the righthand snow bank Larry discovered with horror several wads of used toilet paper. Reeling around as I bent over, "chopsticks" in hand, Larry laughed as he warned, "That's human!"

Two years and several hundred scats later we had a pretty good impression of the food habits of Wisconsin's newly returned wolves. As we had expected, the fundamental ingredients of the wolf's diet are deer, beaver, and snowshoe hare. Seasonal shifts in the relative contributions of deer and beaver were evident. During winter deer are the mainstay, while beaver are locked safe and sound beneath the ice in their watery world, unavailable to the wolves.

The scat study revealed that beaver was the meal of choice in spring. I had suspected as much. Like clockwork, in early March of each year our radioed packs would alter their usual travel patterns and begin following the many creek drainages that transect each territory, intent on "visiting" the many beaver lodges scattered up and down the streams. The wolves would bound to the tops of the beavers' stout, wooden lodges, which were still draped in a blanket of snow, and make futile attempts to dig down through the vent to reach the occupants. The pilots and I were left with the distinct impression that by spring the wolves had grown sick of venison and longed for a change in menu. As the snows receded, the wolves' movements became more and more associated with the stream banks—they were seizing the opportunity to ambush an unsuspecting beaver, who also was out and about to welcome the dietary bonanza spring brought. Thirty-five percent of the spring droppings consisted of beaver.

In summer deer fawns are the wolves' main repast. In the fall beaver reappear in significant numbers in the wolves' diet, before wintry winds glaze over the ponds and seal these large aquatic rodents from the wolves. Snowshoe hares appear uniformly in the diet throughout the seasons, at the rate of about 10 percent of the scats. Notably absent from the droppings were livestock.

The scat study revealed what is empirically evident: winter is the season when wolves in the heavily forested upper Great Lakes region are most dependent on deer. Beaver and other small game are unavailable then. The only other dietary option for wolves is the three-pound snowshoe hare—good for snacks between meals but hardly sufficient to sustain an individual wolf, much less a pack. The wolves' dependence on deer in winter—when wolf kills are most easily detected by humans—earned the wolf the enmity of early sport hunters.

Deer begin arriving in their wintering yards in late November. They trickle in at first, but the number of arrivals increases as winter weather tightens its grip on the land. Does bring their fawns, who learn the tradition of yarding from their mothers' example. By the end of December even the most studly of bucks has entered the yard. And the wolves know where to seek dinner.

As the deer congregate, their metabolism slows. The accumulating winter snows confine their movements. Their fat reserves, built throughout autumn, slowly become depleted. Prolonged cold weather and deep snows accelerate the fat depletion, taxing the deer's already-stressed condition.

Deer bide their time in this deadly endurance race. When winter lingers, the deer succumb, one by one, or in droves.

In the winter of 1978–79 snow depths reached nearly four feet in the Bear Lake deer yard. The magnitude of the winter's effect on the deer herd didn't hit me until one fine day in mid-February when we were trailing three or four Bear Lake Pack wolves through the alder-infested tangle called the Empire Swamp. As the wolves approached the firs that rimmed the swamp, a cloud of ravens flushed. Three or four hundred of them.

The wolves' trail entered the forest and the deer yard that lay within. The wolves walked by the carcasses of three dead deer in the space of four hundred yards. Judging by the signs, long before these wolves had arrived, the deer had succumbed to exhaustion from wading through shoulder-deep snow and simply trying to endure the bitter cold temperatures. The deer we encountered had simply collapsed and died of hypothermia when they could no longer exert themselves.

The wolves walked past many deer carcasses without stopping. Further down the trail they dug one out of the snow and consumed it. The hundreds of dead deer in this yard provided a veritable smorgasbord for the ravens, coyotes, local bobcats, chickadees, woodpeckers, bald eagles, and wolves.

That winter the wolves did not have to kill. Mother Nature took care of that task for them. Wisconsin lost eighty-five thousand deer to starvation and exposure.

In the hundreds of hours we accumulated "flying wolves," however, we never saw them make a kill and only once witnessed a chase. That single chase provided Jim Dienstl and me with a glimpse of how hunting wolves work as a team.

The land beneath us was locked in the dead of winter. The snow was deep, as much as twenty-five inches on the bare hardwood ridges. We were flying over a small drainage on the western edge of the Moose Lake Pack's territory and were dropping down, homing in on the signal of wolf 1189.

The signal was getting louder, and just as I told Jim that we were close, I noticed a deer through the rotating propeller. The deer had just emerged from a stand of firs so thick that we could not see through it. Then it ran through some aspen at the edge of the marsh. Ten body lengths behind it a wolf emerged in hot pursuit.

The deer vaulted laboriously, its movement slowed by the deep snow. The wolf was also having problems, bounding through nearly chest-deep snow in an effort to gain on its quarry. Suddenly, the deer veered out into the marsh, hoping the deeper snow in the open would shake its pursuer.

The wolf started to cross, then retreated to the high ground, stopping to catch its breath and watch as the deer neared the far side of the marsh. As the deer reached the cover of the forest, another wolf bolted from beneath the boughs to greet it. Less than five yards separated the deer from certain death, and it turned abruptly in midair. Forced back out into the marsh, the deer bolted for the other side. Streaking after it was the second wolf.

The deer's first pursuer, meanwhile, was already weaving along the edge of the marsh, anticipating where the deer would reach high ground, and rushed forward to block the deer's escape. The deer made the high ground just ahead of the first wolf and lit out through the conifers, gaining precious ground as both wolves waded through the deeper snow on the edge of the marsh. Both wolves trailed three body lengths behind now, intent in their pursuit, but the second wolf was tiring and starting to lose ground.

We followed the chase through the conifers as best we could, but the dense spruce and fir boughs concealed the outcome of that hunt.

We had witnessed one of evolution's primal processes, this drama of predator and prey. Jim held out that the wolves won. I believe the deer escaped. Only the conifers, the wolves, and perhaps that deer know for sure.

Our winter flights also revealed why some people, especially hunters, have such a problem with wolves—the hunters hate competing with wolves for game. Some hunters (happily, a minority today) believe that wolves will either kill off all the deer or cause them to leave an area. During an extreme winter, hunting by humans and wolves can cause a significant decline in the deer population. But at least one study has shown that during a severe winter, hunting by humans, both legal and illegal, and the weather itself, killed more deer than wolves had. Nonetheless, some people have developed an almost irrational hatred of the wolf, an emotion handed down in some circles for generations.[1]

During a four-year period we located and inspected the remains of twenty-six wolf-killed deer. Although our sample was small, Wisconsin wolves appear to be concentrating on fawns and older-aged deer. Thirty-eight percent were fawns. Yearlings and two-year-olds, generally the most fit members of the deer herd, accounted for only 9 percent. Fifty-three percent were senior citizens.

Wolves faithfully capitalize on the slightest weakness. They select fawns because they are small and do not offer much resistance. They are also inexperienced at detecting and escaping from predators. Fawns are also the most abundant age group in the herd and thus most available.

Older deer comprise the smallest segment of the herd (three-year-olds and older age classes collectively comprise less than 35 percent of the herd). They suffer from the cumulative effects of a harsh life: diseases, parasites, teeth worn so close to the gum line that they no longer chew food into particles small enough to digest properly, harsh winters that take a toll on muscle as well as fat stores, and the stress associated with providing milk for newborn fawns. Wolves prey on older deer in disproportion to their abundance because their debilities make them vulnerable.

Advocates for wolves sometimes misuse wolf-kill statistics in their zeal to show that wolves are really not such bad characters. For instance, some wolf advocates wrongly proclaim that wolves kill *only* the sick and the weak. While that often is the case, one of the first wolf-killed deer that I found provided a perfect example of how an apparently healthy deer in its prime becomes a meal for a pack of wolves.

On a cold day in early March 1978 I found the trail of the Bear Lake Pack as it crossed a fire lane within the Bear Lake deer yard. I decided to follow their back trail. Within a half-mile of the road I encountered a kill site. As I carefully circled the area, I was able to piece together how they made the kill.

A two-year-old doe had bedded down on the lower slope of a glacial kettle within a glade of white cedar. Perhaps it had selected this spot to block out the cold northwest wind or to take advantage of the early morning sunshine. But her selection proved her undoing.

That same night the Bear Lake wolf pack, consisting of seven wolves, happened to cruise that deer yard, and their course led them directly to the bedded deer. Until the wolves crested the hill, they were not aware of the deer. Her life was over before she even detected those silent runners. The wolves had pounced on their unsuspecting prey from above, bringing the deer down twenty feet from its bed. This doe appeared to have been healthy, based on what I was able to tell from her remains.

Opportunity was on the side of the wolves that night. The healthy deer became a death statistic because of fate and her selection of a site that did not allow her to detect danger in time to react. Simply put, she was in the wrong place at the wrong time. Neither wolves nor deer care the slightest for statistics or the manipulations of humans interested in swaying public opinion. Healthy deer do get killed and manage to become meals for wolves on occasion.

A commonly held belief is that single wolves cannot kill deer. This is not true. On a blustery day in early December 1982 Jim Dienstl and I homed in on Sharon, then a yearling, as she slowly moved west, away from her natal Moose Lake territory. Near the western edge of Minnesota's Nemadji State Forest, we spied her standing over a freshly killed fawn, roughly the same size as Sharon. She had killed it.

Many people are fascinated by the methods wolves use to kill deer. They kill deer any way they can. Wolves are far more interested in gaining a meal than in determining the most effective way of bringing it down.

I have inspected a few fresh kills in my career. Typically, the wolves grab the deer by the throat and body-slam the animal off its feet. The rest is just mop-up work. I especially remember the first freshly killed deer I inspected. I had been working with Larry Prenn, Ron Schultz, and Ron VanderVelden, Kaukauna High School's environmental education teacher, in Lincoln County's New Wood country. VanderVelden bumped into the kill and hollered for me to join him. He stood watching intently as a chickadee perched defiantly atop the rump of the deer, vocally chastising Ron for having disturbed him at his meal.

The only marks on the deer were a severe bite to the throat and an area surrounding the anus. The damage near the animal's rump was the result of wolves feeding and had nothing to do with the manner in which they had taken the deer down. Sign in the snow indicated a wolf had run abreast of the deer, grabbed it by the throat, and slammed it to the ground. Once it had the deer off its feet, the wolf had clamped its jaws firmly around the deer's windpipe and suffocated it.

Wolves will occasionally kill livestock (and pets). As knowledge of their return to Wisconsin spread, complaints of depredations began. Most were without warrant.

On a cold day in mid-March 1981 I stopped by to chat with Joe Davidowski, a warden stationed near Superior. Joe had just returned from inspecting a livestock depredation complaint a few miles south of the city of South Superior. He had learned of the complaint while watching television the previous night. A Duluth TV station had aired a clip of a farmer who had found two dead calves in his pasture. The farmer had recently learned that a timber wolf pack roamed Douglas County and decided they might be the culprits.

March is typically a slow news month in Duluth. The station had learned of the farmer's story and decided to make an issue of it.

But the farmer's story didn't add up: we knew of no wolves within twenty miles of South Superior. Back at the Gordon Ranger Station that night, I alerted Fred Strand, the wildlife manager, and called Steve Fritts. Steve handled the Minnesota depredation control work for the U.S. Fish and Wildlife Service. I was counting on his expertise to get to the bottom of this one. Both biologists agreed to inspect the farm the following day. Joe Davidowski alerted the farmer and informed the TV reporter who had handled the story.

The next morning we converged on the farm, situated in the tag-alder flats a few miles southwest of town. While no timber wolf packs were known to be living in the area, one could have wandered in and gotten into trouble there.

The TV crew was already on hand when we arrived. The farmer was cordial and seemed to be fairly level-headed. He had about forty-eight head of cows in the pasture, and most had already begun lactating. He simply wanted to know what had happened to the two dead calves.

We found the carcasses forty yards behind a small hay shed at the edge of a fenced pasture overgrown with tag alder. Both calves were tiny. Not much remained. Scats on the surface of the snow indicated coyotes and domesticated cats had fed on the remains.

Steve and I inspected the hooves of the calves while the camera crew filmed. Fleshy sheaths that looked much like translucent bootlets covered their hooves. The sheaths are designed to protect the uterus of the mother while the calf is still inside.

In a subdued voice Steve said, "These sheaths aren't even worn. They're usually worn off within the first twenty-four hours of life. I'd say these calves were either stillborn or died shortly after birth."

We looked at the exposed rib cages and gut cavities. The viscera had been entirely consumed, and shreds of meat clung to the ribs. Wolves would have eaten the whole thing, bones and all.

"Definitely not the work of wolves," I said as Steve, Fred, and I turned the carcasses over to look at the underside. We walked back to the farmer, who was standing next to Joe behind the television crew.

As Steve began to speak, the TV crew shoved a microphone in his face. "Sir, it appears these two calves were either stillborn or died shortly after birth. Little is left of the remains. It is next to impossible to tell what caused their death. I can say they were definitely eaten by coyotes and at least one of your barnyard cats," he told the farmer and pointed to a cat that was squatting beneath a plank beside the hay shed.

I added, "The timber wolves you heard of roaming Douglas County live some fifteen miles south of here. We've got 'em radioed. None of these packs come closer than that. Their ranges lie considerably south of here. Despite that, it is possible a young wolf searching for a mate and a new place to live might go through here and kill your stock. Like Steve said, we can't tell you what caused their deaths, but we can tell what *wasn't* responsible. Timber wolves would have had no trouble eating the entire carcass of each of these calves. There have been no timber wolves in your pasture.

"If it's all right with you, I'd like to take one of the calves back with me. After it's thawed, I'll skin it to look for sign of teeth marks and blood beneath the skin. This would indicate a predator attack."

The farmer nodded his consent. After some additional conversation, the farmer thanked us and accepted our explanation. The news reporter wanted some interview time with Steve and me.

I explained that the timber wolf was an endangered species within Wisconsin, summarized our survey work, and stressed how few wolves were found in the state.

"Only one case of livestock depredation has been confirmed since the wolves returned to Wisconsin in the mid-1970s. Keep in mind that the situation in our state differs from the experiences of Minnesota, where wolves are fairly abundant and they do cause damage to livestock. We are concerned about the potential for problems in Wisconsin, but, thus far, as in this case, we haven't experienced any trouble."[2]

The reporter thanked us, reminded me to call her as soon as I'd inspected the carcass, and turned to the farmer for a final impression.

Back at the station I waited until the carcass had thawed sufficiently and peeled the skin off the calf. I found no evidence of subcutaneous hemorrhaging, an indication that a predator had attacked. I called the television station with my report, making sure I talked to the reporter who had conducted the interviews.

Retiring upstairs, I plugged in my portable TV, adjusted the antenna until I could discern images through the fuzzy snow on the picture screen, and curled up in my sleeping bag with book in hand, confident the reporter would vindicate the few timber wolves roaming the Douglas County forest lands.

I was wrong. She had taken the angle of pitting big-time government employees against the word of a local farmer who was simply trying to make a living. "While representatives from the DNR claim they have proof timber wolves weren't involved in the deaths of two calves, they had trouble convincing one area farmer."

I was flabbergasted. From our conversations with the farmer after our inspection, I convinced the reporter had taken his story out of context. Sensationalism makes for high ratings by attracting plenty of viewers but it is mighty poor journalism.

Sadly, not all the people who saw the sensationalized version would learn the facts, which DNR's public relations department set out in press releases. The misinformation in this one newscast might well shape the public's view of the wolves' return to Wisconsin.

While the wolves had not caused any problems in the area immediately surrounding Superior, a few people did raise livestock within the area that the wolves occupied in western Douglas County. In 1980, I conducted an aerial census to determine how many farms actually existed within the study area.

On a bright, clear day in early October we flew high above the land and counted 32 residences with livestock within the 380 square miles of occupied wolf range. In all, we counted 28 horses, 152 beef cattle, 284 dairy cattle, 40 sheep, and 6 hogs. The majority of these farms lay on the edges of occupied wolf territories, where wolves were likely to spend the least amount of time. However, problems can arise anywhere that wolves and livestock comingle. Thirty-five percent of the farms lay within or on the edges of the eighty-five square miles of the Moose Lake Pack's territory. And in 1982 that pack encountered cattle.

In late July the pack moved its pups to a new homesite, a location the wolves would occupy throughout August and intermittently into late October. Their first rendezvous site had been at the den site, along the headwaters of Cranberry Creek, adjacent to a washed-out beaver pond.

Their selection of a late summer homesite was less than ideal. The family was now on the northeastern edge of its territory, in a forest next to a pasture of about twenty head of black angus.

The farm and its surrounding eighty-acre field had been carved out of the forest at the end of a town road. Other farmers farther up the road had either stopped using their fields or had abandoned their farms after years of struggling to tame the stubborn land. From the plane we could clearly see the shells of their farm structures, now thoroughly entangled in the forest brush that was reclaiming the scarred landscape.

The farm family was aware of the wolves and tolerated their presence. They even enjoyed watching the comings and goings of the wolves at morning and evening twilight. Two different collared wolves stood out in particular, the family claimed, because these two frequently trotted up the fence row that separated the outer pasture from the farm buildings as they made their way back to the vast forest to the west.

As for the cattle, they generally ignored the wolves. The pack gradually abandoned the site in September and returned to the more isolated forests within the core of their territory.

But they periodically returned. Pilot Fred Kruger and I witnessed one such foray. On this particular flight in early November 1981 we were experiencing technical problems. The coaxial cable leading from the antenna attached to the left wing was not functioning, so I was able to listen only off the right wing. In order to determine from which direction a signal emanated, we had to complete a succession of circles, intently listening for peaks in the volume of the radio wave.

We gradually approached the farm site from the southeast, but I had assumed it no longer held any interest for the wolves, and I expected the source

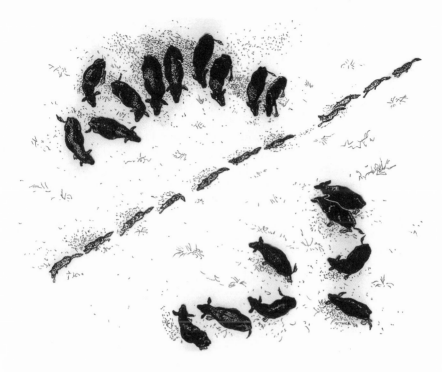

of the radio signal to lie beyond the site. As we circled the pasture, which stretched out far beneath my right side, I gazed down and saw eighteen black angus cattle that had bedded down and were rising to their knees as twelve brown critters waltzed out of the woods in the northeast corner of the pasture. Deer, I thought, as I returned to fidgeting with the receiver dials. As the plane banked away from the site, I suddenly realized those deer had very long tails. I turned my head in time to see twelve timber wolves walk right through the herd of cattle. The cattle all stood and faced the wolves as they sauntered past, paying the cattle no mind at all.

Screaming to Fred to bank right, I momentarily lost sight of the spectacle as the plane's tail blocked the view. Fred turned the plane by diving and slipping to the left, but by the time our cameras were up, the wolves had made it to the far end of the field. The sight made me feel confident that the Moose Lake wolf pack, at least, had no taste for beef.

People who do suffer losses from wolf depredations in Wisconsin should not have to bear the cost of the wolves' recovery. Thanks to a program implemented in the early 1980s by the state legislature, Wisconsin residents may make a voluntary contribution to help preserve endangered species through a checkoff on their state income tax return. A portion of this money is reserved for payments to people who have suffered property damage from endangered species. Most Wisconsinites who lose livestock to wolves have come to accept the compensation program as a reasonable solution.

Wolves are consummate predators, a role so important in nature that humans will never grasp the complete story behind predation. Predators sometimes keep prey populations in check. Predators sometimes merely take advantage of an available resource. In such situations, the availability of the animals they eat controls the number of predators. Populations of predators and prey ebb and flow together.

Scientists measure and quantify, then draw conclusions. Mother Nature keeps no score card.

All in the Family

I remember it vividly. Jim Dienstl and I were homing in on the radio signal of wolf 1189, of the Moose Lake Pack in early December 1981. A fresh snow blanketed the world beneath our seats. The signal was coming from somewhere along the east fork of the Moose River. Our plane followed the brown waters as it spilled over logs and boulders that failed to obstruct its flow.

Jim shouted, "There they are!" as we approached a large marsh. A small glacial knob, cloaked in balsam firs, rose up from the basin one hundred yards from the junction of two rivulets that formed the east fork. Scattered on the new-fallen snow between the knob and the confluence were seven timber wolves.

The plane roared past the group. They paid us no notice. Two were standing; one was a large, well-furred brute. The rest lay sprawled out or curled up in the snow. We slowly circled upward to avoid disturbing the pack while we were observing this intimate view of family life.

Shortly, a small wolf arose from its bed and sauntered over to the big one, tail wagging nervously from side to side as it approached. With lightning speed the first wolf leaped upon the small wolf, pinning it to the ground. The small wolf rolled over, placing its front paw on the nape of the large wolf. The big fellow turned, looking away, then lunged and snapped at the wolf lying at its feet. The small wolf flinched, then poked its nose, daggerlike, into the rump of the large wolf, and fled, darting back and forth as the larger wolf playfully chased after it.

Soon enough, the large wolf stopped and returned to its former post, resuming its stance as guardian of the sleeping wolves. We peeled off in search of other radio signals. I turned around to watch the pack lying peacefully in its private world for as long as I could, till the wolves faded from view.

Several months later I was sitting in the living room of Bernie Bradle, the retired Wisconsin Conservation Department biologist. We were talking about wolves.

123

Gazing momentarily out the living room window of his home in Crandon, Bernie said, "Wolves are family." Those uncomplicated words were marvelously descriptive. As an afterthought, he added, "Few other vertebrates in Wisconsin have family."

His voice seemed distant. I knew where that comment came from. He was thinking back about forty years, when as a young man he had studied a much-beleaguered timber wolf pack in Forest County. I heard his words and understood them perfectly. I started thinking about my recent brushes with Oneida County's Bootjack Pack, Douglas County's Moose Lake Pack, and a host of other timber wolf family groups that lay scattered across the state's northern hinterlands.

After a long, silent pause Bernie turned and looked at me, a warm, broad smile on his face. I returned that smile, nodding acknowledgment. Three generations separated our life experiences. Our common thread was a lifelong interest in and a deep-seated regard for this maligned species. Here, in the comfort of his living room, we spoke a language that spanned the generations.

Bernie's enchantment with the wolf's family ways reflected the observations of a man way ahead of his time. His reverence was borne from personal experiences observing wolves. The books of his day never mentioned the wolf's family life. Through the years, as I went about the business of monitoring the wolves that had recently returned to our state, my mind would reflect upon Bernie's words on many an occasion.

Douglas County's Moose Lake Pack was an exemplary family unit. Its cohesiveness was impressive. Over a six-year period the pack produced a litter each year. A total of fourteen pups from these litters survived to midwinter (an average of 2.3 pups a year). Theirs was the best record, both for longevity of pup production (six continuous years) and total number of pups surviving to midwinter, of all the Wisconsin packs studied between 1979 and 1989.

The Moose Lake Pack's alpha wolves were very successful parents. One of our first glimpses of their pups occurred on a cold day in early January 1981 as Jim Dienstl and I were working a site from which we were hearing the radio signal from 1189, a member of the Moose Lake Pack.

Shallow snow depths only partially obscured the yellow-brown marsh grass, making it difficult to pick out our quarry. Jim spotted them on the third pass.

I spied wolf 1189 lying comfortably on his side in the sun, much like a dog, and paying us no mind. About three body lengths away was a pile of wolves. They were bunched up so tightly it was impossible to count them.

"Look like a stack of cord wood, don't they?" Jim hollered. It was frustrating. In plain view yet we were unable to obtain a count. They were literally stacked on top of each other. We could see the writhing mass of bodies. Evidently, they were lying close together for protection from the chilly arctic air.

Three passes later Jim looked back at me and shouted, "I'll fix their wagon!"

He angled the plane away from the site in a broad arc. I temporarily lost sight of them as we banked sharply to port. Maneuvering the little plane around, Jim came squarely in on their position, dipping down to within four hundred feet. Just as we rushed past them, he reached over on the console, flipped a toggle switch, and blasted the wolves with his law enforcement siren.

The pile disintegrated. Wolves peeled off, running helter-skelter in all directions. Hitting the throttle, Jim pulled up and deftly turned the plane around so we could view the gang beneath. "Seven wolves, including 1189. You seen enough?" Jim asked as he put the plane in a lazy ascending spiral. The technique was admittedly not kosher, but we did manage to get a count.

We'd seen a family. Five of the six wolves in the pile were pups, the same pups Bob Welch, Tom Meier, and I had heard that enchanted evening eight months earlier. The other wolf in the pile was the mother. I never did quite figure out whether wolf 1189 was the dad. Another adult lived in the pack, though it was absent that day.

I did not pay much attention to the Moose Lake Pack until the summer of 1981. The death of 1187 and struggle of his mate, Gimpy, kept me preoccupied with the fate of the Bear Lake Pack that winter and spring. So I did not immediately recognize the significance of the opportunity that our observation of the Moose Lake group presented.

The fascination caught up with me shortly after Steve Fritts and I managed to catch two Moose Lake Pack yearlings within the northern perimeter of the neighboring Bear Lake territory in May. They were among the wolves that Jim and I had seen stacked like cord wood about five months earlier.

It was not difficult to determine the pack affinity of one, wolf 003 (whom we never named), and another, Jamie Bond (007), whom we had caught within the Moose Lake Pack's territory. Shortly after being collared, they both turned up at the decrepit, grassed-over beaver pond–summer home of the Moose Lake Pack.

Mailrunner was another story.

He roamed all over the map. On one flight in early June 1981, Dienstl picked up the Mailrunner within a mile of the Moose Lake homesite. On the very next flight our delivery boy was twenty-five miles to the west, within two miles of the suspected den site of the Stateline Flowage Pack. This game continued for more than a month.

The riddle was solved on a warm, humid day in late June. Ray Marvin was piloting the plane.

We left Shell Lake airport at about noon, heading north beneath a heavy concentration of cumulus clouds. Scanning the horizon, I was able to find only a few patches of sunlight penetrating the darkening sky. Isolated downpours occurred here and there as we headed north. This was typical of summer afternoons in northern Wisconsin.

We found the radioed wolves in the other packs first, then headed northeast to the Moose Lake country. I was unable to find Mailrunner. We cruised along at ninety-five miles an hour, sandwiched between the nearly solid ceiling of clouds—actually, the base of developing thunderheads—and the waving sea of treetops one thousand feet below. At any one moment I could spy a half-dozen blurry gray regions where downpours of rain obscured the horizon.

We approached one squall straight on. The rain being squeezed from the clouds caused a release of thermal energy, creating zones of uplift on the edges of the downburst. As we slipped beneath the edge of this active storm cell, the plane lurched up, then slipped sideways. Ray quickly compensated. Rain began beading off the plane's Plexiglass windshield. Harder and harder it came. Beneath us fingers of steamy fog reached up through the trees, where they were immediately and summarily battered into oblivion by horizontal wind gusts that punched violently through the swaying treetops.

Ahead of us an opaque wall of gray appeared. As we neared it, the rain beading off our windshield lessened and then stopped altogether. The ominous form became backwashed with sunlight from rays peering over the top of the storm cloud we had just passed beneath. Far below us I noted that the gravel surface of the Jackson Box Road was dry. Moose Lake lay ahead. The static on my radio receiver diminished and, scanning through the dials, I picked up wolf 1189, wolf 003, Jamie Bond, and the alpha female 009. Although I did not believe for a moment that my effort would be fruitful, I tuned in to Mailrunner's radio frequency. Ping! His signal rang loud and clear.

At that moment Ray fed the weather band into my headsets. While I'd been listening for wolves, he'd been alert to changing weather reports. It wasn't good news for us. The adjusted forecast called for locally strong storms until 4 or 5 P.M. We'd just slipped through one that was only then gaining momentum. Our present search pattern placed us directly in front of its path, which meant we'd likely be entertained by a repeat performance very shortly.

"Let's make this quick," Ray shouted to me.

"I've got 'em all, Ray," I hollered back, still fidgeting with the dials, trying to determine who to home in on first. We'll pick on Mailrunner first, since he's the most difficult to find, I decided.

We overshot him. We swept past the Peterson Road and were nearly over Solon Springs when a signal that burst off the port side told me he was to our left. I looked behind, eyeing the storm to figure out about how much time we had till the rain hit us. Not much more than two or three minutes.

Ray cranked the plane left, angling northwest toward the homesite of the Moose Lake Pack. The old beaver pond had been a good choice, made by the breeding female. It was about four acres in size and a mile from the nearest road. It was surrounded by dense balsam fir on the east, south, west, and northwest rims and by a very marshy black ash swamp to the northeast, an ideal spot for raising pups.

Curiously, a large glacial boulder rose up out of the marsh grass near the south edge of the eastern lobe. Last summer I'd seen a wolf standing atop the big stone, intently monitoring the movements of our plane. A small island of spruce and fir adorned the western lobe. Trails made by the wolves radiated out in several directions from the island through the sedge meadow to the surrounding forest.

The pack's rendezvous site was in sight as we swept in on Mailrunner's signal. I looked to my left and realized time had run out. Our thunderhead had caught up with us. A sheet of rain stretching from cloud to forest arced back toward the menacing squall. Rain pelted the windshield and the plane jerked up, then down.

We zoomed in on the site, straining to see five wolves scattered about and lying on their sides, oblivious to the rain and thunder crashing around them. Three lay on the little spruce island with their backs up against the trunks of balsam firs, legs stretched out. The rain intensified. One wolf glanced lazily at our plane as we rushed past, eight hundred feet above, then casually dropped its head back to the ground.

We swung back through dense vapor clouds and got another view of the family. Another wolf lay next to an old stump on the isthmus between the two lobes and still was tucked just beneath the boughs of a fir along the southeast rim of the meadow. Mailrunner was on the island, slumbering within sight of two other Moose Lake Pack wolves.

Mailrunner was home. We had seen family.

Including Mailrunner, we were monitoring the movements of five of the seven Moose Lake Pack wolves in the early summer of 1981. In mid-July things changed. Pack mates chewed the collars off both alphas and Mailrunner. The alphas would never be recaptured. Mailrunner continued to be the prodigal son, meandering between his natal pack territory on the eastern edge of my Douglas County study area and the western edge, where farms fringed the Nemadji State Forest on Minnesota Highway 23 beyond the Stateline Flowage Pack.

Mailrunner died in October.[1] With these losses I was down to monitoring two Moose Lake Pack yearlings: male 003 and Jamie Bond.

Yearlings are just plain unreliable for keeping tabs on midwinter pack activity because, in the years of my study, most of them didn't stick around. These two yearlings were already traveling widely, going their separate ways. If I was going to maintain contact with the Moose Lake Pack, I needed to trap and radio-collar another wolf. With luck, I might catch an animal that would stay and provide a count of the pack in winter.

Bob Dreis consented to a fall trapping campaign, although fall trapping was outside the bounds of our earlier agreement. Hoping for an alpha, I settled for the female pup we ear-tagged 013 and named Lucky 13. Keeping track of the two radioed yearlings and the pup was no small chore. I was about to learn something of the incredible dynamics of life within the pack.

Only two days after we collared Lucky 13, we obtained an accurate count of the pack—the highest it would be throughout the upcoming winter. Bob Dreis and I accompanied Jim Dienstl for the flight. Dienstl used the push-pull that flew at greater speeds than we got from our regular plane, the old Piper Cub.

As we approached Moose Lake, I scanned the frequencies of the three wolves. I picked up the signals of 003 and Jamie Bond; they were together and ahead of us by about four or five miles. Lucky 13, on the other hand, was off our right wing and about five miles away.

I chose to check Jamie Bond and 003 first. Within a mere ninety seconds we were over them. Looking out the starboard side, I canvassed the landscape beneath. In the distance stretched the tamarack lowlands outlining the southern rim of Cranberry Creek's flowage. A ragged fault line of black ash trees broke the carpet of conifer trees, weaving lazily eastward and cradling the small trickle that nourished the waters of the flowage. The little rivulet was choked with beaver ponds, some old and grassed over, others of fairly recent vintage. All were lined with thickets of aspen whose mantles lit up the woods with hues of yellow and gold. The aspen were the backbone of the north woods fuel economy and offered food for deer, beaver, hare, and grouse.

Overtaking the signals, we lifted up, banked right, and returned on the mark for another sweep past the radioed wolves. We spotted them, stretched out single-file and running across a beaver meadow, golden sunlight bathing tawny coats. The pack was in full run. The tails of some flowed gracefully behind them, whereas the tails of others bobbed awkwardly up and down, indifferent to the rhythmic movements of their owners. "Twelve!" I exclaimed, not believing my eyes. Jim concurred.

We returned a third time, but only five remained, motionless, out on the blackened floor of a beaver pond that had recently ruptured. Their soft tawny and rufous coats stood out in contrast to the dark brown layer of mud upon which they were standing. Shadows of twilight were rapidly overtaking the scene, and they faded from view as our plane raced on to find Lucky 13.

We found her by herself two miles east of the pack at the old kidney-bean–shaped rendezvous site the pack had used in early summer. She was thoroughly familiar with this spot, the place of her birth. The den was located beneath the partially upended roots of an ancient balsam fir within the forest just off the southeast corner of the sedge marsh.

Obviously, Lucky 13 had become temporarily separated from the pack after her capture and had returned to the place she recognized as home, hopeful the pack would come looking for her. That made a minimum of thirteen wolves, a very large pack supported on a diet of deer and beaver.[2]

The following week Lucky 13 was back with the pack at a site south of the Tom Green Road. Wolf 003 and Jamie Bond were also in the vicinity. I decided to do a little howling that night near the site, to try to determine, from the timbre of their voices, how many pups were in the pack.

The aspen leaves had turned brown and dropped to the ground. The maples on the ridges still held their crimson leaves, but nightly rainfalls were gradually taking their toll. Autumn was subtly acquiescing to the approach of winter.

On this night, October 14, autumn weather still prevailed. It had been cloudy and about 50 degrees throughout the day. Shortly before sundown a clearing appeared along the northwest horizon, the leading edge of the promised cold front. The wind shifted from the south to northwest. Brief, intense gusts knocked a profusion of brightly colored maple leaves to the ground among the tangle of brush and roots on the forest floor. Then, as the final embers of light faded away, the wind puffed itself out.

I stood alone in utter silence atop a hill where an old woods trail left the Tom Green Road and led toward the wolves' rendezvous site. I quietly opened the receiver and slowly hooked up the antenna. A barred owl startled me with its *Whoo-oo . . . cooks . . . for. . . you-alllll* hoot, not two hundred yards from where the edge of the hill and a swamp forest met.

I let a few more minutes pass, then scanned the wolves' frequencies. Lucky 13 was nearby, probably not more than a quarter-mile off. I heard not a peep from the frequencies of Jamie Bond or 003. After placing the gear at my feet on the gravel surface of the fire lane, I straightened out, cupped my hands together, and took in a deep breath, preparing to howl. A few milliseconds before I let out my howl, I heard a far-off crash resounding through the forest. I stopped and listened. Again, the noise . . . like footsteps in the crisp, newly fallen leaves.

Whatever made the noise was some distance off, down over the crest of the hill. It was too dark to see anything except the faint silhouette of bared maple branches against the Milky Way. The sound ceased. I waited three minutes. Nothing. Cupping my hands, I sent forth a blast, wavering low, climbing high, then descending and ending abruptly.

The sound raced off, returned as an echo, and dwindled away. A few seconds followed. Then . . . *R r r r r r r o o o u u u u u u u u u u u u a a h h.* A lone wolf answered from Lucky 13's direction. Within seconds a cacophony of howls, utterances, and ululations erupted. So many gave voice simultaneously I could not count them or distinguish the voices of any pups. Just as suddenly, the pack quit. Silence encroached as echoes carried the pack's song to the farthest reaches of the forest.

The footsteps returned. Precisely from where I last heard it, I thought. It was heading diagonally past me, moving toward the pack. I strained my eyes, staring off into the black forest, but I could see absolutely nothing. It stopped, started, stopped again. Suddenly, I heard *R r r u f f f f,* followed by whines, which announced the presence of a timber wolf less than a hundred yards off.

I whined. It whined, then barked, and hurriedly ran off, the sound of its pounding paws retreating to the south, gradually fading into the void.

Somehow that wolf had detected my presence and had stood motionless, inspecting me as I prepared to howl. By the amount of noise it created, I felt certain it was a pup. It probably had been out for an evening stroll when my presence interrupted its return to the pack.

I stood in that dark maple forest, mesmerized by the experience. Some time afterward an eerie glow along the eastern horizon presaged the appearance of the harvester moon that sullenly crept over the skyline, its bulky, radiant surface casting greenish-white beams throughout the forest.

Reluctantly, I packed up the gear. Walking softly so as not to disrupt the solitude, I retraced my route to the car and headed back to the warmth of the sleeping bag on the floor of the Gordon Ranger Station. Another day in wolf country had come to a magical end.

The next morning I returned to the hill where I'd gotten the pack to howl and rechecked Lucky 13's signal. She was gone. I walked a mile along the fire lane, hoping to find some evidence of where the pack had gone. I found two fresh scats a quarter-mile to the west. Evidently, they had moved out sometime during the night.

Dienstl and I found them that afternoon. Lucky 13 and Jamie Bond were with the pack on a deer kill about six miles from the rendezvous site. Wolf 003 was gone.

Wolf 003 was experiencing growing pains, spending increasing amounts of time away from home. Throughout most of the summer months he acted much like a slicked-back teenage boy on the prowl, roving within the other two wolf pack territories. His forays centered primarily around the northern reaches of the Empire Swamp, the very core of the Bear Lake Pack's territory.

Up until fall, wolf 003 had kept his distance from Gimpy, the surviving mate of wolf 1187 and the Bear Lake Pack's surviving alpha. Whether this was by accident or design I could not tell, but I was nonetheless certain they were aware of each other. Their paths had to have crossed, and among animals with keen noses like wolves, she had to be aware of his periodic presence in her territory long before they were formally introduced.

Throughout that fall 003 spent more and more time in Bear Lake territory. Could this be the beginning of a romantic relationship? Or would Gimpy chase 003 out of her territory? I looked forward with intense anticipation to each flight, impatient to learn the destiny of these two wolves. Each time Dienstl and I flew, the two wolves disappointed us by being in separate places.

Finally, in late October the long-awaited event occurred. We found the two wolves together along the headwaters of Tamarack Creek, which sluggishly drains the southern portion of the Empire Swamp. Although we couldn't see them from the comfort of our lofty seats high above the stream bank, their signals came from the same spot. Bliss at last (for me, at least).

After the very next flight Jim Dienstl called to inform me that 003 and Gimpy had separated. Gimpy remained within her territory and 003 had headed back to Moose Lake. Confused though I was, I was beginning to realize that these highly developed social creatures had very complicated and sophisticated relationships—the kind that took time to develop and mature. These two wolves had entered the "getting to know you" phase of their relationship.

By this time it was early November. Another deer season was just around the corner. Privately, I found myself rooting for love to find Gimpy. Once again I grew nervous. Would 003 return, sweep up his sweetheart, and settle down to a comfortable existence with her in the Bear Lake Pack territory? Or would he pull the typically stupid teenage male trick and blow a perfectly good opportunity for a good life?

Once again, autumn winds battled for air supremacy, as the final remnants of summer gradually receded and Old Man Winter claimed the land. Early November turned cold. Several brief snowfalls dusted the forest floor, glazing the fallen leaves and dormant herbaceous layer. The wolves didn't mind. The cold released a kind of wanderlust within their veins. They moved more extensively. Joyously and flamboyantly, they trotted through their home territories, seeking unsuspecting prey and frolicking with each other in the splendor of early winter. Wolf 003 stayed with his pack while Gimpy remained at home, solitary matriarch of the Bear Lake territory.

The 1981 deer season quickly arrived. Bright and early on opening day, Dienstl and I climbed into the cramped Piper Cub, taxied onto the sole runway at Shell Lake, and shot into the sky, heading north to check in on the status of our radioed wolves.

We found Lucky 13 and Jamie Bond almost immediately. They were separated by four miles. Where was 003? We sailed west, scanning the frequencies of 003 and Gimpy. Somewhere over the eastern stretch of the Empire Swamp we suddenly encountered the telltale pinging of their signals. They appeared to be together.

As we skimmed the northern rim of the swamp, it soon became evident the signals were farther west, *beyond* the territorial boundary of the Bear Lake Pack. Jim glanced back with that "Gosh, I'm still learning things about these wolves" expression. We found both of them, almost three miles outside the western boundary of the Bear Lake territory, across Highway 35 in the heart of the Belden Swamp, nearly a mile or two within the territory of the Stateline Flowage Pack.

Thick cover extended in every direction beneath us. Jim asked whether I wanted to go lower, his suggestion breaking our agreement not to drop below three thousand feet during deer season. "Sure," I replied. But before we did so, Jim and I carefully canvassed the surrounding region for the blaze-orange garments of hunters. Satisfied none was nearby, we began a slow downward spiral.

The dusting of snow revealed flat, flooded ground, tangles of downed wood in thickets of spruce, black ash, and alder so dense a snowshoe hare would find difficulty maneuvering. I guided Jim in toward a small beaver pond, iced up and coated with a thin layer of snow. Wolf tracks marred its surface. Jim revved the engine, climbed up, banked left, and brought us over the scene once again. Out stepped our wolves, Gimpy and 003. They were on the prowl, moving in and out of the tangles, temporarily disappearing from view, reappearing unexpectedly here and there.

They approached an opening studded with the poles of long-dead spruces, yellow tufts of grass carpeting the floor. Gimpy adroitly approached an old stump, arched her back, and raise-leg urinated on it, expressing to other canines that she was a dominant female and damned proud of it.

Gimpy and 003 shot through the Stateline Flowage territory over the next week or so, making a kill on the northern edge of that pack's boundary near the end of deer season. Gutsy, I thought. On a Sunday morning Jim and I caught a glimpse of the two before we wrapped up our activity for deer season 1981. Gimpy was in the lead, trotting down a snow-covered fire lane that wound through a Minnesota maple forest south of Net Lake. A mile to her rear we found 003 coursing down the ice-covered highway of a stream studded with beaver dams. He was following her tracks.

Nearly two weeks later I returned to the field. I was eager to catch up on the latest in this affair. I found Gimpy's signal in the center of the Stateline Flowage Pack's territory. We noticed a pickup truck very close to her location. A trapper was working some beaver sets on a rivulet off the Summit Trail. Too close—something's fishy here, I thought, as Jim jotted down a description of the vehicle, complete with the license plate number, which he obtained by looking through a pair of binoculars.

We found 003 twenty-five miles west of Gimpy, fifteen miles beyond the Stateline Flowage Pack territory. Something was wrong. Of late, 003 and Gimpy had been tight. Since leaving the Bear Lake area, they had acted as a pair. It was time to close in on her signal.

The next morning Larry and I crawled down the deeply rutted, beat-up Summit Trail, cussing every rut and sinkhole in the fire lane. It took more than an hour to make the five-mile journey off the blacktop. We parked our truck in a wide spot on the lane, on a bend just south of where the trapper's truck had been, quickly assembled the radio gear, stuffed our packs, and tuned in to Gimpy's frequency. *P-I-N-G!* The strength of the signal told us she was very close.

Following the signal, we entered the forest. Winding between aspen trunks, we covered ground quickly, coming to a crescent-shaped pocket of alder and marsh grass. Two sassy ravens took to the air, croaking loudly their complaints of our intrusion. They had been dining on Gimpy.

Blood lay spattered for eight feet in every direction from her body. Fur blew aimlessly on top of the snow. Gimpy had arched her rear end up against a protective clump of alder brush, but in the end it had done her no good. A heavy wolf trail left the scene, coursing southeast, dipping down off the aspen-covered slope, and vanishing in the shadows of a dense copse of fir. The assassins had left the scene in that direction. She had paid the ultimate price of a foreigner who had dared to trespass in a territory occupied by another wolf pack.[3]

The Moose Lake Pack had a litter in 1982, but the den was moved. I suspect that alpha female, 009, had died or left the pack in 1981–82 and was replaced by another, but I was never able to prove this. The pack would never again use the kidney-bean–shaped denning and rendezvous site near the banks of the Moose River. The new denning ground lay near the washed-out beaver pond where we had seen the pack the previous October. While I never caught and collared another alpha female in the Moose Lake Pack again, I regarded this pack and its breeding female(s) as the most successful, and certainly most prolific, of the four or five packs I regularly monitored over the ten-year period.

By 1985 the Moose Lake Pack's alpha female was recognizable even though she was not radioed. Her coat was whitening; she was getting on in years. The pilots, Larry, and I affectionately called her "the Old Bag."

The Old Bag's world came tumbling down that year. A dreaded and highly contagious viral disease, canine parvovirus, which is spread among all canines through feces, ravaged the Moose Lake Pack in the spring of 1985. In May we caught two female yearlings and they were severely underweight. One weighed forty; the other, forty-one pounds. Fecal and blood serum samples, examined later, told us these two wolves had been in an acute stage of infection when we caught them. Their feces were shedding virus in amounts great enough to infect other wolves.

I became worried. Throughout summer these two yearlings spent considerable time at the pack's rendezvous site where we heard the pack's pups. In August one of the yearlings died. We recovered its radio in late September, wedged into the hollowed-out base of a dead elm tree on the east fork of the Moose River. (We never learned how that wolf died—the collar was not chewed off, and we never found the body.) That same week, however, we managed to find tracks in the ruts of a woods trail that definitely showed that pups still survived in the pack.

In October we captured and radio-collared a healthy female wolf pup that we called Dolly. Her blood samples showed she had somehow escaped exposure to the disease.

On a very cold week in mid-December 1985 the era of the Moose Lake Pack drew to a close. We picked up Dolly's signal on a small island blanketed in spruces within the Moose River Valley, not far south of where we had captured 1189 six years earlier. I hadn't managed to see her from the frosted windows of our plane but had noted a wolf bed, a likely place to find and collect some droppings for our parvovirus study.[4]

That night Larry, Mary Sagal, a student at the University of Wisconsin, and I braved 20-degree-below-zero weather in an attempt to howl to the wolves. We walked a mile down the poorly plowed Tom Green Road and selected a spot where it dips down into the Moose River Valley. Despite repeated attempts at raising the pack, we heard no replies.

We were tired from a day in the cold and decided to head back to the station. Our pickup truck was a half-mile to our east. I stared at the uneven white surface of the snow, trying to focus on anything but my exhaustion as we trudged back to the truck through shin-deep snow.

Suddenly, the forest was bathed in radiant white light. Looking up, we caught sight of the tail of a great meteorite gliding through the night sky, silently arcing its way across Orion, hunter of the winter heavens, and through the dog stars before it snuffed itself out. The light was brilliant—an awesome spectacle.

The performance revitalized me only temporarily. Just as I began slipping back into a stupor, a second shooting star illuminated the forest. Following the path of the one before it, the celestial debris went out in a flash high over our heads. Magic in the wolf woods, I thought, what a glorious end to a beautiful day.

The next afternoon Mary and I returned to the spot, intent on retrieving some wolf scats from the beds I'd noticed during the flight the day before. The temperature was a stinging 20 below again and promised to plummet dramatically soon after nightfall.

This was Mary's first experience on snowshoes. As we slipped off the ridge forming the eastern rim of the Moose River Valley, I noticed several ravens diving in and out among the trees on the opposite rim.

"Watch that spot, Mary. Probably a wolf-killed deer in that thick stand of balsam firs. If we have time, we might swing back up that way and check it out."

Dropping down into the alder-choked bottoms was no problem, but negotiating a way through the brushy thickets proved time consuming and laborious. Eventually, we entered an open area that paralleled the iced-over stream.

The marsh grass was buried in twenty-five inches of snow. I moved toward the spruce copse, estimating the distance at less than four hundred yards.

I edged past the northern end of the island, staying in the open area just to the east of the spruce trees. Mary was a good fifteen paces behind. As I rounded the south end of the little spruce knob, I expected to see the beds and instead startled a timber wolf, which groggily rose to its feet to confront the disturbance less than ten feet away.

Placing my hand behind my back, I frantically waved for Mary to hurry up while I backed up slowly to give the wolf some room. The wolf was tall and sported a well-furred grayish coat. Despite the intense excitement, I noticed that its muzzle was heavily caked with a pinkish frost, and pink stalactites drooped from its lips.

The wolf staggered, as if unable to move. I glanced quickly at its feet, sure it had to be caught in some coyote trapper's trap. All four feet were fine.

Within seconds Mary approached and stopped behind and a little to my right. She let out a muffled exclamation. With great effort the wolf lurched forward, turned to its right, and headed west, away from us and toward the ice of the river.

I looked back at Mary, hollering, "It's sick!" and sprinted after the wolf.

It kept just ahead of me, walking down a well-worn wolf trail. It gained the ice and wobbled upstream, disappearing beyond a meander in the thickets. I stopped, not daring to cross the untested ice, which could be thin and brittle.

We walked back to the wolves' beds, excitedly replaying the event that had just occurred. No doubt about it. The wolf was sick. Very sick. And it seemed there was nothing we could do about it.

I gathered up a few wolf scats, placed them in plastic bags, and pocketed them, thinking the wolf's malady was surely caused by the dreaded canine parvovirus. I returned to the river's edge. A well-worn wolf trail, carved into the ice when its surface had been slushy, indicated that it was probably solid enough for us to cross. I was interested in checking out the deer kill, if we could locate it before the fading afternoon sunlight disappeared. Gingerly, I walked across. Mary followed.

We entered a thicket of aspen and fir on the far side of the stream and followed the bank north until it bent northeast through a nearly impenetrable thicket of alder. We moved along at a slow pace, impeded by the morass of branches. Within twenty-five yards the heavy wolf trail left the ice and entered a dark, dense fir stand.

"Here's the feed trail."

I left the stream bank for the forest, ducking beneath fir boughs and weaving around alder bushes, Mary following behind.

Within the conifers the light was nearly gone and I soon lost the trail. It seemed to veer to the west. Bobbing my head up and down and sideways in the hope of seeing something, I spied the kill site—a padded-down area where the pinkish snow was as hard as concrete.

I whispered, "Kill" to Mary. Turning back, I noticed a movement on the far side of the kill site—a gray shadow staggering out of view and heading away from us. It was our sick wolf.

Glancing at Mary, I hollered, "I'm going after it!" and lit out through the branches of the fir trees. Despite the foaming, I was not worried that the wolf could be rabid; rabies is not known to occur among wolves in the upper Great Lakes.

The wolf plowed into the deep snow in an effort to escape, loping laboriously. The plume of its breath arched across its back before dissipating.

I soon sensed the wolf was out of breath—but so was I. My lungs felt as if they could not clutch enough air to satisfy my body's demand for oxygen. The wolf slowed, then collapsed ten feet from me. I stopped too and leaned up against the trunk of a tree, grateful for whatever moments I had to catch my breath.

Soon enough, the wolf was on its feet, strenuously plunging through the snow again. I followed. A hundred yards later it again collapsed in its tracks, panting heavily. I foundered too. Again, it was no more than ten feet from me. I was too spent to bridge the gap. Mary was somewhere behind me, out of sight, her thrashing nearly inaudible.

My lungs were close to giving out. I had no more energy. I realized that this next round would determine the outcome. My intentions were to pin the animal down, somehow try to incapacitate it, and haul it out to a veterinarian. In order to carry through with this ridiculous plan, I needed a long, stout stick. Three feet to my left I spied such a device—a dried white cedar pole about six feet long and nearly two inches in diameter. I reached out and grabbed it just as the wolf jumped up and resumed its flight.

Throughout the pursuit the wolf had been making a great arc to the right in a circle that led gradually back to the padded, concrete surface of the river ice. I was running out of options. I thought to myself, when next it crashes, I'll put on the afterburners and close the distance, pinning it with the stick.

The wolf was tiring too. It didn't go far this time. When it folded, I was still ten feet behind, my lungs burning for mercy. But I leaped through the air, snowshoes and all, and came to rest two feet behind my quarry. I used the stick to push the wolf's head deep into the fluffy snow.

The wolf and I stayed there, both paralyzed by the lack of oxygen reaching our overworked lungs. I understood why I was disabled. I was not accustomed to running through twenty-some inches of loose "flour" snow, and I had always performed dismally in endurance runs. The wolf, however, had to be extremely sick to be incapable of outrunning a human on snowshoes. What could be wrong with this animal?

I loosened my grasp on the stick, allowing the wolf's face to resurface. From my vantage point (the wolf was looking directly away from me), I could make out the pinkish frosty foam that coated its muzzle. The wolf behaved as though it were asthmatic. It couldn't seem to gasp sufficient air and suck it into its lungs.

Mary approached slowly from behind. In a muffled voice I told her to advance cautiously.

Now she stood behind me. Incredulous, she asked, "What do you intend to do?"

Still attempting to catch my breath, I whispered, "I don't know."

The wolf lay before us in the snow, the sides of its chest heaving. Steam poured from its nose, condensed, then froze along the side of its face and eyelashes.

Hauling this thing out would not be easy. As I tried to figure out how to do it, I came up with another idea. "Let's ascertain its sex," I told Mary.

"Mary, I want you to slowly reach down, lift up its tail, and slip your hand between its hind legs to feel for either a vulva or a scrotum."

Her expression turned from incredulous to stupefied, but she crouched down, took off her mitt, and slowly reached forward. The wolf was still out of breath, panting heavily. I regripped the stick, ready to use whatever force might be necessary should the wolf react.

Gently, Mary moved the tail aside and slipped her hand into the dense underfur of the groin.

"I don't know. I can't tell."

We switched roles but not places. While Mary held the stick, I removed my glove. The frigid air rushing over my fingers immediately stiffened them. Then I felt an intense burning as the wolf's body heat warmed my fingers as they awkwardly combed through the thick fur. I felt a bulbous protrusion beneath the anus and declared it a female as I quickly retracted my hand. The wolf lay still throughout the ordeal.

"What next?" Mary asked.

"We have to figure a way to haul it out of here. They're predicting minus-35-degree temperatures overnight, and in its condition, this wolf won't be able to survive another night like this."

We had to muzzle the wolf and then hogtie it, but we had no equipment. Shoelaces, I thought, we can use my boot laces to fashion a muzzle, if only they're strong enough to hold those powerful jaws.

I instructed Mary to bend down once again and unlace my boots. The wolf seemed to have caught its breath and had turned its face slightly to its right, eyes alternately focused on us and the open space in front of it.

Mary stooped down. Wha-a-a-m! With lightning speed the wolf turned about, grasped the end of the cedar stick, and pulverized the end of it. Mary flew three or four feet backward, landing upright in the snow. Simultaneously, I slid my hands back to the end of the pole, while firmly grasping it and shoving it forward in the mouth of our unwilling and now fully alert patient.

The eyes of wolf and wolf biologist met. I glanced away, unwilling to challenge a wolf that clearly held the advantage. Over what seemed minutes, the wolf and I were locked in mental combat while continuing to hold opposite ends of the pole.

The wolf let go first. I pulled the stick away from its neck yet clung to it in the event I needed a defense. Slowly, the wolf gathered up its legs and wearily leaped to its feet. With a furtive sideways glance back at me, the majestic beast lumbered forward, coughing out quantities of pink foam. It moved off twenty-five feet, stopping at the padded-down site where the deer kill had been. Freed from the burden of deep snow, the great wolf circled twice, then plopped down, tail covering its muzzle, eyes looking obliquely in our direction.

The wolf had made its decision. It had been born in the wild. It had made its living in the wild. And it was here, in the austere surroundings of the Moose River, that it chose to die. It would be a dignified finale and one I had neither the power nor the right to alter.

Though disheartened, I looked at Mary and asked her to follow the sunset, gain the high ground, and wait for me. She left. The wolf continued to stare in my direction but did not move. In the stillness of the evening, as the fading light stole from me the image of that wolf, I bade it farewell.

Mary and I returned to the Tom Green Road. Orion was already visible in the twilight. At the base of the hill a wolf stepped out onto the road. Sensing our presence, it darted across the snowy trail for the safety of the forest on the opposite side. The old wolf won't die alone, I thought. Its pack mates know where it is and will be with it. Family until the very end.

The next morning we returned and recovered the wolf's body. I had been wrong in declaring it a female—it was a male. (I'd like to think my misdiagnosis was from numb fingers, but I had simply made a mistake.) The wolf was the mate of the Old Bag, which we knew from the process of elimination, and therefore was the pack's alpha male. He died of complications from canine distemper. His lungs were shot.

A few weeks later we found the other collared yearling wolf, dead from malnutrition and a heavy parasite load. Although it had not died of parvo, its immune system had been so taxed that it was incapable of fighting off the intestinal parasites that sucked the energy from its bowels.

The Old Bag roamed throughout the Moose Lake territory for the rest of the winter without a mate. She traveled with remnants of her pack, the two pups she had managed to keep alive.

A pack's success is measured in the number of pups produced and offspring that survive long enough to contribute genes to the next generation. Pups who manage to survive spend nearly two years learning from their parents how to be wolves. As they approach sexual maturity at twenty-two months, most yearling wolves gradually break ties with the family and leave their natal pack, as wolf 003 did.

Young wolves venturing out on their own are known as dispersers. Their journeys take them in search of unoccupied suitable habitat and/or a mate. They accomplish the latter either by roaming within suitable habitat until they bump into another wolf of the opposite sex or by attempting to integrate into an existing pack that has recently lost an alpha of the same sex.

A less common strategy involves what's known as biding. Young wolves elect to remain within the pack of their birth to await the death or departure of the alpha of their sex. They may thus gain reproductive status but generally only if the surviving alpha is not their parent. Biding is rare and seen more frequently in later litters. During ten years of study in Wisconsin I witnessed biding twice. Both resulted in successful matings.

Eight radio-collared offspring of the Moose Lake Pack would take the hike of life, as I called it. Four radio-collared yearlings ended up in Minnesota. One was Sharon, born in 1981.

We caught her in May 1982 near the center of the Moose Lake Pack's eighty-five-square-mile territory. That July and August she made several exploratory excursions for short distances outside her parents' territory. She'd typically stay in a small area—probably a kill site—for perhaps a week and then skedaddle back to the Moose Lake Pack's rendezvous site. There she would loaf around for two or three weeks before hitting the trail once again.

Eventually, her extraterritorial excursions increased both in frequency and duration. One day in late November Sharon left for good. Her journey would last four months, take her ninety miles from home, and end in her death. Sharon was killed in March 1983 south of Hill City, Minnesota, by a resident timber wolf pack, evidently because she was trespassing.

Two sisters from the 1983 litter of the Moose Lake Pack, Ratzo and Barb, also dispersed into Minnesota. Ratzo started south in early December 1984 and made it nearly to Spooner in a couple of days. This was farm and forest country, a far cry from the vast forests of her birth. Apparently, she was uncomfortable, for she turned west and unknowingly headed deeper into farm country.

Ratzo moved only during the hours of darkness. We found her during our daylight flights, curled up within small woodlots surrounded by open pas-

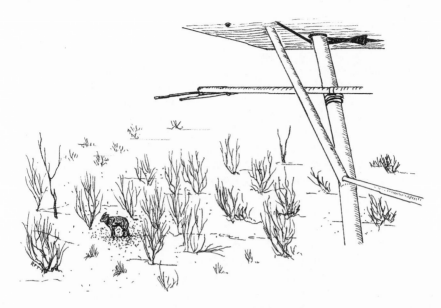

tures, farms, and town roads. During this portion of her journey Ratzo aver-
aged twenty miles a night. Her sojourn took her past Hertel and Grantsburg in
Wisconsin; then she crossed the St. Croix River and went beyond Sandstone,
Minnesota, to the eastern shores of Mille Lacs Lake.

Between January 4 and 20, 1985, Ratzo localized her movements in the
vicinity of Tamarack, Minnesota. She was now fifty miles west-northwest of
the Moose Lake territory. We were nearing the peak of breeding season. The
pilots and I began to suspect Ratzo had settled into this area because she had
found a boyfriend.

We anxiously strained our eyes to catch a glimpse of her in the rather bleak
swamplands dominated by tag alder that stretch literally to the horizon. We
were rewarded several flights later, at the end of January, when we spied her
weaving in and out of the alder brush and followed closely by a larger, much
darker, wolf.

I was elated. In four years of work I had already followed the wander-
ings of six yearlings from the Moose Lake Pack and several yearlings from
other radioed packs and had yet to witness a success story. Here, finally, was a
wolf who had succeeded in making a dangerous journey through a landscape
strewn with humans and their activities. A wolf who had managed to find a
patch of habitat and in that patch a prospective mate.

My enthusiasm was a bit premature. A little over a week later I received
a call from a Minnesota wildlife biologist. A wolf bearing Wisconsin ear tag
numbers 037 and 038 had accidentally been snagged in a coyote trap. Tem-

peratures that night had plummeted to 35 degrees below zero, and the wolf's paw had frozen. The trapper had sought help from the local game warden, who inspected the wolf, saw that its foot was useless, and radioed the biologist for his opinion.

He had decided, for humane reasons, that Ratzo must be killed. The biologist called me a day later to explain the situation. I posthumously concurred with the decision, as disappointing as the information was. It was the only humane thing to do.

Ratzo's sister, Barb, left the Moose Lake Pack shortly after her littermate. She too headed west toward Minnesota but became detained in a coyote set east of the state line. This trapper reported his dilemma to the warden, who went out and released the wolf with the aid of a forked stick.

Barb moved on. Within two weeks she was near Sandstone, Minnesota. Apparently frightened at the prospect of having to cross Interstate 35, which connects Duluth and the Twin Cites, she returned east. She marched through her natal pack territory and moved northeast. By April 1985 she had reached the shore of Lake Superior at the tip of Wisconsin's Bayfield Peninsula.

There she stayed in a thirty-five-square-mile area until the following fall, when she returned to the wolf packs bordering Douglas County. She occupied space between several wolf territories to the west of her natal pack.

In April 1986 she took off again, heading east. Barb was now three years old. We lost her signal for two weeks, but pilot Fred Kruger managed to pick it up east of Butternut, ninety miles east of the Moose Lake Pack. We stayed on her from that point on.

After a brief stint in central Iron County, Wisconsin, Barb slipped across the Michigan state line and headed for the shores of Lake Superior. She roamed an area south of the Porcupine Mountains for perhaps a month, then drifted slowly southeast, ending her sojourn in the eastern portion of the Ottawa National Forest north of Watersmeet, Michigan.

Barb stayed put, evidently establishing a home range. Jim Hammill, a Michigan DNR biologist, believed that a male wolf was living in the area Barb settled. We waited patiently for winter snows to return so that we could learn whether he was right. On the first day of October we obtained our last radio fix on Barb. Her collar had been on for two and a half years. The batteries evidently gave out. We were left in the dark.

On the Monday after Michigan's deer season opened, I received a call from a biologist at Ottawa National Forest. The local taverns were buzzing with talk that someone had shot a radio-collared timber wolf on opening day. The local authorities opened an investigation and recovered Barb's carcass from the shed of a local man. He was not prosecuted. He claimed to have found the carcass, hauled it back to his place, and simply kept it there until he fig-

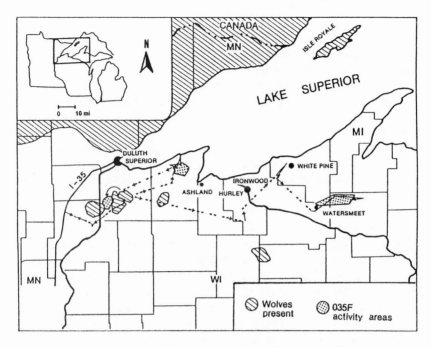

Dispersal movements of Barb (wolf 035F) during her "hike of life," 1985–86 (Wisconsin Department of Natural Resources)

ured out what to do with it. The investigators agreed that prosecution would be futile because it would boil down to his word against ours.

Thus ended the hike of life of another Moose Lake yearling. Barb had shown us some significant aspects of wolf ecology. She had traveled at least 240 miles since leaving the Wisconsin–Minnesota border country and had moved 145 miles east of the place of her birth. Further, she demonstrated that it was possible for wolves as far away as Minnesota to reach the Upper Peninsula of Michigan. Her sojourn sparked hopes that wolf recovery would one day occur in upper Michigan as well.

By 1985 I was really curious to learn how many pups it took to "replace" parent wolves. Biologists define *replacement* as surviving long enough to reproduce at least once and thus succeed the previous generation. The trick was to determine the fate of as many radioed offspring as possible. When the Moose Lake

Pack's alpha male died, I had already radioed fourteen of his offspring. This included Dolly, whom I would have to follow until she was sexually mature. Either the radios had failed on all the other Moose Lake Pack yearlings or the animals themselves had died.

In May 1986 Larry Prenn captured the other of the Old Bag's two surviving pups, now a yearling. Dolly and Tube, as Larry named the newly radioed male wolf, would answer the question of replacement. These sibling wolves used different strategies to achieve reproductive status.

In 1986 the wolf population within the Minnesota–Wisconsin border region was at the lowest point since monitoring began. No males were available to replace the dead Moose Lake alpha male. Tube, Dolly, and the Old Bag roamed the Moose Lake territory throughout summer and fall. In late January we found the trio together for the last time.

On our first flight in early February 1987 we found Tube twelve miles west of Moose Lake, coursing through a cedar swamp on the northeastern rim of another pack's territory. The radioed alpha female of that pack, Maryanne, had unexpectedly left a month earlier. She had been wandering around an unoccupied strip of space east of that pack's territory.

Maryanne had lost her litters in 1986 and 1987. I suspected canine parvovirus. Perhaps she thought her old man was incompetent, because she was the one who left (there *is* divorce among wolves).[5]

Between February 12 and 17 (the peak of breeding season) Maryanne and Tube met. They were inseparable from that moment until their radios failed in 1990. The only hint of a litter raised by the two was a few observations of four wolves lying together in December 1987 and January 1988. Tube was successful.

Dolly and the Old Bag stayed together throughout the winter of 1986–87 and the summer and fall of 1987. In January 1988 a third wolf appeared in Moose Lake, but we were unable to identify its sex until January 1989. It was a male.

I was curious what the Old Bag would do. Obviously, any serious rivalry for the attentions of this male would be gained at great cost. The competitors were the Old Bag and Dolly, her daughter. At stake were the Old Bag's breeding rights, her continued status as the alpha female, and the keys to the territory, which the Old Bag had so expertly handled throughout her career.

A novel solution developed. The male and Dolly pair-bonded. They stayed primarily in the western two-thirds of the Moose Lake Pack's territory, while we continued to see the tracks of a single wolf—presumably, the Old Bag—in the eastern portion of the pack range.

I last saw the Old Bag's tracks in the mud of a woods trail in November 1990 within a mile of where her mate had died. I like to think her bones lie

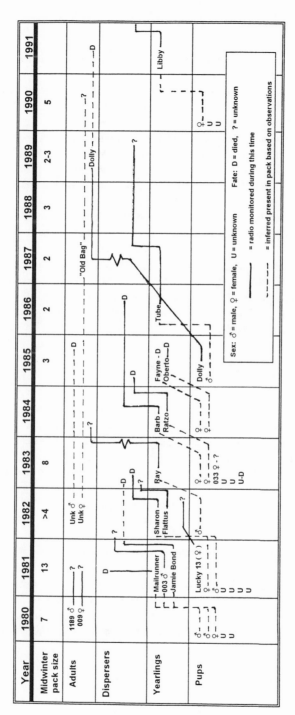

Moose Lake Pack family tree

hidden among the fallen maple leaves on some remote ridge in the depths of the Moose Lake Pack territory.

In February 1989 we obtained our last signal from Dolly. Her radio had outlasted any other placed on a Wisconsin wolf, having functioned for 1,220 days—three years and nearly four months.

We heard nothing of Dolly again until May 12, 1991. An area resident found Dolly's partially decomposed remains within the Moose Lake Pack's territory. She had been shot. She had managed to succeed her mother, producing a litter in 1990 and probably again in 1991, although her untimely death probably doomed her pups.

In the spring of 1991 we captured one of Dolly's yearling pups and named her Libby. Libby was recovering from a gunshot wound, probably inflicted by the same person who had killed Dolly. Libby dispersed from Moose Lake in the summer of 1991 and integrated into a previously undiscovered pack that straddled the St. Croix River on the Minnesota side. She became that pack's alpha and was killed by a car there on June 30, 1992. Thus the line of the Moose Lake Pack wolves, traced by monitoring radioed wolves for more than ten years, came to an end.

The Moose Lake Pack had produced at least twenty-three pups between 1980 and 1985. Of the fourteen offspring that we radio-collared, five disappeared and we never learned their fates. Eight dispersed. They went in almost every direction; some remained within Wisconsin, while others journeyed into Minnesota and upper Michigan. Seven died before they reproduced. Two managed to have litters.

The average age at death of the radioed offspring was two years, five months. Mailrunner died at one year, five months, and Dolly died at age six. Most died before they were old enough to reproduce.

This family's reproductive history seems representative of the other wolf packs that struggled for existence in Wisconsin during the early to late 1980s. At that time pup mortality was inordinately high—probably because of disease—and adult mortality was also steep. It seems remarkable that the Moose Lake Pack, the Bootjack Lake Pack, and Averill Creek Pack managed to survive against the odds and create a succeeding generation, usually many litters later.

Murphy's Law

Everyone has days when nothing seems to go right and circumstances seem to spiral out of control, preordained by some twisted demon of fate. Each year colleges faithfully prepare thousands of wildlife biology majors for the rigors that await them in the real world. These students of the outdoors must commit to memory many rules and laws of the natural world. There is Allen's Rule, Lieblig's Law of the Minimum, and a host of others.

But college professors never discuss one law, the one that can have a profound effect on a person's day-to-day routine: Murphy's Law. Simply stated, Murphy's Law predicts that anything that can go wrong will go wrong.

Ol' Murph and I had several run-ins on the wolf project.

Take, for instance, my first flying experience. Shortly after I began work on the project and before we had any radioed wolves to check on, I decided to get a bird's-eye view of the wolves' forested habitat along the rugged border between Douglas County, Wisconsin, and Pine County, Minnesota, just south of Duluth-Superior. I had made arrangements with the pilot, Jim Dienstl, to pick me up at the Solon Springs airstrip.

At the appointed hour Jim touched down in the Piper Cub, the small two-seater that puts the passenger (me) in cramped quarters behind the pilot. I'm a big guy, and with winter clothing on there wasn't much room to spare.

Jim made sure I was in, then jumped into the front seat and prepared to take off. It was cold—damned cold. And, although he had flown forty-five minutes to get to Solon Springs, the plane's engine refused to start. Nonplussed, Jim declared he knew another way to get the thing going and jumped out, preparing to hand-spin the propeller and force the engine to turn over.

After adjusting the throttle and fidgeting with several other dials and levers, all meaningless to me, Jim gave me a quick lecture on where the foot brakes were. He stressed that I must keep those brakes depressed. There was one problem. I had bulky Sorel boots on. The brake pedals were tiny. I had to straddle each side of the pilot's seat to depress them. I couldn't find the pedals because I couldn't feel anything beneath the soles of my feet. Jim moved my legs, placing the tips of my boots over the pedals.

He slid the front seat back so he could hop in easily when the time came. I twisted and contorted my body to counteract the crushing sensation of the front seat being placed on my lap.

147

That is precisely when Murph paid his visit. I didn't know a Piper Cub could be flown from the backseat. When Jim slid the seat back, my elbow accidentally bumped the backseat's throttle wide open. Of course, I didn't feel that, because of the thick winter coat I was wearing.

Jim walked forward. He grabbed the prop and gave it a downward jerk. It didn't turn. He tried again. Everything started moving—*very* fast. The prop spun. The engine fired. The plane shot out like a rock loosed from a slingshot. Jim quickly dove backward and sideways to avoid the spinning prop and hit the deck to avoid getting his head knocked off by the right wing as it passed by him. An overwhelming look of surprise was plastered all over his face as he disappeared in a cloud of snow whipped up by the churning propeller.

The red-and-white plane sped off like a rocket toward the far end of the field. I did not want to accept the reality of the situation that I suddenly found myself in, but I forced myself to peer out the windshield and saw the edge of the trees at the end of the runway. The little plane and I were gaining on them. Quickly. I looked back, hoping by some miracle that Jim would be right behind the plane, poised to put an end to my first flying lesson. As I twisted back, I saw Jim pick himself off the pavement and start running after the airplane.

Great, he'll be of no help. I remember saying "Holy sh-h-h-i-t!" as the plane cruised down the runway, gaining speed. Desperately, I began slamming my boots on the floor alongside the front seat. Where were those damned pedals? Through my left sole I felt something. I pounced on it frantically, but it was only a spring protruding from beneath the front seat.

The tree line at the far end of the field was getting closer, and Jim, still chasing the plane, was losing the race. Fat chance he'd catch up.

By now the little plane was halfway down the runway. The jack pines at the far end were coming up fast, and the plane was still gaining speed. I became concerned that I would either crash into the trees at the far end of the runway or the thing would actually lift off the ground and clip the trees.

All at once my right foot connected. The plane instantaneously spun to the right and crashed into the huge snowbank that lined the runway. The propeller stalled as it tried to slice its way through the mound of snow. My first (and only) solo flight was over.

Jim was there seconds later. He asked if I was okay and checked the propeller to make sure it hadn't been damaged.

Experience sometimes really can be the best teacher. Thereafter, when Jim had to spin the propeller, I knew where the brakes and the backseat throttle were. I was one "pilot" who sure was thankful that his first solo flight never quite got off the ground.

Florence County's lone wolf, Loafer, must have been a cousin of Murphy's. Murph made two visits while we were working in Loafer's terrain.

The U.S. Forest Service had kindly made the old Purdue Forestry Camp at Lost Lake available for our use during winter months. Larry Prenn and I periodically monitored that wolf for two winters before deciding to try to capture and radio it. We were successful. In May 1983 we collared this giant—he weighed 102 pounds.

Loafer roamed a small area in a remote corner of the Nicolet National Forest. (And I do mean remote—as in more than twenty miles from anything resembling civilization, such as gas stations and pay phones.) In January 1984 we arranged to combine radio flights with ground-tracking surveys to determine whether any other wolves were present.

We invited the wildlife manager, Tom Bahti, to join us as we rambled down countless miles of frozen fire lanes in the pickup truck in search of the big tracks of timber wolves.

Early the next morning we drove over to Halsey Lake, where Dan Doberstein had dropped in by plane to pick me up. As soon as we cleared the trees, I picked up Loafer's signal. He wasn't far away. Dan and I returned in fifteen minutes, and I asked Tom if he would like to go up. He readily agreed, and we traded places.

Tom was all smiles upon his return. He had seen Loafer, only the second time anyone had seen him from the plane. And, although we didn't know it then, it turned out to be the last time we would hear Loafer's radio signal.

By 9:30 we were already cruising sections of fire lane that we had not surveyed earlier in the week. Because it was Friday we broke camp around noon—Larry and I each had three-hour drives to our respective homes in Cable and Tomah. We found no sign of other wolves and returned to the cabin to pack up.

The cabin was three-quarters of a mile off the fire lane. We made several trips in and out on snowshoes, hauling leftover food, sleeping bags, clothing, maps and field notebooks, and a television set back to our vehicles. I decided to warm up the state car, a Renault Alliance, before I stashed the gear I had hauled out last.

A leather pouch issued with the car contained two keys, one for the ignition and one for the doors. I pulled out the door key, unlocked the door, and left the keys dangling in the lock. As I turned around to grab my briefcase and throw it into the front seat, the wind blew the door shut. I saw a flashing sliver of metal drop out of the pouch and disappear into the snowbank.

My heart slumped and I knew Murph was back. The ignition key was now hidden in several feet of powder alongside the car.

I got a pair of snowshoes out of the trunk. For the next fifteen minutes Tom, Larry, and I methodically sifted snow through the webbing of the snowshoes onto the plowed surface of the fire lane.

To no avail. We needed to make a decision. We were all expected home in another two or three hours. It was already afternoon, and we were twenty miles from the nearest American Motors dealership in Iron River, Michigan.

Rifling through the glove compartment, I found the owner's manual, and it contained a surprising piece of luck: the ignition key's identification number was printed right there in black and white. Tom offered to drive me to Iron River on the off-chance the American Motors dealership could help. Larry decided to leave because there was nothing he could do.

The manager at the Iron River dealership was sympathetic but didn't have the equipment to cut a new key. He suggested we try Green Bay—about one hundred miles to the south. Tom was from Green Bay, but he had commitments and couldn't help me over the weekend. The fellow in the garage mentioned that Iron Mountain, Michigan, had another dealership—maybe it could help? Tom figured he'd have just enough time to drive me the forty miles, but it was already 3:30, so it would be nearly closing time by the time we got there. The prospects looked bleak.

(Female readers may well ask why we didn't call the dealer in Iron Mountain, even if that meant asking to use the Iron River dealer's phone. What can I say? Guys *never* ask for help—and fellow guys, like the parts manager, know enough not to offer any help. We guys prefer to do it ourselves.)

As we drove to Iron Mountain, Tom offered to take me down to Green Bay, where I could grab a motel for the weekend, or take me back to the cabin.

After some difficulty finding the AMC dealership, we finally pulled up a few minutes before 4:30. We rushed in and asked to see the parts manager. He listened carefully as we explained our predicament, but he shook his head and told us he simply didn't have that kind of equipment. "Try Green Bay. I hear they got that kind of equipment and can cut you the key. But you'll probably have to wait till Monday."

I was depressed. The sun was already low on the horizon and another arctic blast was enveloping the north country. After a week in the cabin I needed a shower, warmth, and some rest. I didn't have much cash and didn't feel like living in a motel in Green Bay over the weekend. My only other alternative was to stay the weekend (and probably longer because only Tom knew where I was) at the cabin.

We turned and walked out. As we went out the door, we passed a man who was carrying a large traveling case, not unlike the cases the Fuller Brush man used to haul from house to house when I was a kid. He seemed in a hurry to get to the dealership. Just as we reached Tom's car, the parts manager came running, yelling for us to return.

"We just might be able to help you folks," he exclaimed. "This here salesman has a newfangled gizmo for cutting keys." The manager then introduced us to the man we had passed not twenty seconds earlier.

He listened to our story.

When we were finished, he said, "This hand-held equipment is brand spanking new stuff. It's run by a computer. You give me the key identification number, I punch it in, and it'll cut you a replacement key."

"Will it work?" I asked somewhat desperately.

The salesman took in a long, slow breath, considered the question a moment, then replied, "Quite frankly, I don't really know. We jis' got it, and I haven't had time to experiment on it. We were just told to go out and sell it."

My heart began to sink again.

"I'll tell you what. You give me the key identification number, and I'll cut it for free. Won't charge you a cent. If it works, you tell Bud here that it worked, and we'll call it even."

Considering that I had no options, Tom and I gave him the number, and in a minute we were on our way back out to Lost Lake. A half-hour later we pulled up behind the Renault, and I walked resolutely toward it.

I inserted the key in the ignition and gave it a twist. In a few seconds the car's engine was sputtering to life. I was saved. Saved by a twist of fate that placed me at the right time and place to take advantage of a salesman plying his wares.

Tom headed south, and I sat in the lingering sunlight, letting the car warm up. I'd be late getting home, but I'd get there.

Nearly six months later, on a warm June day, I drove down the Lost Lake fire lane and parked precisely at the spot where the key had disappeared. I opened the door and looked directly down at the slightly rusted key Ol' Murph had taunted me with. I placed it in my wallet for safe keeping in case Murphy decided to drop in on me again.

Loafer's radio malfunctioned the week after my mishap with the key. Seventeen months later Ed Wenger, the district ranger, saw our collared friend standing on the Lost Lake fire lane. That was in May 1985, and it was the last time anyone saw Loafer alive.

We searched for Loafer periodically the following winter but found no sign of him or any other wolves. Loafer was gone.

The area he had roamed was wild, so we continued to survey it every year in the hope that another wolf or wolves would make it their home. In January 1988 Larry, Bob Welch, Jim Hammill, the Michigan biologist, and I planned to meet at Lost Lake to run track surveys across the northeastern portion of the Nicolet National Forest and to run some surveys in adjoining Michigan.

The weather turned cold. Very cold. The morning after we arrived, the thermometer at the cabin registered 30 degrees below zero, and my car refused to start. We needed it for the day's work, so we periodically tried to start it while guarding against running the battery down. Jim arrived at 9:30. We used jumper cables to give the battery some extra juice but could not get the engine to turn over.

The engine block was simply too cold. We needed to warm the engine. And by this time we needed to warm our own engines.

We gathered up an immense pile of dried downed wood from the surrounding snow-covered forest floor, placed it in two great piles in the middle of the Lost Lake fire lane, and lit them. We kept ourselves warm at one bonfire and built a smaller fire ten feet from the front end of my car—another Renault.

When the fire in front of the car had burned down to a substantial pile of glowing embers, we walked back, slipped the car in neutral, and rolled it over the coals. We hastily returned to warm our hands while the coals warmed the engine block.

They did. About three minutes later we were standing with our backs to the car and heard a low, muffled "pfoof."

Jim Hammill glanced over his left shoulder, then casually turned to me and remarked, "Jeez, Dick, I think your car's on fire."

I craned my neck and saw smoke pouring out from under the hood.

"By God, Jim, I think you're right."

We ran back to the car. I jumped in, put it in neutral, and the guys rolled it off the coals. Larry popped the hood and opened it. Flames sputtered, and black, sooty smoke rolled out. Bob and Jim grabbed some nearby snowshoes and began shoveling snow into the engine compartment. The snow sizzled and steamed, and the fire went out.

"Piece of shit car, Larry—I'll bet it'll start now," I said as I jumped in.

"No, it won't, Dick." Larry was seldom wrong about cars, but he was wrong this time. It "fired" right away.

After inspecting it, we decided that what had caught fire was a plastic covering beneath the engine block, which probably had collected drops of oil. Because the plastic was not essential to the operation of the car, we declared the vehicle functional.

Two weeks later, as I was driving through the boonies after an evening meeting, the car's electrical system began to fail. When I put the radio, heater, and lights on, I lost power. I drove forty miles in a snowstorm with my lights off, turning them on only at the approach of a car. Thankfully, that stretch of

highway was lightly used, but each time I turned on the lights, the power diminished. I was determined to get it to the nearest DNR garage. But to do that I had to drive through a town—and for that I would have to turn the lights on.

By the time I reached the outskirts of the town, the car's maximum speed was 35 miles per hour. When I hit the lights, the car lurched, sputtered, and slowed to 15 miles per hour. I crawled through the city, made it to the west end of town, and used my lights sparingly until I was once again on a lonely stretch of county highway. Finally, as I neared the town road that led to the garage, the car began sputtering and lurching. If I could just get to the town road, I knew I could roll downhill to the garage. As I made the turn, the car gave one last petrol belch and died. I quickly shifted into neutral, and the Renault coasted down the driveway and came to a stop fifteen feet from the garage door.

A light was on inside. One of the mechanics was working on his personal car. He greeted me at the door. I figured I was in trouble for the stupid thing we had done a few weeks earlier. I explained what had happened. Some electrical wires on the alternator must have gotten scorched in the fire.

He peeked at the car through the smudged glass of the great garage doors. "A Renault. They're shit. Why didn't you do us a favor and burn the whole damned thing up?"

"Next time I'll do a better job," I retorted with a chuckle.

In March 1985 the new director of the state Bureau of Endangered Resources asked me to develop a state-oriented wolf recovery plan, in response to state statutes pertaining to endangered resource management. I had reservations about such an approach. Wolves' problems were a reflection of public attitudes and misperceptions. The only way to help the species was to formulate a plan that had wide professional and public support. And the only way to gain that support is to make all parties a part of the process. I argued unsuccessfully for using a team approach for writing the plan.

By late that fall I had completed a draft. I set up two meetings for comments from wildlife staff in the DNR's northern districts. They were held on two days, back to back, in mid-November.

I stood before wildlife staff members, answering questions and defending the bureau's stance for two grueling days. The primary concern of the staff was that the process did not take into consideration public sentiments and was flawed because it had not been widely discussed.

By the end of the second day I was physically and mentally numb. I needed a day of peace and quiet. Solitude. I drove up to Gordon and spent the evening at the Gordon Ranger Station, intending to get some rest and recuperation in the field the next day.

I woke up around seven the next morning, grabbed some breakfast, jumped into the old 2-wheel-drive wolf-trapping pickup truck, and headed north toward wolf range. I looked forward to spending the day alone, driving the fire lanes, collecting scats. Unbeknown to me, Ol' Murph was there, waiting.

I had not been in the area for more than three months, and I was looking forward to the chance to reacquaint myself with the wolves' environs. I turned off the blacktop and headed toward the Tom Green Road. I turned left and drove along a route that would take me past the Moose River, where we had captured wolf 1189 years before.

As I approached the rim of the valley overlooking the river, I noticed the road was flooded in several places. Other vehicles had gotten through, so I continued on.

Daytime temperatures had stayed well below freezing during the previous three or four days, and several layers of ice had formed where the river washed over the road. The thickest ice was two inches, not strong enough to support the weight of the vehicles that had passed by. They had scattered massive shards of ice over the surface that had then had quickly frozen to the ice on either side of the wheel ruts.

I stopped and assessed the situation. The ruts were a foot deep. The first section of flooded road stretched for forty yards. High ground separated the first section from the second section, a more substantial stretch of sixty yards that extended west to the base of the hill in which the river was ultimately confined. I decided to go for it.

The truck lurched forward, slipped into the icy ruts, and broke through the thick veneer, slowing to nearly a complete halt before gaining purchase from the gravel bottom that was a solid road under more normal circumstances. It moved forward, gaining momentum and crunching ice as the front wheels plowed through the foot-deep trough. As the truck approached the flooded edge, the rear tires spun on submerged chunks of ice. The truck couldn't breach the icy berm. The tires spun, and wet ice became wedged beneath the partially submerged tires.

I slammed the truck into reverse and floored it. The truck raced backward. But I was unable to gain enough purchase to reach the dry ground behind and the tires spun again. As I slammed the gears into drive, the old truck lurched forward through the icy trough, but it couldn't break loose. The truck sailed back and forth four or five times, until it finally gained enough momentum to jump the icy ridge onto the high ground between the two flooded sections of road.

I decided not to push my luck. I turned the truck around, sped back through the hole, and barely gained the high ground on the other side. I parked the truck and decided a long walk along several of the fire lanes would do just fine.

The weather was crisp and very windy. A beautiful day for a walk in the woods. I did not encounter a single human being and managed to collect a few wolf scats. It was late in the afternoon when I returned to the truck.

I placed the scats in the back, jumped in, and started the engine. I suddenly remembered I had to take a leak, so I opened the door and jumped out. That's when Murphy struck. As I opened the door, my left elbow depressed the door lock. Only I didn't realize it.

As I walked off to the side of the road, a gust of wind hit and blew the door shut. Minor annoyance, I thought, until I returned and tried to open the door. It was locked.

I ran to the other side and it too was locked. I stared in at the keys perched peacefully in the ignition, while the truck's engine happily idled away.

I was still frazzled by the previous days' tensions and was in no mood for Murphy's tricks. The nearest road, and help, was a four-mile walk. By the time I got to a phone, the guys at the ranger station would be home. Deeply frustrated, I decided to break the window and deal with the consequences later. I selected a stout aspen stick and swung at the passenger window. The stick shattered.

Just then I remembered I had a roll of wire in the back that we used for trapping. I fashioned a hook on one end of a piece of wire, and on the third try the hook caught, and I was able to unlock the door.

I threw the wire in the back and, with arms outstretched, looked skyward and hollered, "I get the point. I'm going home now, okay?"

Although it was only Thursday, I'd had enough for one week. I returned to the Gordon Ranger Station, packed, and headed south for home. I did not want to take a chance at tempting Ol' Murph again anytime soon.

Boy, Would I Love Your Job!

Some people are infatuated with wolves. Wolves are wild. They are secretive and mysterious, and they are indifferent to the ways of humans. Wolves travel silently in cooperative groups, ranging quickly and effortlessly over great distances in remote landscapes, usually at night. They must kill the food they eat. These qualities invoke awe and admiration, and some members of our society hold wolves in near-religious esteem. Thus some people attach a certain amount of prestige and romantic charm to the profession of wolf biologist.

About nine months after taking the wolf job, I gave a talk in Madison. Two students from the university approached me afterward, and both introduced themselves by saying, "Boy, would I love your job." It was a comment I would hear repeatedly through the years.

I agreed. My job was great. I loved the opportunity to work with wolves. I even loved working with many of the people I'd encountered in both government and private sectors. However, sometimes being a wolf biologist was not so pleasant.

I experienced some uncomfortable situations in taverns on a couple of occasions. Patrons of these institutions are not especially noted for their self-control and discretion.

The winter of 1981–82 was rough on the deer herd in Douglas County. For starters, an early storm dumped fifteen inches of snow on the Douglas County wolf ranges. Unlike most storms early in the season, this snowfall remained until spring.

Snowfall the rest of that winter was average, but the early storm greatly stressed the deer, causing about a 10 percent decline in the herd. By winter's end, wolves were the talk of the town in every crossroads tavern throughout the region.

The old duffers knew the deer season of 1982 would not be good. Many a sudsy speech was given about the villainous conduct of wolves who, even as the speaker was slurring his words, were diminishing the chances that he and his buddies would be able to bag their bucks next fall. Feelings ran high.

I absentmindedly pulled into one of those back-road establishments one evening to lubricate my parched throat. As I sidled up to the bar, I drew gawking stares from the locals. The stares tapered off and conversation gradually resumed as I paid my fifty cents and settled in to a cold glass of beer.

Eventually, the man to my right began a conversation. I explained I was just driving through and was thirsty. This bar seemed like a quaint place, so I decided to stop and wet my whistle.

My newfound partner, a fellow in his early forties who sported a three-day stubble on his face, was jovial enough. Our conversation rambled on aimlessly until he eventually, and inevitably, came around to the DNR and its deer program. Experience had taught me not to reveal the source of my employment. I was glad I kept my mouth shut.

He gathered momentum as the minutes slid by.

"Damned DNR shot out all the does, and now there's no bucks left."

Teasingly, I responded, "Correct me if I'm wrong, but the DNR doesn't do the shooting—hunters do."

"P-f-s-s-t" (sound of beer shooting through front teeth). "Hell, I know that. What I mean is, they issued too many doe tags, an' they allowed too many to be taken."

"Yep," I said, acknowledging his thought, then added, "but if hunters were so all charged up about it and truly concerned that the herd would suffer, then they wouldn't have lined up to get their doe tags."

Got him in a pickle now, I thought—let's see him squirm outta this one.

He thought long, maybe even hard, then said, "It's them damned downstaters and Minnesotans. They don't know, and they don't give a tinker's damn. They don't live here. They come and go as they please."

I let that conversation die. A long silence followed during which we both nursed our beers.

Suddenly, my friend on the right and two fellows to my left launched into an emotional conversation about how the DNR sold doe tags merely to make money. Then one of the gents new to the conversation mentioned wolves. They launched into a babbling and slightly slurred diatribe about how these devils had taken over the countryside, wreaking havoc on all God's poor creatures.

"I saw two bucks taken down by wolves while locked together, fighting during the rut."

I kept my mouth shut, privately musing that, if they were really locked, they would have exhausted themselves and died anyhow and been lost to you orange-coats, so what is the point?

The conversation heated up considerably. By then I was considered one of the boys, albeit a relatively quiet one. The three traded horror stories of how the wolves had chased all the game out of the country. There were no deer left. And the DNR was to blame.

"How so?" I asked.

"Hell, they stocked 'em. I seen it myself. They have a biologist hired to put 'em back. Name of Dick Thiel. He's been on TV. He was the guy I seen driving the Minnesota DNR flatbed truck down the West Moose Road. The truck had twenty-five crates with timber wolves in 'em, already collared and ready to go."

I nearly spit out my beer. I was shocked and truly impressed that my modestly inebriated friend had correctly named Wisconsin's wolf biologist. For some inexplicable reason, however, he was unable to recognize the one and the same Dick Thiel sitting on the stool beside him. (I felt it wise not to introduce myself and feigned acceptance of his story with a muffled "uh-huh.") I quietly finished my drink and left.

I got into a similar situation six months later. In Wisconsin all hunters who bag a deer are required to tag it and register it at a registration station. Hundreds of stations are scattered across the state. DNR biologists run about eighty of these and obtain ages on deer by inspecting the animal's lower teeth. Data obtained from the aged samples aid deer management officials in determining the size, growth, and condition of the herd.

During the 1982 deer season the local wildlife manager wanted to obtain ages of hunter-killed deer in the deer management unit that included the Douglas County wolf range. I agreed to help and was assigned to one of the few deer registration stations in that area, the White House bar near Lyman Lake.

I pulled into the parking lot around two in the afternoon on the opening day of the season. The lot was already full. Blaze orange dominated the interior of the bar. Most had been giving their elbows considerable exercise already, judging from the condition of most of the patrons. And most hadn't gotten their deer yet. Hard to kill a deer from a bar stool, I mused to myself.

I introduced myself to the bartender, a woman in her late fifties. I told her that I worked for the DNR and that I would be aging deer. I offered to register the deer while aging them. She readily accepted the offer (private enterprises get a commission from the DNR for each deer registered, but they have to interrupt their regular work to tag each deer and do the paperwork at the end of each day).

I let the patrons sitting near me know I was a DNR employee and that I was there to register and age deer as hunters brought them in. They accepted my explanation and continued their conversations. About every twenty minutes a party of hunters would stroll in, and, amid excited greetings and traded insults, I would follow the lucky ones to their vehicle to age and register their deer.

After a while the local stool huggers warmed up to my presence and gradually included me in their discussions. One fellow offered me a drink, but I politely declined, reminding them that I was on duty and that it was not proper for a state employee to drink on the job. As the crowd grew, the locals started telling hunting stories—big bucks that got away and other yarns of bygone seasons (clearly, few had been in any position to gain new stories). Every so often I would leave the raucous crowd to go out to the parking lot and register deer as actual hunters drove in.

By 4:30 a steady stream of hunters was converging on the little bar in the woods. I was kept fairly busy for an hour. When I finally came back into the bar, the conversation had taken a dark turn. The boys were talking about wolves, and none of them was in a happy mood.

One of the newcomers had not been successful.

"Damned DNR. I was sittin' on my stand from 5:30 to 8:30 this morning. Never saw a thing move. I went back to my truck for a sandwich and a drink out a' th' thermos. Then went back an' sat til about 10:30.

"I hears this sound—see—comin' from beyond the rise down in the swamp. Deer, I thinks to myself.

"Th' sound keeps comin' slowly. Stops. Comes again. Makin' its way in my general dirikshun. Iss still too far and thick for me to make out what it tiz. All of a sudden I hears this roar, an' a plane swoops outta nowhere glidin' right over the treetops passin' right above me."

"It was the DNR trackin' plane. You know, the one that's trackin' them damned wolves! I had a mind to shoot it outta the sky. But I didn't want to spook whatever was out there. It didn't matter. They spooked the deer an' I never heard it again."

"We gotta do something about them damned wolves. Not only are they killing off all our deer, but them damned researchers in the DNR are ruinin' our hunts."

He went on, claiming he was going to make a complaint to the Federal Aviation Administration. One of his buddies asked whether he had seen the plane's identification number, because the FAA would need some means of identifying who was flying the plane. The disgruntled hunter had been unable to make the numbers out because of dense fog.

One of the bar stool steadies suddenly remembered that I worked for the DNR.

"Hey, he works for the DNR."

In unison a dozen hunters turned to me. One said, "Is it true, the DNR's flying them wolves on *opening day?*"

Once again, I found myself in an uncomfortable situation. I decided, in the interest of personal safety, not to reveal my identity as the DNR's one and only wolf biologist unless asked. I did feel it was necessary to answer the man's challenge head-on with some facts.

"Where'd you say this took place?"

"Why, I was hunting south off the Hunter's lane near where County Highway A bends at the Tower Road."

"Funny, I was hunting *south* of Highway A between the Empire Swamp Trail and Summit Tower Road, and I saw that plane too. It wasn't the DNR plane, though. I heard the pilot canceled the flight this morning on account of the fog," I told him.

"That plane was darn low and circled the area several times before drifting off to the east. My immediate thoughts were some guy had hired a pilot to spot deer for him, radio positions to the ground to move the hunter in close for a shot. That's illegal, you know."

This miffed my interrogators, who were raising their eyebrows and grunting and groaning when another hunter interrupted by asking me to register his deer. When I returned, all eyes were locked on my form, glaring coldly at me. I think I'm in trouble, I thought to myself, as I quietly returned to my seat next to the window.

The boys were thoroughly riled up. And several more people had joined the conversation. Wolves.

"We should kill 'em all," one fellow barked as others indignantly traded stories of how they had encountered deer slain by the wicked, slashing teeth of wolves.

Another hunter came in, and I left to register his deer. When I returned, the place was fairly quiet. Some of the boys had picked up their hats, said their goodbyes, and left. Others returned to their seats across the bar. I was left with five or six hunters, including some of the diehards who had greeted me four hours earlier.

I ordered a diet soda from the bartender. As she went to retrieve a can, the fellow whose hunt had been interrupted by the plane turned to me, squinted, and said, "You're the wolf biologist, ain't you?"

As I groped for a tactful, life-saving way to answer his question, his buddy said, "Why, Arnie, lay off him. He ain't no more the wolf biologist than you or I is. He's jis' tryin' to do his job. Leave him alone."

Thank you, God, I thought, and with gratitude I bought them both a beer.

"Boy, would I love to have your job." Those words echoed through the very frozen recesses of my brain on Thursday morning, January 19, 1984, at the end of the coldest week I had ever spent in a cabin. Jim Hammill, the Michigan wildlife biologist, and I had planned to conduct some joint surveys along the Michigan–Wisconsin border areas during the winter of 1983–84. For one of those surveys Jim had made arrangements for us to use a private cabin on American Can industrial forestland ten miles north of Amasa, Michigan.

Larry Prenn, Dan Groebner, a temporary assistant with the wolf study, and I drove up on a Monday and spent the better part of the afternoon cruising backwoods fire lanes in the eastern Ottawa National Forest with Jim. Jim showed us the way to the cabin, which lay a mile off a plowed fire lane. By the time we arrived, it was dark.

We had at our disposal a single snowmobile. With it we began hauling in our personal gear. This took some time, and because we were all cold, tired, and hungry, we rigged up a rope with several hand loops. Dan and I donned skis and our backpacks, grabbed a loop, and Larry towed us behind the snowmobile in the dazzling moonlight to our cabin.

Jim showed us how to light the liquid propane space heaters and lanterns, then bid us farewell until the next morning (he lived only fifty miles away, so he headed for home). It took only three hours to warm the cabin to the point where we could take off our coats. We heated up cans of Dinty Moore stew, ate, and crawled into our sleeping bags with books in hand. Larry found a thermometer hanging from a spruce tree outside the door and at 8:30 P.M. reported the temperature at 24 degrees below zero. It was going to be cold come morning.

At 7:45 the next morning we were out on the fire lane. Both trucks started but just barely. Jim met us fifteen minutes later and we began a cold day of cruising for sign of wolves.

We worked the whole day in the Michigamme Flowage country, a wild region of forest that stretches for about forty miles north of Crystal Falls. Tracking conditions were ideal. Frigid temperatures drained every bit of moisture out of the dry sky each night so that frost fell like snowflakes under a clear sky. But we found no evidence of wolves.

The next morning one truck refused to start. Larry, Dan, and I piled into the remaining truck to cruise the eastern Ottawa National Forest in the Perch Lake country north of Iron River. But once again we found no sign of wolves. Our route back to the cabin took us through Iron River, and we stopped at a nice little restaurant called the Chalet for supper because none of us wanted more lukewarm canned stew. The thermometer on the bank at the center of town read 24 degrees below zero at 6 P.M.

Larry woke up at 5:30 the next morning. I was too cold to move in the darkness. I could hear him groping for the matches. I could also hear the sharp crack of trees exploding in the forest outside. Larry eventually managed to light a gas lantern. He went outside, and when he returned, he casually said, "The thermometer tacked to the tree goes down to 48 degrees below, boys, and the mercury is entirely within the bulb."

I peered out of the top of my sleeping bag through a frosted window. Moonlight bathed the forest in a blanket of dead light. Eerie. No shadows beneath the trees. Cold. Unforgivingly cold.

I mustered the energy to get up and confront the very real possibility that neither the snowmobile nor the trucks would start. The previous day's weather forecast had said that a Canadian high pressure system would stall out over Lake Superior, providing the region with plenty of sunshine and bitterly cold temperatures.

It was time to make a decision. Working in these temperatures could be life threatening, especially if we had to deal with equipment failures. None of us fancied staying in the cabin another night. It was too cold. We decided to pack our gear out, and if the trucks started, we would grab a motel room and finish the week's work. If the trucks did not start, we would work on them until they did and then head for home.

Larry packed quickly and braved the weather in an attempt to start the snowmobile—our most certain means of transportation back to the road (our skis would be difficult to use because we had left our poles in the truck—we didn't need them when we were being towed).

From inside the cabin I heard a sputter, then a cough, followed by a protracted pause of some fifteen seconds before another cough followed. Larry's laughter reached the interior of the cabin, which was hovering somewhere between 32 and 40 degrees with space heaters running full blast. I scraped frost off a window pane and peered through the smudged glass to see a great cloud of blue smoke rising from the snowmobile's exhaust pipe. A cough—a cloud—a pause of several seconds, then another cough, repeated by a cloud and another pause. The engine was firing but only once every few seconds.

Larry came in. "No use standing out there watching that thing try to warm up," he said as he shut the door. The snowmobile continued to sputter at that pace for a full fifteen minutes before the engine block had built up enough heat to warm the oil, which freed the piston to do its work.

In ten more minutes we were headed out. Our thick woolen gloves were no good. By the time we reached the trucks, our faces and hands were burning cold. The moisture from our breath froze to our mustaches, eyelids, and eyebrows, and we all appeared as white as old St. Nick. And, as we suspected, neither of the trucks budged.

Jim Hammill arrived at 8:30. His truck barely started, although it had spent the evening in a garage. We decided to cancel the remainder of our surveys for the week and concentrated on getting the trucks started. Boy, I thought, as we monkeyed with the trucks in 40 degrees below zero, this sure is a fun job.

Bureaucracy is another beast that can cause one to question one's sanity. Not long after our new bureau director arrived, I realized he knew little about biology. He was one of the DNR's old boys and would finish out his career there.

Even before the wolf project began, it was obvious the wolves in Douglas County were part of an interstate population that straddled the state boundaries between Minnesota's Highway 23 and Wisconsin's Highway 53 south of Duluth. This population was separated from Minnesota's primary wolf range, which extended north of Duluth and Grand Rapids. And, of course, no barrier separated Minnesota wolves from Wisconsin wolves. The Stateline Flowage Pack actually roamed 160 square miles of the interstate wilderness.

It would have made no biological sense to study the population dynamics of wolves living *only* on the Wisconsin side of this insular population. To obtain a complete picture of wolf ecology in this region, the Wisconsin DNR obtained permission from the Minnesota DNR to collar and study wolves on the Minnesota side.

This agreement was subject to renewal every March. And, besides being truly cooperative in spirit, such agreements qualify both states for federal grants under Section 6 of the Endangered Species Act, administered by the U.S. Fish and Wildlife Service. So each March, I dutifully wrote a reminder and attached a memo drafted for the secretary's signature and sent it to the bureau director. All he had to do was put the memo in the bureaucratic pipeline to the secretary. The request for renewal would go out under the secretary's signature to the Minnesota DNR's secretary for approval.

A week or so after I wrote the memo and sent it to the new bureau director, I happened to be in Madison working in the bureau, and the director called me in to his office.

He offered me a chair. I sat down. Following some chit-chat, he mentioned the memo. "Why," he asked, "are you planning on trapping and collaring wolves in Minnesota?"

I explained that the population was fairly small and geographically isolated. Half the population was in Wisconsin, while the other half was in Minnesota. His expression remained unchanged.

"You realize you are a *Wisconsin* DNR employee, and not a Minnesota DNR employee?"

Uncomfortable as to where this conversation was going, I simply replied, "Yes."

"Then why should you be concerned about wolves living in Minnesota?"

I responded, again using biological rationale as the basis for our involvement in Minnesota, hoping that reason would prevail. He remained unmoved.

Sensing that this fellow was about to seriously compromise our efforts to understand the dynamics of wolves living at the edge of their continental range, I changed tactics. I pointed out that we had been studying the entire population for three years, and no one in that time had thought anything irregular about the arrangement, *including the DNR secretaries of both states.*

He budged only when I reminded him that interstate cooperation was a criterion for gaining the Section 6 money, which was the primary means of support for the program. Leaning back in his comfy chair, he crossed his hands in front of his face, contemplating these last pointers. After a pause of perhaps thirty seconds he issued his edict: he would let us continue working in Minnesota. However . . .

"I am not comfortable with the fact that you are doing this work as an employee of the state of Wisconsin. I may change my mind in the future."

I walked out of his office, eyes rolled far back in my head. On the two-hour journey home that evening, I reran this conversation in my head, chuckling at the thought that anyone would want to be in my shoes. I knew then and there that the wolf project was to endure many a trying moment with this fellow at the helm.

The phone message tacked to the door of my office "bedroom" at the Gordon Ranger Station stated, URGENT: CALL ARLYN LOOMANS IMMEDIATELY.

One of the fire control boys peeked around the corner of his office door down the hall and shouted, "You get that message? You're to call that fellow right away."

"Thanks," I hollered. I put my gear down, found a phone, and called the North-Central District wildlife supervisor, thinking that perhaps he was going to tell me that a wolf had been killed.

That wasn't it.

"Whatever you're doing, you have to drop it and be in Madison at the State Capitol tomorrow morning at 10 A.M. sharp," Loomans told me.

"What?"

"The secretary's office has tasked you and me with being at the rotunda of the Capitol for the unveiling of the wolf display. . . . You know, the one that was shot in Lincoln County.[1] State senator Tiny Krueger has devised some type of news media conference. I am to deliver the wolf display and represent our district. You are to be there to answer questions about the plight of wolves in the state."

I was fairly naive about departmental politics, which I despised, so I was reluctant to accept that I had no choice in the matter.

"Can't someone else do that? For God's sakes, I'm in the middle of important fieldwork up here and can't simply break away on less than twelve hours' notice."

"Where the secretary's involved, and when it involves a powerful person like Krueger, you'll be there," Loomans replied.

Madison was a seven-hour drive for me. I thanked Loomans for delivering the message and packed up for the drive home.

Shortly before ten the next morning, February 9, 1982, Loomans and I were ushered into a small room off one corner of the rotunda. A member of the secretary's staff briefed us on the upcoming news conference and why we were there. The state assembly had just passed Bill A303, the Income Tax Checkoff for Endangered Species. It had been delivered to a state senate committee for review, and the department's legislative liaisons were not sure it would get out of committee. The wolf display would be a symbol for support for the bill; DNR administrators hoped the news conference would stimulate public support and thereby move influential state senators to endorse its passage.

As the staffer left the room, he nearly collided with a slick young fellow in a three-piece suit who had been looking for us. He introduced himself as an aide to Senator "Tiny" Krueger, a Republican representing the Merrill area just north of Wausau. He said Krueger had not yet decided which way to vote on the bill. A few seconds later the state senator himself entered the room. His aide suggested I brief Krueger on the status of wolves in the state before we stepped outside to meet the press. Krueger seemed unconcerned as I described the precarious existence of *Canis lupus* in Wisconsin.

Meanwhile, maintenance employees had delivered the stuffed wolf to the rotunda. The DNR staffer, Arlyn Loomans, and I escorted Tiny, a behemoth of a man, and his entourage to the wolf's glass tomb. The press had not yet arrived.

Senator Krueger walked over and leaned against the case, one arm perched atop the great structure. Shortly, a pair of elderly tourists walked up to the display. After gazing upon the wolf for a few seconds, the man mumbled that they were all killers. The senator looked at the couple and responded, "Yes, they certainly can be destructive."

The couple moved off and were replaced by another couple less than a minute later. Tiny maintained his perch at the corner. This couple exclaimed,

"It's a shame they're almost all gone," to which the great politician answered, "They should be preserved."

The news conference began ten minutes later. A reporter asked whether the display of the wolf had been timed to garner support for Assembly Bill A303. The senator replied, "No, the appearance of the wolf here at the Capitol is merely a coincidence in timing with Bill A303. It really symbolizes that times are tough and serves as a reminder to everyone in the legislative body that the wolf is at the door. I'm sure you all know to what I refer: the projected $450 million deficit which is presently confronting state law makers."

They Shoot the Messenger,
Don't They?

The exposure I had to Tiny Krueger's political posturing was innocuous compared to what another politician put me through three years later.

During the early 1980s, when Wisconsin's wolf project was still in its developmental stages, wolf biologists had no means of measuring the physical attributes of wolf habitat. The federal government's Eastern Timber Wolf Recovery Plan, approved in 1978, listed four factors crucial to wolf survival. Among these were the two attributes that determine wolf habitat: large tracts of wild land with few people and minimal access, and adequate supplies of prey.

Wolves are recognized as "habitat generalists." That is to say, they are found where they know they'll find dinner, regardless of climate variations. Wolf prey is widely distributed throughout North America (some species, such as moose and white-tailed deer, are actually more abundant now than they were two hundred or more years ago). Thus wolves occupied an incredibly large geographic range before they were both bountied and squeezed out of their U.S. range by humans between the Civil War and World War II.

The primary factor limiting wolf distribution in the world today is the presence of people. By the early 1980s biologists had long understood the inverse relationship between the presence of humans and the presence of wolves. However, biologists lacked the means to evaluate whether an area from which wolves hade been exterminated in an earlier era could now support wolves. They needed some way to measure the level at which human use of a landscape caused a collapse in the wolf population.

Now that wolves were protected, land managers charged with maintaining their habitat would certainly find such a tool useful. More important, they could use it to determine which areas wolves might find agreeable and therefore where recovery would have a chance of succeeding. Obviously, this tool would have a great influence on our efforts to restore a wolf population to Wisconsin because it would provide clues to whether permanent recovery was possible.

I had been intrigued by this problem since my high school days after reading a passage from Dan Thompson's treatise on the plight of Wisconsin's wolves in midcentury Wisconsin: "In the timber wolf range, the opening of each new section of closed fire lane area to public travel has jeopardized the existence of the wolves. Trappers then drive into an area with a carload of traps where formerly they had to hike in with only as many traps as they could carry in a packsack."[1] Thompson was describing the basic tenet of access. Access allows people to get closer to wolves. As access increases, exploitation of wolves increases. At some level access creates overexploitation, and the wolf population falters, leading to the species' extirpation.

Clearly, access was related to how people shaped wolf range, making landscapes uninhabitable for wolves. It seemed to me that measuring the level of access would provide the standard we needed to objectively ascertain whether an area could support wolves. If this was true, the relative level of access within areas inhabited by wolves should be different from areas devoid of wolves. Further, I hypothesized that areas with wolves would have lower levels of access by humans than areas without wolves.

We could measure access by determining the average number of linear miles of road per square mile of habitat. These were really measurements of road density. By comparing values in wolf-occupied areas to areas where wolves were absent, I hoped to be able to spot a trend.

Wisconsin actually was perfect for such an analysis: a few scattered enclaves of occupied wolf habitat amid vast areas of "wolfless" habitat. Further, I decided to review historical wolf distributions from Wisconsin when fellows like Bernie Bradle and Dan Thompson were lamenting the imminent demise of Wisconsin's original wolf population.

I compared period road maps of counties maintained at the State Historical Society of Wisconsin's Map Archive section to historical records of wolf pack distribution from the 1920s through the 1950s.[2] I also used what I knew of roads within areas occupied by wolves, as well as within similar but uninhabited areas adjacent to pack territories. I asked the same question for each decade: At what level of roading (in other words, road density) did wolves disappear? For the current data I asked, Is there a difference between the road densities within territories occupied by wolves today and adjacent areas that remain wolfless?

I was especially pleased to find that the answers for the pre-1960 data and the post-1979 analysis agreed because the two events (annihilation of wolves before 1960, and the return of wolves since the mid-1970s) were unrelated, or "independent" of one another. The answer was roughly one linear mile of road per square mile of habitat. More miles of road = no wolves. Fewer miles of road = wolves. Simple. Magic? No, merely applied science.

The study, published in 1985, was closely followed by similar analyses conducted by other wolf researchers in the eastern Upper Peninsula of Michigan

and in northern Minnesota.[3] The Minnesota and Michigan results echoed the Wisconsin findings. Wolves tended to vanish from, or failed to occupy, areas where road density exceeded one mile of road per square mile of habitat. The limit was termed the *threshold*.

Although this tool was supposed to aid wildlife officials in preserving wolves and their habitats, most people misunderstood its utility and failed to recognize its limitations.

One misconception prevalent among professionals and the public was that wolves fear and loathe roads, as if they were somehow allergic to them. In reality, wolves love roads and use them for the same reason that we build them. Roads provide a convenient means of travel through terrain otherwise difficult to maneuver. Wolves minimize their contact with humans by being mostly nocturnal. But they occasionally use roads in broad daylight.

Loafer, our radio-collared wolf in the northern Nicolet National Forest, chose the height of the summer tourist season in 1983 for one of his public day-time strolls. Pilot Ray Marvin and I were homing in on Loafer's signal under a blazing sun.

As we neared Loafer's range, I turned the receiver on and immediately noted that we were very close to him. Highway 139 appeared a mile ahead of us, with the tiny village of Long Lake off to our right. I motioned to Ray that we were close. He nodded. As we approached the two-lane highway, I asked Ray to veer to the left. As we flew over, we noticed a commotion of sorts below. Two cars were stopped and the occupants of one were spilling out, running up an embankment, and excitedly pointing into the woods. The dense foliage prevented us from seeing what they had seen. Because this was rather queer, I switched to the right antenna, and the ear phones nearly blasted clear of my head. Loafer was right there.

I was afraid he had been hit by a car, which is what I told Ray and asked him to circle. The people noticed our plane, gawked into the woods for a few more minutes, and left. We really did not know what to think or do, so we followed the car until we obtained a description and license plate number, then returned to the site and continued circling.

About a mile off, we saw a logging truck heading toward the spot that Loafer's signal was coming from. All of a sudden Ray shouted, "There he is!"

Peering below, I saw Loafer lope out of the woods, walk confidently onto the blacktop, and begin walking down the yellow line — straight at the oncom-ing logging truck that two enormous hills obscured from the wolf's view. The two inched closer as the moments passed. We prayed they wouldn't meet at a hillcrest. Fortunately, the trucker reached the top before Loafer did. He saw the wolf and slammed on the brakes. Loafer sidestepped off the blacktop, loped up an embankment, and stood at the edge of the forest while the truck crept past him.

Once the logging truck was out of sight, Loafer continued on. Another ve-hicle, a green station wagon with U.S. Forest Service decals pasted on the front doors, appeared about a half-mile behind him. A minute later the car crested a hill. The occupants must have had a clear view of Loafer as he reacted with surprise and ran off the road, this time for good.

I couldn't wait to land and call my friend, Tony Rinaldi, the biologist for the Nicolet National Forest, to tell him that I had witnessed two of the national forest's staff people as they encountered Loafer on a road. It turned out he was just as excited to get hold of me: he was in the car.

Perhaps the greatest misconception about the road density work was that the threshold level of one linear mile per square mile of habitat would remain static, or frozen in time. When first introduced to the concept, most foresters and wildlife managers did not embrace the notion that it was possible to quantitatively measure wolf habitat. And they vehemently rejected the notion that wolves required such low levels of roading, fearing it would have a severe effect—and perhaps curtail—important management activities on public lands. In fact, their fear that protecting wolves meant barring people from public lands was somewhat justified because a majority of the publicly managed lands in Wisconsin, Michigan, and even Minnesota had higher road densities.[4] What the managers did not understand was that the threshold actually is an indirect measure of the prevailing attitudes of humans toward wolves. As such, the threshold is subject to change, given a little time for education programs and other public awareness efforts to work.

Today, more than fifteen years later, it is clear that both public support for wolf recovery and attitudes toward wolves have improved. Wolf packs have colonized areas of Wisconsin that exceed the original threshold limits. This is a result of two events: as territorial packs have saturated the best habitat, wolves have had to colonize less suitable areas with higher road densities; and humans' greater tolerance of wolves has increased the total amount of habitat that wolves find suitable. Another way of looking at it is that the population of humans who think the only good wolf is a dead wolf has gotten smaller over the years.

Yes, it was possible to misuse this tool to demand that wildlife managers shut down extensive road systems and manage the land exclusively for the benefit of wolves, but most regarded doing that as extremely threatening to the survival of the wolves. Closing down roads would undoubtedly so rile the public that the wolves would be more at risk than ever—vulnerable to retaliatory killings and legislation. And that is what nearly happened.

In 1986 the director of Wisconsin's Endangered Resources Bureau created a state timber wolf recovery team and charged it with developing a recovery plan. I was appointed to head the team. These new responsibilities would compete with and supersede my fieldwork for the next three years.

We were to generate a scientifically defensible goal, one that, it was hoped, would restore the wolf in numbers that would make its population viable. We were also to develop management strategies that would help achieve that goal. At our first meeting the team—composed of wildlife managers, foresters, endangered species biologists, and public information specialists—recognized that any plan developed within a bureaucratic vacuum would not receive widespread public acceptance. Failure to win public acceptance would doom any plan that we came up with.

We needed to involve the public from the beginning. The director reluctantly agreed. Throughout the summer of 1986 we worked feverishly to prepare for our initial public forums, set to begin in mid-September.

By sheer chance, just as we were getting ready for a media blitz announcing our invitation for public comment on wolf recovery, the U.S. Forest Service was preparing to release its final management plans for both the Chequamegon and Nicolet National Forests—massive documents that had been subjected to intense public scrutiny in their draft phases. Because wolves were on the federal endangered species list, both federal forests were compelled to devote some attention to managing wolf habitat. Our team knew that the sudden appearance of two unrelated government actions, both dealing with wolves, would be confusing. As it turned out, that would be the least of our worries.

In early August 1986 a reporter for the *Vilas County News Review* wrote a story about the sections dealing with wolves from the soon-to-be-released national forest management plans. The *Vilas County News Review* report was picked up by the Associated Press, and on August 10 it ran in the *Milwaukee Sentinel* and other papers throughout the state. The timing could not have been worse for the wolf recovery effort. The *Sentinel's* banner headline screamed MAKING WAY FOR GRAY WOLVES: NICOLET FOREST PLAN WOULD CLOSE SOME LOGGING ROADS. The lead said: "Nicolet National Forest managers have proposed closing about 500 miles of logging roads crossing 100,000 acres of forest land to reduce human impact on the endangered gray timber wolf." And a sidebar quoted a Nicolet forest planner as saying, "Wolves and humans just don't get along. We aren't saying there will definitely be wolf packs flourishing between Eagle River and Florence, but we are providing the habitat. Without roads, human contact with the wolves would be reduced."

What had happened was that the *draft* version of the forest management plan produced by the forest service had proposed to *accelerate* road building. Meanwhile, to meet the federal mandate to protect an endangered species, the Wisconsin DNR and the U.S. Fish and Wildlife Service had recommended that the U.S. Forest Service produce less ambitious plans for development and even close off some minor access roads within the two national forests. And that, combined with intense criticism and threats of legal action from environmental advocates and the public, had forced the U.S. Forest Service to modify its road-building program for the final forest management plan.

But the boys in power at the Nicolet were still hell-bent on having their roads. My guess is that someone at Nicolet, well aware of what the local re-

action would be, leaked the final management plan to the *Vilas County News Review* reporter.

The story in the *Vilas County News Review* about the inch-thick management plan focused on road closures. The article made it appear as though major access roads, and perhaps even some highways, would be affected. This was far from the truth. The sensationalized article had its intended effect. Loggers, the powerful timber products industry, local hunters and state hunting groups, and people living in northern communities—many of whom had little cause to oppose wolf recovery—reacted with fury.

The local reporter also had an outdoors column, which fed public animosity when it appeared three days after the story broke statewide:

BOTTOM LINE: WOLVES WON'T SURVIVE HERE

The controversy over restricting public access to improve habitat for timber wolves in the Nicolet National Forest has two distinct sides: a philosophical viewpoint and a practical look at the matter. . . .

Those who cater to a philosophical view look at the timber wolf as a mystical animal which has been virtually absent from Wisconsin since it was driven out by hunters and trappers more than three decades ago. They envision the wolf . . . as a symbol of the wilderness. . . .

I would not condemn the Forest Service's proposal to close roads based on any dislike of wolves, or even a dislike of the philosophical viewpoint. . . . I might even support some road closings, regardless of what is good for wolves, to isolate some hunting and hiking areas from four-wheelers. . . .

Hurt most by this proposal are those few, unique outdoorsmen who hunt bear with hounds. They use logging roads, especially those remote areas that would be highly rated wolf territory, to find fresh tracks of bears. . . .

. . . The only sensible reason to oppose the Forest Service's plan to close roads would come after answering the practical question: will humans allow a wolf pack to survive in eastern Vilas and Florence counties? . . .

. . . For all practical purposes, there are still too many people who don't want a wolf pack roaming the Nicolet National Forest.

The bottom line is that it makes little sense to close 500 miles of logging roads for an animal that is almost certainly not going to thrive here.

. . . Some road closings would be acceptable, but not for the sake of timber wolf habitat. Like it or not.[5]

Within fifteen days individuals representing several state agencies were entering the fray. In October I received a call from the governor's office. Some officials outside the DNR were reviewing the possibility of filing an appeal of the Nicolet National Forest's final plan, in partnership with several environmental organizations, to seek greater protection for the wolves. The powerful timber products industry also had mobilized on the roads issue and viewed the Nicolet National Forest's final management plan as a threat to its economic viability. The enemies: environmentalists, wolves, and a certain wolf biologist. Democratic governor Tony Earl lost his reelection bid that November, and, although I heard nothing more from his office, the public intervenor (a sort of ombudsman for social and environmental issues) and the state attorney general were getting interested, to the annoyance of the governor-elect. But after the new governor, Republican Tommy Thompson, was sworn in, the state withdrew its support for an appeal of the forest management plan. Two Wisconsin environmental groups vowed to carry on.

The road issue was being blown way out of proportion.

In December state senator Lloyd Kincaid, a Democrat from the heart of Nicolet country, began a tirade against the wolf program, telling the *Vilas County News Review*, "The obvious motive underlying the State appeal of management plans for federal forests in Wisconsin is a foolhardy attempt to reestablish timber wolves in our state, and it is the major factor in the conflict of interest move by the Attorney General's office, encouraged by Governor Earl, to block most of the timber harvest on federal forests in our state."

Kincaid, well known for his scorched-earth tactics, told the Vilas County paper a week after the story broke, "At the root of this movement is clearly an unrealistic idea that enough acreage can be reserved without the roads needed to carry on logging, and large blocks of the forest set aside without any logging at all to encourage the reestablishment of timber wolves in the two national forests in our state."

And wolves weren't the only thing Kincaid wanted run out of state on a rail: "I am asking that the Department of Natural Resources reconsider the activities of a DNR timber wolf specialist who has been working with the Sierra Club leaders, and other militant environmentalists, seeking to drum up public sentiment to favor establishment of habitat for timber wolves."[6]

Meanwhile, the state wolf recovery team convened to review public comments from the first round. In an effort to clear the air the team decided to draft a news release explaining the role of road management and logging in maintaining wolf habitat

And Kincaid's comment on the foolhardiness of wolf recovery was evidently causing something of stir itself. Just before Christmas the *Vilas County News Review* outdoors columnist did some quick backpeddling on behalf of the good senator:

> I really don't think State Sen. Lloyd Kincaid, a Democrat from Crandon, meant exactly what he said recently when he called the DNR's wolf recovery program a "foolhardy" attempt. . .
>
> The "foolhardy" criticism comes into play when state wolf experts and their most avid supporters, such as members of the extremist Sierra Club, attempt to prioritize the timber wolf ahead of the economic stability of an entire region.

The columnist included information from our news release on logging, roads, and wolves:

> In pushing for the closing of a 100,000-acre area in the Nicolet National Forest to vehicular traffic and all logging, the Sierra Club has argued the timber wolf needs such an area to survive.
>
> The facts prove quite the contrary. According to Terry Valen, a member of the DNR's wolf recovery team, many people hold the misconception that wolves require wilderness to exist.
>
> "Because of this misconception many people believed logging should be restricted if not eliminated from some areas in an effort to promote and protect wilderness," Valen said. "Yet to maintain suitable wolf habitat, deer are necessary. To maintain deer, trees need to be cut to promote growth of such tree species as aspen—the primary food source for deer."

The columnist concluded, "Now it becomes clear that the Sierra Club and the Wilderness Society don't care much about wolves, they just used the animal as a way to push for more wilderness."[7]

Our press release got wider play after Christmas. It read, in part:

> While the wolf is certainly at home in a wilderness setting, it can, and often does, do well in environments dominated by humans. . . . If wolf recovery occurs in Wisconsin, the wolves will live in an environment dominated by human activities. . . .
>
> Wolves prey predominantly upon large-hoofed mammals such as deer. . . . Deer thrive in disturbed habitats—habitats characterized by young stages of forest growth. Wildlife managers and foresters enhance deer habitat in northern Wisconsin through timber cutting programs. That means . . . what's good for the deer is good for the wolf. . . .
>
> So why all the commotion over roads and wolf habitat requirements? . . . Access facilitates . . . illegal killings. . . .
>
> Roads themselves are not the problem; human attitudes are. But, until attitudes towards the wolf change, open roads are a key to wolf survival. . . . While some roads are necessary to carry out timber cutting activities, it is important to limit human access. . . .

This marked the beginning of a gradual change in attitudes toward roads and wolves. It would take more than a year to educate the various interest groups that the thrust of a road management policy was not to shut down roads or trails open to the public but to limit the number of roads developed in the more remote forested areas of the state.

The state wolf recovery team eventually gained the trust of the timber products industry, hunter advocate groups, the state's snowmobile association, and the County Forest Administrators Association. With their aid the DNR developed a road management policy that was accepted by a majority of people who had expressed concern. No landowner would be forced to comply with the terms of the road management policy of the Wisconsin Timber Wolf Recovery Plan. The policy was totally voluntary, relying on cooperative agreements between the department, various county forest administrators, and private industrial forest managers.

On a sunny day in the late spring of 1987, about the time that the road controversy began to die down, I walked into the DNR's headquarters in downtown Madison. I had been ordered to meet the director of the Bureau of Endangered Resources about an important matter. At the appointed time he ushered me in to his office and asked that I close the door. I complied.

He asked whether I had brought a paper and pen. I replied in the affirmative. He then asked me to pull up a chair. All of this seemed rather peculiar.

"I am going to dictate a letter and I want you to copy it down," he told me.

I glanced furtively over my right shoulder to see whether his assistant was sitting at her desk in her little cubicle. She was. Very odd, this behavior. Did he really call me down here to take dictation?

He began:

"Secretary—DNR: This is to inform you that I have been wrong in promoting road densities as measures of wolf habitat. After reviewing the data more carefully, it appears there is no relationship between roads and wolves. The data I used was flawed and the conclusions are in error."

In shock, I put my pen down as he continued to speak. I heard none of the words that followed. A deadeningly cold, numbing sensation gripped me. This man was part of the department's power structure. I wondered whether he thought I had any integrity. To expect I'd go along with this scheme was absurd. It was also career suicide for me to defy him. I knew right then and there that my career as a wolf biologist was over. The only question was when.

Because he was engrossed in his phraseology, he didn't notice until he was well into his second paragraph that I had stopped writing.

"Is there something wrong—you didn't catch something?" he asked.

"Yes, sir, there is something wrong. Your intention is that I retract the findings of research I conducted, which withstood rigorous scrutiny in a refereed scientific journal and was duly published. The work, while controversial, is accepted by the scientific community as valid. You are instructing me to send a letter up to the secretary that renounces my own work. You are essentially asking me to *lie*."

"You mean to tell me you are defying me?"

"I am telling you I will not be a party to this. You can write this letter and place your name on it. But I will not. I will stand by my work. And if people ask me to explain the department's about-face, I will tell them I back truth: the truth that road densities are a useful gauge in identifying wolf habitat. I am well versed on the topic. You are not."

I thought he'd lower the boom right then and there. Perplexed by my insubordination, he merely excused me.

Road management is now considered a reliable wolf management tool in the states of the upper Great Lakes. Wisconsin approved its timber wolf recovery plan, which relies on road density, in the fall of 1989. A number of recent regional studies, using powerful geographical information system computers, looked at a host of other factors, including human densities, forest cover, livestock distribution, and so on. They concluded that the most important predictor of wolf habitat remains road density.[8] The Chequamegon and Nicolet National Forests still have roads. And they have wolves.

Two major environmental groups pursued their appeals of the federal forest plans. I lost track of who won. In this vicious political fight one discipline of resource management (forestry) was pitted against another (wildlife). The battlefield: roads and wolves. The casualties: one DNR biologist.

I doubt the bureau director ever wrote a retraction of my road density study. I do know the result of that pivotal meeting. They *do* shoot the messenger. However, sometimes the messenger survives the shooting.

Life in the Shadow of Civilization

August 16, 1988. Five of us were sitting in a van on the Sheep Ranch Road at 8:44 P.M. A metal pipe "mast" ran out the roof, its base perched on the floor after passing through the center of a compass rose glued to a makeshift table. Atop the van the pole sprouted out in two directions, supporting a massive, seven-element radio antenna. An identical van with a similar number of occupants was parked one hundred yards behind us. A few people stood outside the vans to catch a few last quiet moments.

This night was a treat for me. Two years of intense preoccupation with the state's timber wolf recovery plan had left me feeling like a stranger to the very fieldwork I supervised. For the past several months I had been busy piecing together and writing the final draft of the Wisconsin Timber Wolf Recovery Plan. Now it was finished and high time for a little treat.

I was commenting to the person sitting next to me how remarkable it was to be sitting in the woods at dusk *without* being assaulted by hordes of hungry mosquitoes. Then it began. Somewhere to the east, among the deepening shadows of twilight, a lone wolf gave voice. Low and throaty, its howl climbed an octave, held its note ever so briefly, faltered, and was lost in an explosion of whines, yips, barks, and howls as the rest of the Bootjack Lake timber wolf pack chimed in with exuberance. We all sat silently, waiting for the action to begin.

We were members of Northern Michigan University's EarthWatch crew, led by a graduate student who was a former part-time assistant to the wolf project, Dan Groebner. Back in the fall of 1983 Dan had spent time in a cabin deep within the Bootjack Lake Pack's territory. One day he asked me whether it would be feasible to follow the wolves by *ground tracking* them, using a couple of vans with antennas mounted through their roofs. I told him that was absurd. The roads were too few and far between, and the wolves' signals would be blocked by the dense forest. Granted, he would get an occasional signal when the wolves were close to him, but he would not be able to accumulate enough contacts to get any meaningful data.

"If this were feasible, Mech or somebody else would have been doing it by now," I said as I dismissed the idea.

Dan didn't give up. To my delight, he not only proved me wrong but brought about a real shift in the approach to studying wolves. Because he lacked sufficient funding necessary to develop the ground-tracking system he was researching for his master's thesis, Northern Michigan University contracted with EarthWatch, an environmental action organization, to run a vacation study program for people interested in participating in a scientific project. Dan conducted several summers of wolf research in the Ely, Minnesota, area before returning with his crew of enthusiastic EarthWatch followers to find Wisconsin's Bootjack Lake Pack.

The howling ended as abruptly as it began. The leafy treetops above us trembled as the last daytime breeze fell victim to the night.

Silence. But only for a moment.

From within the van came the muffled voice of the person monitoring Big Al's radio collar, "She's on the move! Everybody in!"

No sooner had the howl died away in the night air than Big Al commenced her nightly jaunt. She was headed west, away from her pups and toward us. Five minutes later she slipped across the road on which we were parked. She was headed for a rendezvous with a radioed yearling wolf—probably her son—named Sparky. While we would *officially* be monitoring her radio this evening, we were also listening to Sparky's frequency. His favorite haunt was Fould's Creek, a drainage area lying west of us.

For his master's thesis Dan studied the daily movements of radioed wolves by obtaining fixes at fifteen-minute intervals during a twenty-four-hour tracking bout. He and his study assistants followed the wolf's movements as closely as possible along forest roads, parking at points that were pre-plotted on maps. The radio person in each van then rotated the great antenna's mast until it was pointing in the direction of the wolf and read the bearing. Crews in each van precisely timed each reading by communicating through walkie-talkies. Between readings the crew leader plotted the locations for each van, entered on a map the bearings taken from each van, and determined the location of the radioed wolf by noting where the two sets of data intersected.

Fifteen minutes after she left the pack's homesite on the headwaters of Buck Creek, Big Al's signal merged with Sparky's. They were together. And, judging from their signals, they were on the move.

For the next forty-five minutes the wolves' signals danced up and down the drainage. Shortly before 10 P.M. Big Al's signal became stationary.

"She's probably nailed a beaver," someone said, giving voice to what nearly everyone in our van agreed was going on. Five minutes later she headed *straight* back to the pups. "Feeding time," we agreed.

Our eight-hour shift ended at four in the morning. Big Al had stayed back at the homesite for an hour, then headed back over to Fould's Creek to resume hunting. At 10:30 the next morning, when the last crew's shift was over, Big Al was still at Fould's Creek. This was fairly typical of the day-to-day routine of the Bootjack Lake Pack family and other wolves living in scattered locales throughout northern Wisconsin.

The Bootjack Lake Pack wolves, like wolves everywhere, are indifferent to the antics of humans. They operate in a world of their own. Their only desire,

I suspect—if indeed wolves have desires—is to be left alone to carry out their ecological mission: to survive as long as possible as individuals and as a species on planet Earth and, to that end, eat as many deer, elk, and moose as they can.

Unfortunately, wolves today live in a world dominated by human beings. Sometimes that works to their advantage—the information we glean from studies such as Dan's can help us help wolves survive. But for wolves, life on the edge of civilization more often is fraught with hazards: fragmented parcels of suitable habitat, contact with coyotes and dogs that serve as vectors for disease transmission, contact with dogs that threatens the wolves' gene pool, humans armed with rifles, bureaucratic political jockeying that changes rules that protect wolves, and the unintentional "conditioning" of wolves to recognize livestock as a source of food. These were but a few of the issues that complicated the initial comeback of wolves in the area south of Lake Superior during the 1980s.

In my years of watching the wolves I grew partial to the yearlings, wolves between the ages of one and two years. Yearlings occupy an especially awkward place within wolf society. Within their second year, as the months slip by, these juveniles bridge the gap between the dependence of puppyhood and the independence of adult life.

Necessity probably drives their initial experiences at independence. When wolf pups reach their first birthday, their parents are focused on the newborns. Whether suddenly or gradually, they stop giving the yearlings handouts. Yearling wolves learn that in order to eat *enough* food, they must rely on their own hunting skills, however unrefined those skills may be.

Most yearlings ultimately leave their natal pack, searching for a niche of their own. Life for these nomadic wolves is tough. They must seek food and shelter in unfamiliar areas. They must ferret out places not occupied by resident territorial wolves. If the yearlings are fortunate enough to find a patch of suitable habitat, they try to attract the attention of would-be mates that may happen along.

In places such as northern Minnesota, where resident wolf packs dominate the landscape, unoccupied space is at a premium. However, in Wisconsin, finding unoccupied wolf range is easy. Finding *other* wolves, and avoiding people, is an entirely different matter.

Between 1979 and 1989 Wisconsin's wolf researchers captured twenty-four yearlings. We were able to learn something of the fates of fifteen of them. Ten left their natal pack and traveled an average of one hundred miles in their quest for space. Nine of the ten dispersed during their yearling year. Only six of the fifteen (40 percent) lived to see their second birthday. They commonly left their parents' territory in autumn, during the fall hunting seasons, which might explain such dismal survival rates.

The importance of dispersal to wolves is somehow lost among the facts and figures scientists construct to describe it. What role do these wandering wolves play in the scheme of things? And of what relevance are these dispersers to the recovery of wolves in places like Wisconsin?

The paws of these wandering loners have carried natural wolf recovery along, step by step, for more than twenty years. Dispersers essentially form a pool of unattached and available breeders. That they generally end up far from their natal pack ensures a degree of genetic variation. In areas like Wisconsin, with its fragmented patches of suitable wolf habitat, dispersers are the vital link to wolf recovery because they are capable of colonizing isolated tracts far from established wolf range.

The Bootjack Lake Pack had a particularly hard time of it over the years. This family group of wolves had made me aware of a disease that was killing entire litters of pups in most of the state's few wolf packs.

The Bootjack Lake Pack roamed an uninhabited bit of forest land that straddles Price and Oneida Counties. On the Price County side was the Park Falls Unit of the Chequamegon National Forest. To the east lay the desolate lands of the Nekoosa-Edwards Paper Mill Company. The pack roamed one hundred square miles of this region. And they were isolated from other wolf packs. The nearest — Lincoln County's Averill Creek Pack — was located thirty-five miles to the south, and the Douglas County groups were eighty-five miles to the west-northwest.

In February 1982 we officially verified the existence of the Bootjack Lake Pack and named the group. The following July we captured two female timber wolves, the alpha, which we named Deborah, and one of her pups, Big Al. Summer howling nights told us that Deborah had had three or four pups that summer, but the following winter the pack consisted of only four animals, including Deborah and Big Al.

The trouble began the next year. In late July, Ron Schultz, Dan Groebner, and I moved in on the pack's rendezvous site near the headwaters of Buck Creek and strung out a series of traps. The following day we caught two wolves. One was a small yearling female — which we named Carol after Ron's wife — and a sibling of Big Al's. Though small, she appeared in good shape. The other wolf was a male pup that Groebner decided to name Ea. This wolf was underweight and full of lice. We processed both wolves and released them.

Dan and I returned to Douglas County to resume our wolf studies there, and Ron remained behind to monitor the Bootjack Lake Pack and Lincoln County's wolves. Thirty days later I received a call from Ron. Ea, the pup, was dead.

"The pilot reported his signal coming from the same exact location two flights in a row," Ron exclaimed.

I knew from Ron's comment that the wolf had been in the same spot for at least ten days because recent budget cuts had forced us to reduce the number of flights to three per month.

"I decided to go in on it. All we found was a pile of bones, matted hair, and the collar."

"Any indication other pups are with the pack?" I asked.

"No, we haven't been able to obtain howls from the group recently because of rainy weather and the fact that Deborah is in a fairly remote area."

This wasn't good news. On a howling survey in the area shortly after we caught these new wolves, Ron had glimpsed three pups and an adult as they walked down a woods trail at twilight.

Despite repeated attempts throughout the rest of the summer and in early fall, we were unable to obtain howls from the Bootjack Lake Pack to confirm the presence or absence of pups. With growing anxiety I realized we would have to wait until the first snows of winter and rely on aerial counts to determine whether any pups had survived.

We didn't spot the Bootjack Lake Pack until after the November deer gun season, nearly December. By then Carol had dispersed. She had traveled slowly south and east, and so far as we know, she never returned to the pack.[1] Now the pack numbered three: the uncollared alpha male, Deborah, and radioed yearling Big Al.

No pups had survived. Had the entire litter died at about the same time as Ea? The loss of some pups in a litter is normal, but at the time we considered the loss of an entire litter unusual. Perhaps the blood samples from Carol and Ea would shed some light on this mystery.

That year (1983) we had begun testing our wolf blood samples for common canine diseases such as infectious canine hepatitis, canine distemper virus, and canine parvovirus. Parvo was of some concern because it had only recently mutated into the dog family and was wreaking havoc among domesticated dog populations. Dog pups were highly susceptible, and we had no reason to believe that wolf pups would be any less so.

The lab results confirmed my suspicions: Ea's parvo titer was extremely high. One veterinary diagnostician who looked at the values believed the animal was sick when we caught him. And, of course, three weeks later his body had been reduced to a pile of bones. I believed his littermates met the same fate.

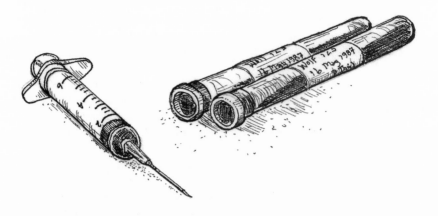

Was the Bootjack Lake Pack's experience in 1983 an isolated case? Or was the entire Wisconsin wolf population, which had been buoyed each year by surviving pups, suddenly being obliterated by a new disease? How was the disease being spread? How did it do its dirty work once an animal became infected? Did *any* animals survive once symptoms began? Would animals build up immunities to parvo?

The questions piled up. No money was available, and few other wolf biologists working elsewhere were seeing any problems among wolves in their study areas, although they had found antibody responses to the disease in some blood samples from their wolves.

My first task was to document whether any of the other Wisconsin wolf packs had lost entire litters. Only two other Wisconsin packs had produced litters in 1983—the Moose Lake Pack and the Averill Creek Pack. We were unable to locate more than two wolves in the Averill Creek Pack during the following winter (1983–84), although it had boasted as many as twelve members in 1979–80. The lack of pups could be explained by the undetected loss of an alpha before the previous year's breeding season or any of a dozen other causes.[2] By winter's end I realized I would have to wade through another summer's pup-rearing season and closely monitor the activities of the other Wisconsin wolf packs.

As fate would have it, the federal government slashed funds in the middle of the spring trapping season. I was forced to cut back on flights and to temporarily lay off my seasonal help. Ron Schultz, working on his own, continued to monitor the activities of the Bootjack Lake Pack. From the scant flight data we surmised that the alpha female, Deborah, had denned. In late May she moved away from the den and settled in at the Buck Creek homesite, a pattern typical of previous years. But in late June she suddenly abandoned the homesite and began moving throughout her territory without so much as a visit to the Buck Creek headwaters. I knew her pups had succumbed, but scientific protocol required that I await the winter months and confirm that no pups were present—that is, if the radios on our collared wolves continued to transmit.

Big Al, now two, had not dispersed like her sister Carol and most yearling wolves. I wondered why but was too preoccupied with the case of the missing pups to pay much attention to her. On October 31, 1984, we recorded Big Al's radio signal for the last time, near the western edge of her parent's territory. She had been on the air for a record 834 days.

Deborah's radio, now our sole contact with the Bootjack Lake Pack, continued to transmit. We were flying only twice monthly because of the budget cuts, and I was very concerned that each flight would mark the last contact with Deborah. Deer season came and went. Initial winter ground-tracking surveys indicated that, as during the previous winter, no pups were present in the Averill Creek Pack. The Moose Lake Pack once again had pups.

On a cold wintry evening in early January Ron Schultz called to report that the pilots thought something was wrong with Deborah. She hadn't moved from a spot they had recorded for her at the end of deer gun season a month earlier.

The next day we recovered her body. She had been shot. I felt terrible because, as far as I was concerned, her death meant the demise of the Bootjack Lake Pack. But even in death we were able to extract a crucial bit of information from Deborah. On the inner surface of her uterus the pathologist found three crisp black placental scars, signifying that she had borne a litter of three pups in 1984. She *had* denned and subsequently lost her pups.

The winter census confirmed that the decline observed in Wisconsin's wolf population for the past few years had continued. A pair of wolves roamed the Averill Creek area, and lone wolves roamed portions of remote forested lands once ranged by the Stateline Flowage and Bear Lake Packs. Pack integrity had disintegrated. The only pack with more than two members during the winter of 1984–85 was Douglas County's Moose Lake Pack. This single pack accounted for half of the fifteen wolves counted in Wisconsin that winter.

Because we were aware that parvovirus was the probable culprit, we began several studies with support from the U.S. Fish and Wildlife Service in an effort to determine whether biologists could intervene on behalf of the wolves. Over the next several years we gradually learned that nothing short of a Herculean effort could prevent wolves from contracting the disease. We knew the initial wave had run through the continental wolf population between 1980 and 1984. While we found no *wild* wolves during this period that had actually *died* from parvo, several Wisconsin wolves had died in the months after their bouts with the disease. All had been weakened by starvation and heavy parasite loads, and some were suffering from pneumonia when they died. It seemed that parvo had so weakened them that other pathogens were able to move in and kill them.

Lab analyses of blood samples told us that not all wolves that were exposed to the disease died. Lab studies and anecdotal observations suggested that pups were most susceptible. It stood to reason: their immune system, like other systems within their bodies, was not fully mature and capable of sustaining the onslaught of this nasty pathogen. Yearlings and adults stood a better chance, depending on their condition at the time of infection and afterward. Mortality was also affected by the virulence of the strain of parvovirus.

How did the virus spread from wolf to wolf? This particular virus attacks the intestines and is spread through feces, a perfect medium for transmission between canids because wolves, coyotes, and dogs all use feces—like urinations—as scent posts. Transmission is completed via a sniff that inoculates the nasal passages. To our dismay we learned that the virus was viciously tenacious, remaining viable in feces six months or longer—even after the dropping had long since disintegrated into dust.

Most wolf biologists suddenly realized that wolf territories were strewn with ticking time bombs. Undoubtedly, coyotes and hunting dogs in Wisconsin contributed a far greater share of infected feces within wolf territories than the wolves, and they were spreading the virus in uninhabited wolf habitat as well.

Some biologists predicted that as more exposed wolves survived, the disease would be less deadly to pups and the wolf population would increase. They reasoned that the virus had hit a naive population, and future episodes would create only minor ripples.

I disagreed. Wisconsin had all the ingredients for repeated waves. Wisconsin's dog population (and its coyote population) would act as a gigantic reservoir for the disease. Wisconsin's precariously small wolf populations stood out as virtual islands in a sea teeming with coyotes and dogs. The high turnover rate (time between generations) of Wisconsin's wolves would cause rapid declines in the number of supposedly immune wolves, and these wolves would be replaced by naive ones.[3] I felt certain that parvovirus would continue to infect our canid population and would prove to be a more or less constant presence among our state's wolves. But I also knew we could do nothing to stop it.

In the mid-1980s a vaccine was developed to attack the spread of the disease among dogs. Though it was not approved for use in wolves, we began vaccinating the wolves we captured. Studies on dogs, however, showed that the vaccine's effectiveness lasted for only one year. At best we were vaccinating a half-dozen wolves annually, mostly yearlings. Many were subsequently shown (through blood samples analyzed weeks after their capture and release) to have antibody responses to the disease. This forced us to ask ourselves what we were accomplishing by vaccinating our captured wolves. The

discomforting answer was nothing, and we eventually abandoned the vacci-
nation protocol.

Meanwhile, the state's wolf population began a slow rebound. Wisconsin
had had a high of 27 wolves in the winter of 1981–82 and a low of 15 in 1984–
85. In the winter of 1985–86 we counted 16, and in 1986–87 the population
crept up to 18 animals. As predicted, most wolves captured during this period
had been previously exposed to parvo and had managed to survive. By 1989–
90 the population numbered 34 wolves. Wisconsin's wolves had apparently
weathered the first parvovirus storm.

After Deborah died, I was sure the Bootjack Lake Pack was finished. I was
elated to learn that Ron Schultz had picked up tracks of two wolves within
the pack's territory in late January 1985. One was a female in estrus. Could it
be Big Al?

Ron and I were unable to capture either of the wolves the following summer, and we had a hunch there were no pups, which we verified the following
winter—the winter of 1985–86. It had now been four years since members
of this pack had succeeded in raising pups. We also learned that winter that
only one wolf—which we were unable to identify—remained in the Bootjack
Lake Pack's territory.

During the winter of 1986–87, Ron cut tracks of a pair of wolves in the
Bootjack Lake country, and we were excited to think that *just maybe* the pack
would produce a litter in 1987. We were elated on August 6 when Ron walked
up to a trap he had set on a trail near where Big Al had spent her puppyhood
and spied a feisty timber wolf pup that had managed to get caught. Two days
later Ron captured its mother. It was Big Al.[4]

The Bootjack Lake Pack also figured prominently in deciphering the effects of
the *next* malady to course through the wolf population. Mange. This is particularly nasty stuff. It is caused by a tiny mite that reaches explosive population
levels. The mites burrow just beneath the skin, causing a source of unending
irritation to infected animals. Scratching incessantly and in futility, wolves,
dogs, coyotes, foxes, and other species of wildlife create lesions in their own
skin that eventually become infected. The scratching causes hair loss, and the
oozing of infected areas leads to the matting of remaining hair, which means
a loss in the insulating capacity of the fur. In winter this condition may lead
to death from hypothermia.

Big Al probably died from mange. So did two or three other wolves that Ron Schultz managed to collar within the Bootjack Lake Pack in 1989 and 1990. One wolf, named Bo, was mangy when captured in July 1991. Bo was observed alone throughout the winter of 1991–92 by pilots who marveled at the spectacle of an almost denuded wolf managing to survive the cold.

In February 1992 Bo managed to woo a female, and that spring the Bootjack Lake Pack once again had pups.

After nearly continuous monitoring of a single pack of timber wolves in Wisconsin for fifteen years, we have a fairly interesting reproductive history, one that was interrupted at least twice by disease. The pack either was barren or had no pups that survived until winter in 1983, 1984, 1985, 1986, 1991, 1993, and 1994. Statistically, this represents a loss of twenty-one wolves that would have at least seen their first birthday; some would perhaps have dispersed and colonized other enclaves of wolf habitat. Thus the pace of wolf recovery was slowed that much more.

Our Bootjack Lake Pack, like the other timber wolf packs in Wisconsin, lives in the shadow of civilization. Canine parvovirus probably originated among domesticated dogs, then spread among the wild canids. Although an effective vaccine was developed nearly twenty years ago, the disease is still found in dogs. Our wolves will simply have to cope if they are to have a future within the shadow.

After administrators in Madison finally approved the Wisconsin Timber Wolf Recovery Plan in the spring of 1989, I could focus on fieldwork again. Bob Welch and I had been working out of the Gordon Ranger Station in Douglas County, trying to trap and collar a few wolves in the Stateline area. We'd had no luck.

We returned from the field one afternoon to find a note tacked on our door. A DNR staff member had called from the Spooner District headquarters to relay information that an employee at the Agricultural Extension Service's farm on the outskirts of town had shot a "big coyote." The note said it weighed sixty-five pounds.

I called the fellow, who said he had become suspicious after the extension service employee had told him over a cup of coffee how heavy the "coyote" had been. A pack of wild dogs or coyotes had been plaguing the ag farm lately, killing their sheep. In a final effort to end the depredations, employees shot the adult female and two pups. Thanks to the extension service employee who called us, the DNR had picked up the bodies, which were now stored in the agency's walk-in freezer. Would I be interested in looking at them?

Bob and I were there before closing time. The coyote looked like a wolf. One pup, which weighed roughly fifteen pounds, looked like a border collie mix. The other didn't look at all like its sibling but was about the same size. If the stories of the farm employees were to be believed, the pack consisted of a large rangy dog—presumably, the adult male—the wolfish-looking adult female, and five young that farm employees had seen numerous times.

Was it even *possible* that we were looking at the offspring of a dog and a wild wolf? We immediately went to the farm and interviewed the employees who had seen the critters and who were involved in the shootings. After walking the grounds of the various sheep pastures, Bob and I were convinced of their stories.

Back at the freezer, I pulled out the adult female for a closer inspection. The only deviation from classic wolf that I saw was in the muzzle: the lips were mottled pink and black, and a distinct sharp line separated the dark upper region of the head from the lighter cheek and chin area. Among wolves, the contrast is more gradual change and is not so starkly delineated. I suspected this animal was a wolf-dog hybrid.

Suddenly, we had cause to worry about another problem that could affect Wisconsin's small wolf population: genetic pollution. Unique to members of the genus *Canis* is the ability to mate and produce fertile offspring. Wolf-dog hybrids are the result of captive breedings. Behavioral barriers in the wild generally deter such unions, and the resulting crossings are exceedingly rare.

In the world of pets, however, wolf-dogs represent the ultimate. They are marketed as the supposedly perfect companion for more rustic types. Wolf-dog hybrids also are hot among people seeking the "guard-dog qualities" of several dog breeds and the intense loyalty displayed by wolves. They have become something of a cultish preoccupation, not to mention a lucrative business venture, for numerous Americans. It is not illegal. It is not regulated. And few politicians want to tackle such an issue in this age of individual rights.

How did this Spooner wolf-dog-whatever get out there? We will never know. Perhaps it was the product of a union—in the wild—of a wolf in sexual overdrive and an equally willing and receptive dog. Doubtful but possible, nonetheless. Most likely it resulted from a pet that was either deliberately abandoned or got loose. Either way, the genetic threat to our small wolf population is real.[5]

In the fall of 1979 two wolves—one in Douglas County and the other in Lincoln County—were shot and killed during the nine-day deer gun season. Few among the hunting public then knew that wolves were living within the state. Because Wisconsin's coyote season was open during the deer gun season, and because wolves are easily confused with coyotes, we needed changes in hunting regulations to prevent another wolf killing because of mistaken identity.

In 1980, at my urging and with the backing of the Office of Endangered Species, the Natural Resources Board ended coyote hunting within the deer management units in both counties where wolves were known to be living. This measure would certainly aid the state's *known* resident packs, but it did nothing to help any dispersing wolves that were traversing Wisconsin's northern forests outside these units. Needless to say, I was not content with the limited ban on coyote hunting. Still, the department had taken flak from some elements of the deer-hunting community and had opted to take a stand in support of wolf recovery.

It didn't last long. In early 1983 the Natural Resources Board acquiesced to political pressure from the Wisconsin Conservation Congress, a body appointed by the state legislature to advise the Natural Resources Board, composed primarily of hunters and anglers. In reversing its position, the board reasoned that banning coyote hunting infringed on the "rights" of deer hunters to harvest coyotes as trophies. The DNR, for its part, rationalized that the ban on coyote hunting was no longer necessary because wolves had spread to areas outside of the zones that were closed to coyote shooting. Additionally, the ban did nothing to protect wolves that the endangered species act was not already doing.

Environmental groups loudly criticized the department. The DNR justified its stance by claiming first that a new pro-wolf public attitude meant the ban on coyote hunting no longer was necessary and, second, that continuing to ban coyote hunting would result in a "backlash of animosity towards wolves."

In conclusion, the department's secretary noted, "The coyote hunting closure could be reinstituted if we detect that it is again needed."[6]

In November 1984 Deborah was shot during the deer season. In May 1985 I petitioned the director of the Bureau of Endangered Resources to begin the process of reinstating the coyote closure, citing the recent loss of this breeding female as evidence that rescinding the ban on coyote hunting had been an error. Incredibly, he responded by asking, "What evidence is there that the last one or two deer seasons have resulted in wolves being shot?" Clearly, the DNR was reluctant to butt heads with the Wisconsin Conservation Congress.

While the director and I traded memos, the hunters were busy. On the opening day of the 1986 deer season, a hunter shot another timber wolf. This time the hunter honestly mistook a timber wolf pup for a coyote. The incident occurred in the Averill Creek Pack's territory in Lincoln County.

I received the call on a Sunday evening. Would I be willing to come look at the body and verify it as a wolf? Bill Meier, the wildlife manager, and the warden wanted confirmation.

I made the three-hour drive to Merrill on Monday morning. I was told the carcass would be leaning up against a garage stall in one of the outbuildings behind the ranger station. I caught sight of the animal as I rounded the corner of the ranger station. From seventy-five yards off I could tell it was a wolf. Sad, I thought, this could have been avoided. As I loaded the body into the back of my car, I vowed that this animal's death would not go unnoticed.

That winter the DNR did propose a ban on coyote hunting in the northern third of the state. Predictably, the Wisconsin Conservation Congress was indignant. It voted resoundingly against the proposal, a move that won it the wrath of many state citizens. Among them was the *Milwaukee Journal*'s outdoors columnist, Jay Reed:

> *An open letter to the Executive Council of the Wisconsin Conservation Congress:*
> The reason I am writing you today is because, for the first time in more than 20 years of covering your activities, I am concerned, personally, about an action you have taken.
>
> The other night in Marshfield, you guys stood up and blocked a proposal aimed at providing at least limited protection for the few timber wolves that remain in Wisconsin. . . .
>
> By doing that, you put yourselves squarely on the side of those who will not be satisfied until every last wild wolf in the state is dead. . . .
>
> You will discover, I am certain, that those who have a sincere concern for wolves, and any other wild thing that is endangered, outnumber the total of all recreational hunters in the state. . . .
>
> Maybe you guys think you are a bunch of bull-headed heroes now that you've stood up to save the deer-season coyote shoot. No way. What you've done, instead, is stain the reputation of every person who buys a hunting license in this state. . . .
>
> The DNR will have to learn that it can't speak out of both sides of its mouth. It can't say, on the one hand, that wolves can, must and will be protected and then withdraw proposals aimed at doing just that when the going gets sticky. . . .
>
> Is nine days of coyote shooting during the deer season really worth it?[7]

The ban on coyote hunting during deer season took effect throughout the northern third of the state during the following deer season and has remained in effect since. The closure actually benefited hunters because it kept honest hunters from making mistakes in identification. Its greatest advantage was that it provided protection to dispersers taking their "hike of life," searching for those scattered patches of suitable habitat. Since the closure was reinstituted, Wisconsin's wolf population has experienced unprecedented growth. While the ban on coyote hunting is not the sole reason for the increases in Wisconsin's wolf population, it has contributed to making their comeback possible.

Ron Schultz and I stood at the end of Montrose Road in Lincoln County, swatting a few mosquitoes while waiting for darkness. Bill Meier, the wildlife manager, had had a complaint of a livestock depredation nearby one July evening in 1989. There was nothing for Ron to see when he inspected the site because hungry critters make fast work of carcasses in the summer. A neighboring farmer told Ron that he'd seen some wolves fairly regularly in his pasture in the weeks before the cattle was killed. We suspected the newly formed Ranger Island Pack had moved its pups here to the eastern border of its territory, where it was sure to get into trouble.

A half hour later, we got what we came for. We howled and got a response from a pack of wolves with pups. Now we really had a problem. The farmer wanted the wolves trapped and killed. Federal regulations would only allow us to move depredating wolves. How were we going to move a whole pack?

The farmer was paid for the loss of the cattle—one or two, as I recall. In the meantime we continued to keep tabs on the pack; luckily, the alpha female had been radio-collared a year earlier. Although the pack's rendezvous site was located in a dense mixed hardwood stand immediately north of a beef veal farm (and across the road from where the depredations occurred), no further incidents developed.

I was busy with recovery-planning work and regular office duties, having left the depredation problem in the capable hands of Ron Schultz. Ron called me on a hot, humid evening about two weeks later. He was chuckling as he related the story of his visit to the veal farmer.

"This fellow, Higgins, is definitely aware of the wolves. Get a load of this. I walked in on the rendezvous site from Montrose Road to inspect it. I found a carcass disposal dump in the midst of a balsam fir forest. The dump had the remains of quite a few calves and other livestock. The tractor trail led south through the woods to the pasture just north of this fellow's spread.

"I visited him with the intentions of letting him know that wolves were on his property, and he should beware for his livestock," Ron related as a giggle formed in the back of his throat. "He says, of course he knows they're there. He dumps the carcasses out there 'cuz he likes looking at bears, bobcats, and other creatures. He says in the early morning hours when he gets up, he frequently sees two, three, and sometimes up to five wolves laying in the pasture out in front of the house . . . including the radioed one. Thinks it's the neatest thing."

I gritted my teeth as Ron finished his story. Now we really had a problem. It's one thing to have to deal with an irate farmer who has just found the chewed-up remains of one of his calves or a bunch of mutilated sheep in the back forty. We know what to expect when we knock on the farmhouse door. We can help the farmer out by paying for the losses and perhaps moving the perpetrating wolf or wolves.

In areas where farms intermingle with forested lands, farmers are generally less well-to-do than their counterparts in more southerly latitudes. Poorer soils and shorter growing seasons are a constant struggle. Bush farms, as they are known, are also miles apart.

Livestock disposal companies cannot survive in these regions; farmers therefore must find a way to dispose of dead farm stock. One popular and easy method is to drag the dead animal off to the woods where a host of hungry predators will take advantage of the banquet. Some—wolves and bears— are intelligent and strong enough to figure out that the living critters on the other side of the fence are just as tasty. This is referred to as conditioning.

And that's just what Higgins was inadvertently doing by intentionally feeding the remains of livestock to the wolves. Their newfound taste for beef had already led them to help themselves to the neighbor's steak on the hoof.

Most exasperating is that the farmer who conditions the wolves may never suffer losses. The problem may be manifested miles away, sometimes hundreds of miles away. And, of course, these wolves poison the views and attitudes of humans far removed from the source of the problem.

A particular problem, as studies by Steve Fritts and others in Minnesota have verified, is that pups raised on farms and acquainted with livestock often kill stock while traversing farm country as they take their hikes of life. Because dispersers that kill livestock are here today, gone tomorrow, government officials are nearly powerless to stop them. And, of course, such behavior does not win the wolf any points from farming communities that experience such depredations.

Thus it was definitely in the best interest of the wolves to shut down the Higgins dump. But government agents cannot tell private landowners what to do on their properties. Ron Schultz eventually got Higgins to agree to stop dumping the carcasses and arranged for a local mink farmer to pick up Higgins's dead stock. But all of that did not occur soon enough to prevent further problems.

In early August 1989 Ron captured and collared a forty-four-pound male pup that he named Charley. In January 1990 Charley disappeared from the Ranger Island Pack. In a memo dated October 8 a DNR staff member reported what he had learned about Charley:

He was found dead . . . [near] Hinckley, Minnesota and was thought to have been killed on about June 17, 1990. The location was about 150 miles NW of the Ranger Island Pack. Charley was apparently shot and perhaps also trapped. There were some complaints about livestock depredation in the area, but Charley may have been feeding on livestock already dead. Charley's original capture was near a veal farm where wolves fed on disposed carcasses. . . . Charley's conditioning to feeding on livestock carcasses seemed to cause his final demise.[8]

The factors that led to Charley's death were clear enough. But sometimes, even when we were able to recover the carcass, determining why a wolf had died was a long process. When Larry Prenn and I recaptured 1191 in November 1982 and named her Babushka, the alpha female of Douglas County's Stateline Flowage Pack had aged considerably since I'd last seen her two years earlier.

Her left front leg, which, though healed over, had atrophied and its joints appeared frozen. Despite this, the old gal was still padding the home territory. And for that I was glad.

On a flight in mid-December I spotted her coursing through a stand of aspen, following a deer trail. She stopped momentarily in a small opening deep within her territory, glanced behind her, tail stiffened in a broad arc, and continued on. It was the last time I saw her alive.

She died not a mile from the spot where, years earlier, Bob Welch and I heard our friend Yukon shouting that his group had found wolf sign. Her body lay buried beneath a foot of snow. Not one hundred yards away was a hunter's tree stand.

We discovered a small, blood-stained hole in her rib cage on the side of her body that faced the ground. I was sure she had been shot and left there to rot.

I was wrong. The necropsy showed that the hole was caused by a voracious shrew that had bumped blindly into a prize of great worth while tunneling beneath the snow. Babushka had actually died of a heart attack, the result of a massive bacterial infection that probably was also the cause of the oozing lesions observed on her leg back in 1980 when we had first captured her. But what had caused the injury?

We learned the answer to that question a year later, thanks to the specimen collections housed at the University of Wisconsin Zoological Museum in Madison. The clues to her injury actually came from the hard palate of her skull and the skull of a Wisconsin timber wolf that had been killed in 1945.

Frank Iwen, the museum's curator, and I had been doing some detective work, trying to learn the origin of a timber wolf skull at the museum. The only information the museum had was a notation: "Forest County—November 1945." I had suspected that Bernie Bradle, the Wisconsin Conservation Department biologist, had given the skull to the museum. In reviewing Bernie's notes from that period, I noticed he had visited a noted timber wolf trapper in Forest County in November 1945. Evidently, he had obtained the skull (and hide) of a wolf that this fellow had trapped, and the specimen eventually made its way to the museum.

The Forest County wolf had been trapped. Back in those days, bounty trappers did not much care about treatment of trapped animals, which society had deemed vermin. Sometimes they did not check their traps with any regularity. Occasionally, wolves spent days in traps—so long they were nearly able to extricate themselves. In trying to get free, they would bite at the steel traps and break their gigantic fourth upper premolars, the largest teeth in their mouths.

One of the fourth premolars of the old Forest County specimen had been sheared off beneath the gum line just before the wolf had died. The gaping hole in its skull stood in mute testimony to how it had died.

When I inspected Babushka's skull, I found the same tooth was missing. But unlike the Forest County wolf, she had survived, and the bone had completely healed over the hole.

Babushka had evidently been caught in a coyote trapper's set. In her successful attempt to extricate herself, she also had fractured the long bones in her left front leg. A bacterial infection had set in, interrupting the healing process and grossly twisting and contorting her left front leg into a misshapen and dysfunctional appendage.

I was impressed with how long Babushka had lived. Biologists try to gain information on age and sex ratios of study populations in an attempt to understand reproductive vigor, turnover rates (generation time), and longevity. Biologists usually get their best picture of the ages of individuals in a population by sampling animals that have recently died.

A recurring problem for wolf researchers is that no one has been able to develop a reliable aging technique for wolves. I began working on a way to assess the *relative* age of wolves by looking at the amount of wear on the surface of their fourth upper premolars. I assumed that I would find wear in direct proportion to the age of the wolf. To get some idea of whether I was on the right track, I visited several museums to inspect skulls of wolves whose ages were known. The expected progression of wear was evident.

I developed five "wear classes." Wear class 1 shows no wear, and wear class 5 shows almost total loss of the tooth (through natural wear—not from fights with traps). I was not able to assign absolute ages because this technique is a relative estimator, but given that the lifespan of wild wolves is about twelve years, I came up with a rough conversion for the tooth-wear classification.

How old were some of Wisconsin's wolves when they died? Babushka was in wear class 4. So was the alpha male of the Moose Lake Pack.

I was working with extremely small numbers of animals, and the total population in the state was similarly small. The wear-class technique revealed that

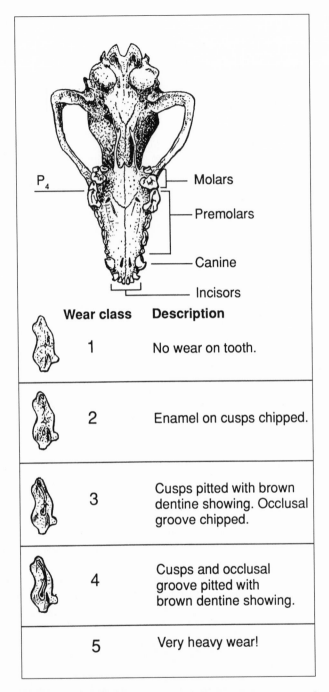

Wear class	Description
1	No wear on tooth.
2	Enamel on cusps chipped.
3	Cusps pitted with brown dentine showing. Occlusal groove chipped.
4	Cusps and occlusal groove pitted with brown dentine showing.
5	Very heavy wear!

Relative age of wolves by wear on teeth (Wisconsin Department of Natural Resources)

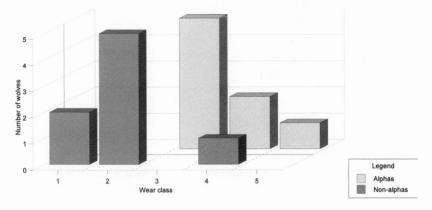

Wear class versus social standing

most alpha wolves were fairly young when they died, fueling a high turnover among breeders.

Most wolves don't become alphas until they are two or three years old (roughly wear classes 2 and 3). An alpha female named Cassie in the Ranger Island Pack produced her first litter when she was two. The Moose Lake Pack's Dolly and the Bootjack Lake Pack's Big Al produced their first surviving litters when they were four.

The high turnover rate meant that most alpha wolves managed to reproduce only one to three times before they died. Dolly had two litters, and the second probably died because she was killed early in the whelping season. Big Al produced four litters before she died at about eight.

The loss of alpha wolves frequently interrupted the annual rhythm of a pack's pup production because of the paucity of available replacements. The Moose Lake Pack did not replace its alpha male for two years. New alphas did not materialize in the Bootjack Lake Pack for three years after Deborah was killed, and another pack's alpha male roamed his territory for two years before he found a new female. No breeding took place in any of these packs during these intervals.

The low numbers of pups each winter, and the small overall size of the state's population throughout the 1980s, were partly the result of the high turnover among breeders.

Despite what seemed to be tremendous obstacles, wolves rapidly repopulated Wisconsin over the next ten years.

Farewell

On a warm day in the fall of 1988 I drove to Madison, summoned once again by the director of the Bureau of Endangered Resources. He had something important to discuss with me. The meeting was brief. He wished to inform me that with the imminent approval of the Wisconsin Timber Wolf Recovery Plan, the agency no longer needed the services of a wolf biologist. I could expect to be out of a job within a year.

I was not surprised. Not coincidentally, my four-year contract would end within a year, and my dismissal at that time would not generate controversy. As an employee in an entrenched bureaucracy, I had to pay for standing strongly behind my convictions and speaking out on delicate issues. The name *Thiel* had been synonymous with the roiling political controversy about road densities and the national forest management plans. This had angered important people within the U.S. Forest Service, certain state senators, and the DNR's upper echelons.

I was astonished, though, that he actually believed the state could implement the wolf recovery plan without someone to coordinate the work. But he was serious, and I was grateful that he had had the decency to warn me of what was coming so that I could line up another job.

The end of the wolf project was finally in sight. I always knew that the job would end. But I was heartsick that it was happening now, just as the real work of implementing the recovery plan was beginning.

The two-hour drive home that evening was a long and tortured one. I experienced alternating waves of intense anger and bouts of separation anxiety. Ironic, isn't it? I thought with a snicker—these feelings are similar to what I felt when I left home one cold, cold morning nearly ten years earlier to begin the wolf project.

His decision forced me to examine critically my employment situation. I had accepted the conditions of employment in order to do the work that I loved. In the ten years I served as the state's wolf biologist, the position was always considered a temporary assignment. As a temporary employee, I accrued no seniority. Others, hired in permanent positions at the same time as I, had been promoted, accrued vacation time and pension benefits, and reaped other benefits. My yearly vacation time was the same as the day I started, and I was not eligible to transfer into vacant permanent positions within the agency. These factors were less important than the mission I had set out to accomplish.

But I was now entering middle age and had yet to hold a permanent position in my adult working life. I had a family and was eager to settle in a secure setting, whether with this agency or some other. My priorities were changing.

When I thought about it, I began to realize that I had accomplished part of what I had set out to do. The blueprints for wolf recovery in Wisconsin were well established. Public sentiment was beginning to soften. Many politicians who had opposed wolf recovery were beginning to see that helping wolves was not detrimental to their more vocal constituents. The barriers to wolf recovery were crumbling. Most important, the wolf population was growing.

One thing I had learned over the years was that education was the key to shaping attitudes and behaviors of people in regard to controversial animals like wolves. I had become very involved in educational activities and found that I liked teaching. When a DNR job for a wildlife educator opened up, I realized it also met my family's needs. I applied, was invited to interview, and was offered the job. The best part: I wouldn't have to uproot the family because it was within driving distance of our hometown. I would begin my new duties in late November 1989.

As the time for me to assume my new duties grew near, I arranged to make one last flight in each of the districts. It would be my private way of saying farewell to the animals I had come to know and care for as one of the keepers of the wolves.

I wouldn't be satisfied merely to fly a last flight. I really needed to see the wolves. Absurd as it seemed, by seeing them I felt I could somehow convey my appreciation for all the rewarding experiences I'd had watching their day-to-day lives. Seeing them one last time would affirm that the species had managed to survive all the knaves who, through ignorance, indifference, callousness, or selfishness, had deliberately or unwittingly fostered the species' demise.

Of course, I knew all this was rationalization. What I was really doing was preparing myself for my departure from the wolf project.

On a Friday in early November I pulled up to the hangar at Shell Lake. I would fly this last flight in the Northwest District with my friend and able

pilot Fred Kruger. The day was clear and cool. Fred maneuvered the plane into the air and pointed its nose toward the northwest and the homes of the Douglas County wolf packs.

The trees had recently shed their leaves. The forest floor lay fully exposed. Still, I knew the chances that we would see any of the study wolves were real slim. Wolves are especially difficult to make out against new-fallen leaves.

Fred and I spied Maryanne and Tube at the northern extreme of their territory. They were curled up, side by side, beneath a huge white spruce, just as we usually saw them each winter. I had known Tube since the death of his father, the old Moose Lake alpha male. Tube was now four. I would never see him or Maryanne again.

Next, we heard Darth Vader's signal. He was outside his territory, trespassing within the southern edge of the area occupied by Tube and Maryanne. From the sounds of his radio signal I knew he was on the move. Miraculously, he too appeared beneath us, gray form gliding effortlessly along a deer trail, not a half-mile from where Greg Sevener and I had encountered the deer hunter while packing that buck's head out nine years earlier.

Darth Vader was probably the last wolf I would ever catch. He sauntered along, stopping briefly to sniff a stump, oblivious to our presence. When we finally left the area, I glanced back to catch a glimpse of this elderly wolf as he drifted beneath the boughs of a stand of firs.

The following Tuesday afternoon I took my last flight with the North-Central District's pilot in search of radioed members of the Averill Creek, Ranger Island, and Bootjack Lake Packs. Luck rode with me on that day too.

Beneath us in a small opening lay Storm, a yearling female collared in Lincoln County's Averill Creek Pack territory. I was elated. On up to the northeast we homed in on the signal of Charley, the pup from the Ranger Island Pack collared in August 1989 by Ron Schultz. We couldn't believe our eyes. There beneath us lay five timber wolves in the middle of a huge sphagnum bog. Fading rays of flaming scarlet sunlight illuminated their luxuriously furred, tawny sides. This was our first count of this pack for the winter season.

Last, we homed in on the Bootjack Lake Pack. I picked up Smokey's signal, but we were unable to see him. I was acutely disappointed because I felt especially close to this pack.

One other Bootjack Lake Pack wolf was radioed—Caesar, the pack's alpha male. He didn't let me down. As we approached his signal, I spied some blood beneath us in the skiff of snow that dusted the ground. Nearby I caught some movement—three wolves tugging at a downed deer. We circled for a few minutes, captivated by the sight of the pack as it dined in the fading light of the forest. I felt exceptionally privileged to see the radioed wolves this one last time.

The next morning Ron Schultz and I visited the kill site, located along Fould's Creek. Before heading into the brush for what I believed would be my last inspection of a wolf-killed deer, Ron and I had scanned the frequencies of the radioed wolves. Sometime after dark Smokey had joined Caesar. Their signals emanated from the forest near where I had marked the deer kill on my map.

It took us a while to make it to the kill site, using the wolves' radio signals as homing beacons. Curiously, no ravens were around to guide us. We spooked the wolves before we could zero in on the spot. Spreading out, we eventually stumbled onto the site. Nothing remained of the deer except a handful of fragmented bones and a hock, the size of which told us the deer had been a fawn. A careful search of both banks yielded no additional body parts.

With us was my eldest daughter, Allison, then seven. She had been out with me on wolf patrol before, but this experience was new to her. When she returned to her second-grade class the next day, she told her teacher she wanted to read to the class a report she had written the previous night.

> We took a receiver and t[w]o of the wolfs were there. And there [*sic*] names were Smokey and Caesar. When my Dad was flying the wolfs thay [*sic*] killed a deer. And the two wolfs were at the deer kill. We walked up on them but thay were not there when we got there. I had to walk by myself. Then we got to the deer kill. And there was only a few bones. And there was lots of blood. I mean there was blood all over the place. We went back to the car [and] started on the three hours of driving [home].

The act of predation leaves a powerful impression. My daughter was obviously impressed. As we tramped back to the car, I thought how ironic it was that grown men would make such a fuss over a pile of deer bones, bones that have littered the humus of our earth for hundreds of thousands of years. Suddenly, it was unacceptable for deer to die to feed wolves. Humans retaliated by spending one hundred or more years littering the soil with the bones of wolves and other predators they viewed as serious competitors for deer. And then, perhaps realizing the errors of their ways, humans did an about-face and spent their resources to learn how to correct the wrongs they had committed. That had been my job.

I was privileged to have witnessed the wolves' secret lives. We had collared fifty-three wolves, and six had been kind enough to pay our traps two visits. About a third of the wolves died while wearing active radios.

We had obtained literally thousands of locations from the collars these wolves wore, and the information they provided gave biologists insights into the world of Wisconsin's wolves that we could not have gained in any other way. We amassed a great deal of information that would help determine how to safeguard the elements that sustain the wolves and their habitats and provide guidance in how to change people's attitudes toward wolves. On that cool morning back in November 1989, when Ron, Allison, and I returned to our car along the fire lane near Fould's Creek, I could not have imagined how successful the program would be.

Wolves in the Twenty-first Century

"Woof!"

The noise shattered the silence of the darkened marshland. It was abrupt, loud, and serious in intonation. Two minutes after I howled a second time, the wolf repeated its single woof. Much closer, I thought. Peering wide-eyed through the blackened night sky, I could barely discern the forms of our daughters, Allison, now seventeen, and Cassie, thirteen. They were sitting on the pavement of Highway 173, which was closed to traffic because of construction. As I looked away from them and toward Deb, I could plainly see the single mercury vapor light that lay low on the horizon, just about where the road disappeared. That light betrayed the tiny hamlet of Mather three miles to the southwest. The light seemed to wink. Allison saw it, and she immediately leaned over and whispered something to her sister, who turned and peered in the direction of the light. I knew Allison was aware that something had passed between us and the light.

Moments later we heard the distinctive sound of nails on asphalt. Click-click, click-click. The sound advanced rhythmically in our direction. Whines softly accompanied the staccato. The nails continued their approach uninterrupted. Allison and Cassie stood up. Deb suddenly leaned forward, began slowly walking toward the oncoming sound, stopped, then started backing up. I moved forward, passing her. The sound of the nails was getting closer. Gazing through the murky darkness, I discerned four long, slender legs pumping pistonlike as they moved forward, not twenty yards away.

Retreating slowly to the car, I reached in, and flicked the headlights on for just a second. The sound of the nails paused abruptly. In the time it took for the flash of light to dissipate, we heard the clicking nails leave the asphalt, prance off the gravel shoulder, and disappear into the marsh grass bordering the highway.

Thus ended our encounter with a timber wolf on September 11, 1999, in northwestern Juneau County, halfway between the towns of Wisconsin Rapids and Tomah in west-central Wisconsin.

When I began my new job as a wildlife educator in late 1989, I believed my active participation in wolf recovery had ended. I was aware that the L-shaped "central forest" region in west-central Wisconsin where I worked was a sparsely populated area of dense forest and expansive bogs and thus was suitable for wolves. But at that time wolves had not moved beyond the northern reaches of the state. None of the radioed wolves had left northern Wisconsin heading south. And between the northern forests and the central forest—a forty-five hundred–square mile area in west-central Wisconsin bounded by Eau Claire, Tomah, Necedah, Wisconsin Rapids, and Neillsville—there was nothing but farmland and intensely active farmland at that. All of which made it extremely unlikely that a disperser wandering south out of northern Wisconsin's wolf range could actually reach the central forest.

On December 1, 1994, several wildlife biologists and I were conducting a winter tracking survey in Jackson County, a rather remote region in west-central Wisconsin, in response to repeated reports by locals of some large canids "too large to be coyotes." A quarter-mile into our route we encountered coyote traffic—lots of it. The coyotes had popped up onto the dike road and sauntered down the middle of it, leaving the road here and there, only to reappear farther on, messing up an otherwise great tracking surface.

A two-inch snowfall the night before had created ideal tracking conditions. I was already losing interest and not paying much attention to the road. I was gabbing with my assistant. For some inexplicable reason I turned my head and peered out the window just as we passed a point where a culvert crossed beneath the road. I could see more coyote tracks in the snow. And in the middle of all that coyote traffic, I thought I saw the imprint of a *large* canid that had crossed the road where the ditch was. I slammed on the brakes, jumped out, and exclaimed, "Why I'll be damned!" Unmistakable. It was a timber wolf's track.

By the end of the day we knew that *two* wolf packs were living south and east of Black River Falls, a small city about fifty miles southeast of Eau Claire, hard by I-94. The following spring we trapped and collared an adult male wolf in the Black River State Forest's Wildcat Pack. Based on conversations with locals, deer hunters, trappers, and even spring turkey hunters, it seems the first wolves drifted into this region around 1990. My arrival at the Sandhill Wildlife Area near Wisconsin Rapids, itself located in the middle of the central forest, predated the wolves' arrival by one or two years. Between 1995 and 1996 another pack formed, and by 1999–2000 ten packs had colonized portions of the central forest.

The appearance of wolves in the central forest coincided with an expansion in Wisconsin's wolf population, which began growing around 1990. State and federal recovery guidelines developed in the late 1980s mandated that Wisconsin maintain a population of at least eighty wolves for three consecutive years. If and when the state met this goal, Wisconsin would be able to "downlist" the wolf to threatened status. In the winter of 1993–94 Wisconsin's wolf population stood at eighty-three, reaching the recovery goal for the first time. In 1995–96 Wisconsin had ninety-nine wolves.

On a bright, sunny day in early April 1997, twenty-five biologists, volunteers, and administrators from around the state gathered in the conference room of the Park Falls headquarters of Chequamegon National Forest to assemble the results of the wolf census for 1996–97. Each person was responsible for reporting on census work within his or her assigned areas. Then they tallied the wolf counts. Wisconsin was home to 150 timber wolves in 1996–97. This represented a milestone in wolf recovery, not only for the state but for the nation. For a third, crucial, consecutive winter the population had exceeded state and federal recovery goals.

As the applause and whooping cheers died down, Ron Schultz, who had been with the Wisconsin wolf project since 1982, exclaimed, "The number of radioed wolves we've been monitoring these past few years exceeds the state's entire wolf population only ten years ago. We have so many wolves on the air right now, it's hard to remember all their names and recall where in the state each lives."

In a presentation at a wolf symposium in New York the previous fall, Adrian Wydeven, the Wisconsin DNR's wolf biologist, had attributed the success of Wisconsin's natural wolf recovery to

1. Its proximity to the very healthy Minnesota wolf population
2. The presence of suitable habitat
3. The abundance of prey populations, especially deer and beaver
4. Dispersal corridors that allow the wolves to move to and from Minnesota's wolf range and to and from the various areas of habitat scattered throughout northern and west-central Wisconsin
5. Adequate legal protection, including hefty state fines and the closure of the coyote season in northern Wisconsin during the deer gun season
6. Educational efforts that seem to have increased public awareness and have been a factor in reducing the incidence of illegal killings

Wolf biologists have noted a remarkable reduction in overall mortality since the early 1980s. Between 1979 and 1985 wolves suffered a 39 percent annual mortality rate, which wolf biologists consider high enough to keep the popu-

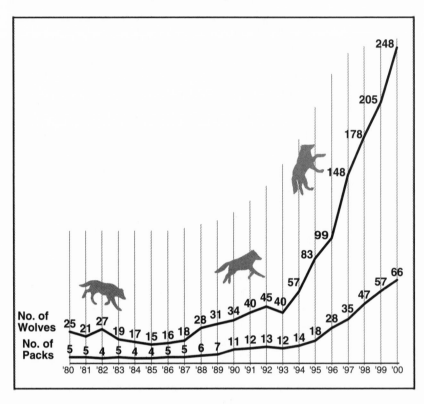

Changes in Wisconsin gray wolf population, 1980–2000 (Wisconsin Department of Natural Resources)

lation from increasing. Between 1986 and 1992 the annual mortality dropped to 18 percent.

The causes of death of radioed wolves are varied. Car kills have become more common, a reflection of the greatly expanded wolf population. And while it appears that shooting deaths (malicious killing) have decreased markedly (45 percent in 1979–88 versus 19 percent in 1989–98), a look at the number shot in each five-year period reveals that the lowest incidence of gunshot deaths occurred in 1989–93. Shooting deaths increased between 1994 and 1998, which may reflect a decreased tolerance of wolves at a time when the wolf population was increasing.[1] Is this increase in shooting deaths an indication that wolves have reached "cultural carrying capacity"—that fine line between human tolerance and intolerance—in certain portions of their Wisconsin range?

With 5.1 million humans living in Wisconsin, it is inevitable that the interests of wolves and humans will clash. This is a fact that cannot be ignored.

To provide a future for wolves in Wisconsin, wildlife officials responsible for their management needed to develop a template—a management plan. In March 1998 the Wisconsin DNR held public forums in ten communities throughout the state on its draft wolf management plan. Antiwolf sentiments prevailed at a number of them. Significant numbers of individuals commented that the wolf population was already at or exceeding tolerable limits—the cultural carrying capacity.

In fact, since the early 1990s hound hunters had been complaining about the expansion of the Wisconsin wolf population. Nearly every year since the late 1980s, territorial wolves have killed hounds used to pursue coyotes, foxes, rabbits, and other game animals.[2] Though hunters are paid for their losses through the depredation compensation program, many feel the cash is no substitute because the hounds are also pets. Other citizens are quick to point out, however, that the state does not pay for hounds lost to bears, coyotes, and other species—and they note that hound hunters do not complain about these losses. Some believe that paying hound hunters for losses to wolves is an unjustifiable and inappropriate use of state funds.

More recently, hound hunters have suffered a series of political setbacks in pursuing their sport. Stiffer trespass laws enacted in 1997 have forced many hound-hunting outfits to rely more on the use of public lands to hunt coyotes, raccoons, bears, and foxes. These are the same lands the wolves have "taken over." The inevitable conflicts resulted in injuries to and the deaths of twenty dogs between 1989 and 1997. Many hound hunters—who tend to view wolves as an unwelcome newcomer—say that the wolves are "putting us out of business." Forced into a corner by circumstances, the hound hunters are increasingly angered by the wolves' return. Many proudly display a bumper sticker depicting the head of a wolf with a slash through it.

The hound hunters are not alone. Livestock farmers worry that wolves will "eat us out of our livelihoods." The number of depredation problems has held fairly steady in Wisconsin, averaging 1.4 livestock depredations per year since 1989. But these figures are rising, and livestock producers do have a point.

The problem lies in the quality of Wisconsin's wolf habitat. David Mladenoff, Robert Haight, T. A. Sickley, and Adrian Wydeven reviewed data on land ownership, road densities, prey densities, forest cover, and human densities within fourteen Wisconsin wolf pack territories. They used this in-

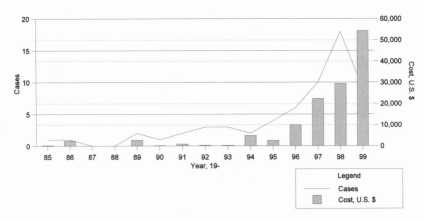

Wolf depredation cases and costs in Wisconsin, 1985–99

formation to produce a template of wolf habitat, then searched the entire state for similar areas. They found six thousand square miles within Wisconsin that contain the characteristics wolves seem to prefer.[3]

However, these six thousand square miles are highly fragmented—scattered across the length and breadth of northern and west-central Wisconsin. In 1998 the three largest habitat enclaves contained eight packs each. Each might be able to hold perhaps ten to twelve packs. Obviously, these enclaves are approaching saturation. Other parcels are barely large enough to support a single pack. And some of the smaller islands of habitat have been colonized in recent years, as the Mladenoff team predicted.

A common misconception is that once wolves saturate good habitat, they will quit breeding. They won't. Instead, their offspring will mature and inevitably disperse into areas where some will feast on livestock and pets or cause other trouble.

Because Wisconsin has far less high-quality habitat than its neighbors, Minnesota and the Upper Peninsula of Michigan, and because of the fragmented nature of the state's existing wolf habitat, Wisconsin's wolves are starting to lose the public relations game. The recent upswing in shooting deaths, and the rumblings heard at public forums, may presage that Wisconsin's wolf population (approximately 248 wolves in the winter of 1999–2000) is approaching its cultural carrying capacity.

The DNR recognizes that at some point it may have to institute a very limited wolf-hunting, or "harvesting," season to curb excessive repopulation. But the very notion of harvesting wolves is highly controversial. Why? Because some people remain unaware that this species is no longer endangered or threatened with extinction. Some deify the wolf. Others deeply mis-

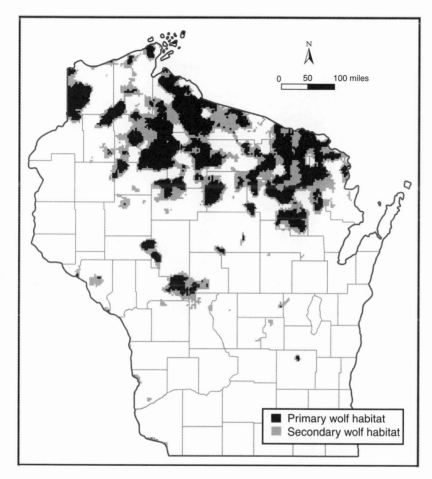

Primary and secondary wolf habitat in Wisconsin (Reprinted by permission of Blackwell Science, Inc.)

trust the ability of government agencies to effectively manage harvest levels. Some suffer from misinformation, mistakenly believing that wolves will "self-regulate" their numbers through interpack killings and low reproductive rates (both have been known to occur when wolves are greatly stressed by limited amounts of food; however, in Wisconsin their food supply—1.5 million deer and even greater numbers of livestock—is essentially unlimited). Some people are unaware or cannot grasp that the areas in Wisconsin where wolves can roam without encroaching on human activities or damaging personal property (livestock and pets) are extremely limited. And still others cannot

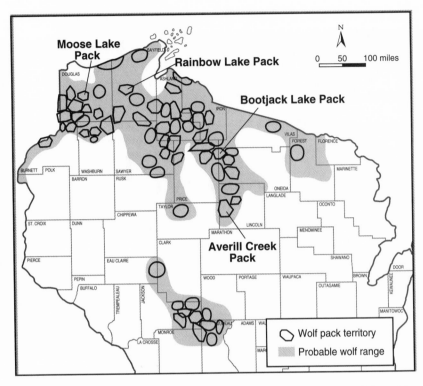

Gray wolf distribution in Wisconsin, winter 1999–2000 (Wisconsin Department of Natural Resources)

accept the reality for wolves that live among people: some die at the hands of humans.

Wisconsin approved a new state wolf management plan in October 1999. The goals included downlisting the wolf to "threatened" instead of "endangered" and removing wolves from any special listing once the population reached 250 animals. The plan called for a population management goal of 350 animals. This figure was based on (1) the amount of suitable habitat, (2) recognition that not all the suitable habitat is or should be filled with wolves because it is geographically fragmented, and (3) an extrapolation of the size of a reasonable wolf population based on calculated occupancy rates and wolf population projections. The plan suggested that a "public harvest be considered" to keep the population within a cultural carrying capacity.

The state's downlisting occurred right after the state approved its wolf management plan. Awaiting approval by the U.S. Fish and Wildlife Service, as this book goes to press, is a similar plan proposed by the federal government to downlist Wisconsin's wolves to threatened. Once the federal government downlists wolves in the state, Wisconsin will have permission to euthanize individual wolves that prey on livestock—a tool sought by biologists and livestock interests alike.

So where do we go from here? As painful as it is to contemplate, Wisconsin must begin a public discussion of the need to limit the wolf population and how to reach a political compromise that everyone—especially the wolves—can live with. If we do it right, wolf advocates will learn to accept that a few individual wolves will have to be sacrificed to ensure the species' survival. And wolf opponents will learn that wolves are a part of the ecosystem, and their existence is valued by many people in our society.

Perhaps one of the biggest problems state wildlife managers will face will be convincing the public that wolves are no longer endangered. In fact, wolves have been restored within suitable habitats in the upper Great Lakes region. That fight is over.

But over the years educational efforts have made the wolf the poster child of endangerment. The public has come to believe that once a species is endangered, it either remains endangered forever or becomes extinct. However, with proper wildlife management many species have actually recovered. Recent examples in Wisconsin include bald eagles, double-crested cormorants, fishers, and wild turkeys. And because of wolves' predatory nature and their tendency to prey on livestock, continuing to manage them as if they were still endangered is not in the wolves' best interest.

Wisconsin's central forest offers a prime example of the problem. Wolves live in a small enclave of suitable habitat virtually surrounded by livestock-rearing regions. Each pack produces five to six pups yearly. Those pups that survive to adulthood will eventually seek their own territory. As Wisconsin's suitable wolf habitat becomes saturated, dispersers will be forced into outlying areas of the central forest where they are more likely to cause depredations.

Farmers cannot be expected to bear the brunt of this conservation success story. This is why wildlife managers will need to be able to "take" (kill) wolves

when and where conditions call for it. If wildlife managers are not permitted to do this, the political backlash that undoubtedly will develop will doom the wolves once more. We need only look to history to understand that this is what will happen.

Our society once sanctioned the destruction of the wolf because wolves were perceived as an economic liability to farmers and an annoyance to hunters. Yet wolves were not annihilated until they became a political issue. This occurred in 1915 when Congress capitulated to constant appeals from influential livestock interests from western states and created the Predatory Animal Control program.

Long before 1915, government biologists had called for the removal of predators only in livestock-rearing areas, arguing against control work in remote areas because wolves in those areas seldom made forays into cattle and sheep ranges. After Congress got involved, the government declared an all-out war against wolves that required "intensive organized effort until the last animal is taken . . . in every state where they find suitable harbors." The war even extended into the national parks because they served as wolf preserves. The political solution left no sanctuary. The political solution was absolute.[4]

Some people in Wisconsin already are calling for the removal of wolves. They say there should be no sanctuary, no space for wolves in this state. If our society fails to acknowledge and address the problems wolves pose, we run the risk that the political backlash will once again lead to the annihilation of the wolf in Wisconsin.

And so it is that we need to begin talking about a public harvest of wolves to curb excessive population growth. This approach is justified for a number of reasons. Because our tax-conscious society demands a level of efficiency that government agencies are unlikely to meet, a regulated public harvest would be the most economical method of addressing the problem. Because state wildlife officials have a great deal of data about Wisconsin wolf populations, they would be able to closely regulate a public harvest by identifying the geographic area(s) where population reductions are necessary, thus also identifying locales where wolves would remain protected. The state would limit the number of permits to the level necessary to alleviate wolf population pressures, just as they already do for turkey, deer, bear, geese, and other wildlife populations. Proper statutory language would ensure that seasons could be closed within twenty-four hours of reaching prescribed harvest levels. Anyone drawing a harvest permit could be required to attend a workshop to learn about treating humanely and ethically the wolves they would harvest. And sensitivity training of permit holders would expose them to the varied views of humans toward wolves.

Animal protectionist groups and individuals who deify wolves are likely to vociferously oppose a public harvest program as a means of curbing excessive population growth. While these groups lack sufficient political clout to prevail, they might attempt to block public harvesting of wolves through the courts. But delays caused by slick legal maneuvers will only increase public intolerance of wolves because the state will be unable to address increasing populations and the problems they create. Thus the only result of litigation would be to fill lawyers' wallets, while wolves continue to die. Although well intentioned, such efforts to "save" wolves would play into the hands of the more extreme elements of our society, those who call for the wolves' annihilation. And those are the people who will use any excuse to take matters into their own hands and kill wolves. You can bet this will have just as much of an impact—if not more—than a regulated harvest. The only difference is that such killings will go unchecked and unregulated.

Wolf management today is complicated by the wide range of emotions that wolves elicit from Americans. Some people hate them with a vengeance. Others are so passionate in their devotion to this animal that it blinds them to the reality of limited habitat.

Somewhere in between lies the viewpoint of the wildlife profession, which places an emphasis on preserving the species over survival of its individual members. Individuals are mortal and come and go, but once a species is lost, its loss is forever.

The movement to save wolves started fifty years ago with visionaries like Aldo Leopold, Bernie Bradle, Dan Thompson, and Bill Feeney. For a brief period I followed in their footsteps. When I left, the responsibility shifted to Adrian Wydeven and other staffers at Wisconsin's DNR, the U.S. Forest Service, and the U.S. Fish and Wildlife Service. That responsibility will shift again when the federal government downlists the wolf from endangered to threatened and allows states in the upper Great Lakes region to use wildlife management principles to determine how best to manage their wolf populations.

In order to preserve the wolf, Wisconsinites must agree that the species is worth keeping. We must also realize that the population will need to be trimmed periodically by removing individuals. These are the choices that confront us because we are all keepers of the wolves.

Notes
Index

Notes

Phantoms of the Forest

1. In winter deer congregate beneath stands of conifers, called deer yards by biologists and woods workers, because the fir branches catch and hold a considerable amount of snow. These areas provide the deer with protection from the deep snows and cold winds that sweep the open poplar, maple, and birch ridges.

2. "Block" is wildlife biology jargon for a large block of forested land largely undisturbed by humans. Members of the Department of Natural Resources and other outdoors types typically use the name of a prominent lake or stream located within the block to identify it as a specific geographic location.

3. In 1979 wolf researchers Fred Harrington and L. David Mech reported their circumstantial evidence that wolves could hear their imitated howls in a forested environment from four miles off ("Wolf Howling and Its Role in Territory Maintenance," *Behaviour* 68 [1979]: 207–49). They believe the maximum human range in forests is two miles (Fred Harrington and L. David Mech, "An Analysis of Howling Response Parameters Useful for Wolf Pack Censusing," *Journal of Wildlife Management* 46 [1982]: 686–93).

4. The Wisconsin Conservation Department became the Department of Natural Resources in 1968.

5. R. P. Thiel and R. J. Welch. "Evidence of Recent Breeding Activity in Wisconsin Wolves," *American Midland Naturalist* 106 (1986): 186–94.

Beginnings

1. Daniel Q. Thompson, "A Preliminary Study of the Timber Wolf in Wisconsin," master's thesis, University of Wisconsin–Madison, 1950.

2. John Keener, "The Case for the Timber Wolf," *Wisconsin Conservation Bulletin* 20, no. 11 (1955): 22–24.

Dust, Mosquitoes, and a Few Collared Wolves

1. Originally a part of the U.S. Department of Agriculture, the U.S. Fish and Wildlife Service was given the responsibility during the early to mid-1980s for trapping wolves that were feasting on livestock in Minnesota. The program was returned to the U.S. Department of Agriculture's Animal Damage Control division in 1986.

2. In the late 1980s we made modifications to our traps that almost eliminated the problem of capturing skunks and other small mammals instead of wolves.

3. Female wolves sometimes display pseudopregnancy and are capable of lactating even though they have not bred.

Trying Times

1. Wolves seem to love their mobility. Their need for a sustainable supply of food may account for their wanderlust. The size of a wolf's territory is primarily related to the relative abundance of food on the landscape. In areas with higher densities of hoofed mammals, wolf pack ranges tend to be smaller. Conversely, where prey exists in lower densities, wolf pack territories are larger. Researchers have recorded territories as small as thirty square miles (Wisconsin) and as large as five thousand square miles (Alaska).

2. Local wildlife staff consented to limited trapping efforts in 1983 only after the Averill Creek Pack declined from twelve to fourteen wolves in 1979–80 to fewer than three in 1982–83. The cause of the crash remains a mystery. It likely was caused by disease, a source of mortality that none present at the August 1980 meeting anticipated. The first wolf in Lincoln County was collared in 1985.

3. Lest readers indict all the state's hunters and trappers . . . by 1979, automobiles had claimed two other wolves.

What's in a Name?

1. Wolves in North America do not recognize humans as potential prey. This does not imply they never have or will never do so in the future. In recent years several attacks have occurred in Algonquin Provincial Park, Ontario, Canada, involving wolves habituated to people near campsites. See R. Rick Stronks, and Dan Strickland. "Fearless Wolves in Algonquin Provincial Park, Canada," abstract 23 from the conference Beyond 2000: Realities of Global Wolf Restoration, February 23–26, 2000, Duluth, Minnesota, published by the International Wolf Center, Ely, Minnesota. The wolf should be respected as a wild animal and capable predator.

2. I have seen numerous places where tree cutters have dropped gloves in the woods. Wolves frequently investigate them, but this wolf evidently had a taste for them.

3. The dental acrylic was messy and cumbersome to work with, and the wolves managed to chew through a few of those collars too. A year later I read an article on wolves in Italy that provided a solution to the persistent problem of loss to collar chewing. To protect their sheepdogs from wolf attack, Italian shepherds place spikes in their dogs' collars (decorative spikes on dog collars in America evidently are a relic of their protective function). Punching holes through our wolf collars and placing hardware bolts in them solved the problem. We never experienced collar chewing again.

4. Nekoosa-Edwards Industrial Forest lands in western Oneida County were sold to another industrial forest corporation in the late 1980s.

Deer, the Wolf's Bread (and Bane) of Life

1. Most hunters today do not feel this way toward wolves or other predators. However, as with any group, a minority will always hold to certain views. Under extreme winter weather conditions the combination of human and wolf predation can cause declines in deer herds (see L. D. Mech, and P. D. Karns, *Role of the Wolf in a Deer Decline in the Superior National Forest*, U.S. Forest Service Research Report NC-148 [Washington, D.C.: U.S. Government Printing Office, 1977]). In a study conducted in north-central Minnesota, where the deer herd was slowly declining, humans (hunting both legally and illegally) and severe winter weather were the primary causes of deer mortality, even though wolf densities were fairly high and wolf predation might be expected to be more significant (see Todd Fuller, *Dynamics of a Declining White-Tailed Deer Population in North-Central Minnesota*, Wildlife Monograph Number 110 [Washington, D.C.: Wildlife Society, 1990]).

2. While this was true in 1980, it no longer is. See my concluding chapter for an update.

All in the Family

1. In early December 1982, more than a year after Mailrunner disappeared, the Madison office of the DNR received a letter. Postmarked St. Paul, Minnesota, it read: "Timber Wolf Killed with bow and arrow on Oct 20, 1981 in Nemadji State Forest near Kerrick, Minn." Attached were ear tags 005 and 006. There was no return address.

2. Mailrunner died several days after we got the count of the Moose Lake Pack, according to the Minnesota letter. Assuming he had left the territory and was not one of the wolves we saw, the Moose Lake Pack contained at least fourteen wolves during the summer of 1981. This remains the largest pack observed in Wisconsin in twenty years of population monitoring (1979–99).

3. With the death of Gimpy, the Bear Lake wolf pack territory would not produce a litter of pups for eight years, although a pair of wolves did recolonize and occupy the area in 1983 and 1984. The disruption brought about by the killing of wolf 1187 could be measured in as many as forty pups that would never be. As for wolf 003, he returned to the Stateline Flowage area in January and joined the pack that had killed his lady love.

4. By 1983 we were aware that Wisconsin and Minnesota wolves had been exposed to canine parvovirus, a disease that causes acute intestinal distress, dehydration, and often death. We knew this by analyzing the blood of captured wolves to determine whether they carried parvo antibodies. Because wolves use feces as scent posts and the disease is spread through contact with contaminated feces, we knew wolves were extremely vulnerable. We began routinely collecting feces to determine where and at what time of year outbreaks of the disease occurred.

5. The following year a radioed female wolf integrated into Maryanne's former pack and raised a litter. Her mate, though never radio-collared, was a large, dark-colored male who looked just like Maryanne's former escort.

Boy, Would I Love Your Job!

1. The wolf had been shot illegally during the 1979 deer season in Lincoln County, killed within the district of state senator Clifford "Tiny" Krueger. It was mounted and placed in a display case for use as a portable educational tool prior to an agreement to preserve specimens at the University of Wisconsin Zoological Museum.

They Shoot the Messenger, Don't They?

1. Daniel Q. Thompson, "Travel, Range, and Food Habits of Timber Wolves in Wisconsin," *Journal of Mammalogy* 33 (1952): 439.

2. For historical data on wolf populations and distribution, see Richard Thiel, *The Timber Wolf in Wisconsin: The Death and Life of a Majestic Predator* (Madison: University of Wisconsin Press, 1993).

3. R. P. Thiel, "Relationship between Road Densities and Wolf Habitat Suitability in Wisconsin," *American Midland Naturalist* 113 (1985): 404–7; W. F. Jensen, T. K. Fuller, and W. L. Robinson, "Wolf (*Canis lupus*) Distribution on the Ontario–Michigan Border near Sault Ste. Marie," *Canadian Field-Naturalist* 100 (1986): 363–66; and L. D. Mech, S. J. Fritts, G. L. Radde, and W. J. Paul, "Wolf Distribution and Road Density in Minnesota," *Wildlife Society Bulletin* 16 (1988): 85–87.

4. The road density technique does not imply that wolves will *never* be found in areas that exceed the upper threshold. It would predict, however, that wolves living in such areas are unlikely to survive for long. Loafer, as an example, lived far beyond the edge of his species' range. The nearest area inhabited by a wolf pack, the Bootjack Lake Pack, lay fifty miles to the west. The road density within Loafer's home range was nearly twice the threshold. He disappeared in the summer of 1984, and we heard rumors that he had not died a natural death. Similarly, in 1986, a year after the road density work was published, we found a pack of wolves living in the Chequamegon National Forest, where the road density exceeded *two* linear miles per square mile of habitat. In January 1988 we heard rumors that the pack's alpha female had been killed by a hound hunter disgruntled at persistent stories that government agencies were going to close off roads as a means of protecting wolves. Radio tracking of the alpha male confirmed the disappearance of his mate around this time. This pack pushed the limit, and evidently unscrupulous individual humans pushed back.

5. *Vilas County News Review*, August 13, 1986.

6. *Vilas County News Review*, December 17, 1986.

7. *Vilas County News Review*, December 24, 1986.

8. D. J. Mladnoff, T. A. Sickley, R. G. Haight, and A. P. Wydeven, "A Regional Landscape Analysis and Prediction of Favorable Gray Wolf Habitat in the Northern Great Lakes Region," *Conservation Biology* 9 (1995): 279–94; D. J. Mladnoff, R. G. Haight, T. A. Sickley, and A. P. Wydeven, "Causes and Implications of Species Restoration in Altered Ecosystems: A Spatial Landscape Project of Wolf Population Recovery," *Bioscience* 47, no. 1 (1997): 21–31.

Life in the Shadow of Civilization

1. She gradually drifted south and by March was near the edge of the territory of Lincoln County's Averill Creek Pack. When last seen, Carol was standing near an old barn within a few miles of the city of Merrill. Her radio signal was never heard again.

2. The Averill Creek Pack in Lincoln County slid from twelve wolves in 1979–80 to one or two in the winter of 1983–84. The DNR authorized us to capture a wolf in July 1983, but it wasn't until 1985 that we finally caught one. As events shaped up, the decision against radioing wolves in Lincoln County, handed down in August 1980 (see chapter 2), may have slowed our efforts to understand the cause of these declines.

3. Deborah provided an example. When she was captured in 1982, she showed a high blood titer response to parvo antibodies. By 1984 she was dead. In theory, another wolf would replace her (had the pack not been so isolated from other wolves). What were the chances that her replacement would be naive?

4. Big Al replaced her mother as the alpha female of the Bootjack Lake Pack. Although she was in poor condition, she managed to bear another litter in 1988. Her radio malfunctioned on December 5, 1988. Ron Schultz obtained reports of a sickly wolf hanging out near the yard of a backwoods residence on the eastern edge of the Bootjack Lake Pack's territory in the winter of 1989–90. He caught a glimpse of the wolf and saw it had a collar. He was sure it was Big Al. She was never seen again, and Ron felt certain she died soon thereafter. Big Al would have been eight—a nice old age for a Wisconsin timber wolf.

5. Between this first incident in 1989 and 1998, wolf-monitoring crews recorded at least twenty other cases in Wisconsin. *Wisconsin Wolf Management Plan*, Publ.-ER-099 99 (Madison: Wisconsin Department of Natural Resources, 1999), 74 pages.

6. C. D. Besadny, DNR secretary, to Brian O'Neill, October 26, 1983, in the author's possession.

7. Jay Reed, *Milwaukee Journal*, January 25, 1987, p. 14C.

8. Adrian Wydeven, "Field Progress Report, July–September 1990," memo dated October 8, 1990, to the Bureau of Endangered Resources, Wisconsin Department of Natural Resources.

Wolves in the Twenty-first Century

1. The mortality data come from Adrian Wydeven, R. N. Schultz, and R. P. Thiel, "Monitoring of a Recovering Gray Wolf Population in Wisconsin, 1979–91," in L. N. Carbyn, S. F. Fritts, and D. R. Seip, eds., *Ecology and Management of Wolves in a Changing World* (Edmonton, Alberta, Canada: Canadian Circumpolar Institute, 1995), and unpublished quarterly and annual wolf status reports, Wisconsin Department of Natural Resources, 1979–98.

2. Wolves are territorial and will often kill intruding foreign wolves, coyotes, and dogs they manage to catch trespassing within their territories.

3. David Mladenoff, Robert Haight, T. A. Sickley, and Adrian Wydeven, "A Regional Landscape Analysis and Prediction of Favorable Wolf Habitat in the Northern Great Lakes Region," *Conservation Biology* 9 (1995): 279–94.

4. See Verson Bailey, "Wolves in Relation to Stock, Game, and the National Forest Reserves," *U.S.D.A. Forest Service Bulletin,* no. 72 (1907): 1–31; David E. Brown, *The Wolf in the Southwest* (Tucson: University of Arizona Press, 1983); Rick McIntyre, ed. *War against the Wolf* (Stillwater, Minn.: Voyageur Press, 1995).

Index